Sequel to *Mountain Meadows Witness*

MOUNTAIN MEADOWS

This picture was taken on the Mountain Meadows by the author,
September 12, 1997. This day marked the 140th anniversary of
the massacre.

Through Bonds of Love

In the shadow of the Mountain Meadows Massacre,

Priscilla Klingensmith,
the eighteenth surviving child of the massacre,
grew-up in Utah where she became a plural wife of
John Urie.

by

Anna Jean Backus

Orem, Utah
1998

————

LIBRARY OF CONGRESS CATALOG CARD NUMBER: 98-93009
ISBN 0-9664471-1-5

————

Printed in the United States of America
First Printing May 1998

AJB DISTRIBUTING
P.O. Box 970351
Orem, Utah 84097-0351

Other books attributed to the author:

*Mountain Meadows Witness, the life and
times of Bishop Philip Klingensmith*, 1995,
published by The Arthur H. Clark Company,
Spokane, Washington; *The Klingensmith
Scrapbook*, 1996, self published.

With gratitude and love
I dedicate this book
to my cousins.

Content

Illustrations

Acknowledgements

While writing this book I felt a responsibility that I deemed a privilege and blessing. My memory was brimming with knowledge retained from writing my first books, and the stories related to me by my mother, aunts, and cousins. This wealth of information burst forth into my writing. Resurrecting history from the past allowed me to feel the emotion and imagine the thoughts of those who I wrote about.

With sincerity and love I thank all who have been involved with the production of this book. Other expressions of gratitude and thanks can be mirrored from sentiments found in *Mountain Meadows Witness* and *The Klingensmith Scrapbook*. Going beyond thanks to my family, friends, and descendants of Philip Klingensmith and his wives, I thank descendants of John Urie, Sarah Ann McMillan Urie, and Priscilla Klingensmith Urie--including a special thanks to Bernon J. Auger, my cousins: Ila K. Robinson, Betty Evans, Mary Urie, Margaret Mills, Brent Ashworth, Simon Benson, Barbara Burt, Mel and Ellen Smith, Norman Rose, Susan Foster, her husband Craig, Helen McBain, Freeda Schofield, Alice Boroughf, Ada Long, Russel Urie, Jack and Samuel Leigh, and the late Ross Urie, Hurschell Urie, and Albert Urie Andrew.

Editor, Ted Stoddard, encouraged me while he, again, accomplished a proficient editorial feat. My thanks go to him for his support and friendship.

Even though Robert "Bob" Clark didn't publish this book he helped me in the technical details, and gave generously of his time to comment on this publication: "*Through Bonds of Love* carries forward the Utah pioneer saga recounted in the author's *Mountain Meadows Witness*. Based on letters and other original sources, this is a dramatic tale filled with historical reality." I appreciate his kindness and interest.

Writing skills were first formulated in my mind by the teaching of Don Norton and were expanded by, Ted Stoddard, Don Q. Cannon, and Robert Clark. My love and thanks go out to all of them.

The opportunity of publishing this wonderful book has given me experience in formatting and design that is gratifying. I am also grateful for the abilities of expert technicians.

Many people have been waiting for this book. It is my prayer they will be pleased with my efforts and know that I did the very best I knew how.

As always,

Anna

Preface

Through Bonds of Love has been written as a companion--which may be termed as a sequel--to *Mountain Meadows Witness: The Life and Times of Bishop Philip Klingensmith.*

Thoughts of writing a history on the life of John Urie, the author's grandfather, were reluctantly set aside after several initial attempts. The writing of *Mountain Meadows Witness*, a documented biography of Philip Klingensmith, who was a participant of the massacre, pushed its way into importance and took over the author's time. The emotion and drive which created *Through Bonds of Love*, were brought about when the importance of Priscilla Klingensmith's history was realized.

When *Mountain Meadows Witness* was begun, Priscilla Klingensmith was important only because she was the author's grandmother. The author was well into writing her first book when her research revealed the hidden secret of where Priscilla came from.

The author's unwavering belief that Priscilla was indeed the eighteenth surviving child from the massacre stands firm. The name Priscilla Klingensmith can not be found on church nor census records before 1857. To this point, pictures and locks of hair are the strongest available evidence that Priscilla belongs to the Alexander Fancher family.[1]

The process of trying to prove with some certainty from which family Priscilla descends, by the process of DNA blood testing, was done by Eccles Institute of Human Genetics, University of Utah, Salt Lake City. Research funds were provided by the Mountain Meadows Association--spearheaded by Ronald E. Loving and fed by an anonymous donor. The results remain inconclusive at this point in time.

---

[1] Known victims of the massacre.

Priscilla Klingensmith
holding son William
Courtesy, Jack Leigh, Washington, UT.

Triphenia Fancher Wilson
*Courtesy, Carroll County Historical
& Genealogical Society & Heritage Center*

Duncan Backus

"Kit" Fancher

William Urie

Introduction

Bonds of love found within this book and the bond of love that tied the author to Philip Klingensmith as she wrote her book, *Mountain Meadows Witness*, made this book possible. Bonds of love prevailed as the author gathered bits and pieces of history from descendants of the characters within this book, *Through Bonds of Love*.

A chapter is included in the book about the Mountain Meadows Massacre with additional documentation pertaining to the incident.[2] The role of Philip is partially dramatized to give further understanding of actual events as they took place in his life.

True characters, from the same span of history, are woven into a faith-promoting love story, which naturally pulls a thread through the massacre that ties the main characters, John Urie and Priscilla Klingensmith, to her father and to the incident. The touching story about their lives conveys the rigors of pioneer living in a remote outpost of southern Utah, found in the heart of Indian country.

Endnotes are used to establish credence to a history of real people, places in time, and actual events. Some dialog is assumed, but most is supported by journals, letters, and histories written by John Urie; his wives, Sarah Ann McMillan and Priscilla Klingensmith; their children; John's parents; and Philip Klingensmith.

The beginning unfolds in Scotland, where John Urie was born. John migrated to America and finally settled in Cedar City, Iron County, Utah. John Urie was a staunch Mormon and always remained a loyal member of The Church of Jesus Christ of Latter-day Saints. He studied the scriptures intently and shared his beliefs with his family in the old country.

The familiar sounds of shrill-toned music played by bagpipers, stories of family predictions, friends, and relatives; and the smell of rich fruit cakes baking in an oven tucked away fond memories in the mind of John Urie--all of which kindled a longing for the beautiful lowlands of Scotland.

John's record keeping preserved a piece of Cedar City history that may have been lost forever. From his homeland, he brought the knowledge and skills of an iron worker, which contributed to the Iron Mission. Because of his strong religious beliefs, he was pursued by the law for maintaining plural wives--a heart-rending portion of the book.

During the infancy of John Urie's first marriage, his sweetheart, Elizabeth Hutcheson, died in childbirth. Subsequently while raising a goodly family by his

---

[2]Since the publication of *Mountain Meadows Witness*, readers have given new information about the massacre to the author.

second wife, Sarah Ann McMillan, John Urie took a companion wife, Priscilla. This time period is where the drama of the love story begins--preserving a faithful portrayal of the characters, dates places, and events.

It was common knowledge in Cedar City that Priscilla was a surviving child of the Mountain Meadows massacre. She remained a mystery to outsiders, but John knew where she came from. He watched her grow from a young child to womanhood. The understanding John had for Priscilla and her love of the gospel drew him to her.

As an adjutant[3] in the Nauvoo Legion during the massacre, John Urie wasn't a participant in the slaughter of Priscilla's parents and siblings. The author wonders what has happened to her grandfather's records of the event.

Priscilla, her Mormon name, is assumed to have been only two years old when she was kept by a Mormon family and raised in Utah. She hadn't formed any thoughts or memories that might call her back to the Ozarks. She was old enough to have felt the love of her parents; but the memories of people, sights and sounds, and places in Arkansas were snatched away from her. Priscilla's posterity never heard ancestral stories that could be passed down through generations--and two branches of lineage were taken away from both her and her descendants.

Priscilla's life, while she was raised as a Mormon girl, was patterned in the direction her Mormon mother and father taught her. She gained a testimony that God lives, and she always remained faithful to the Church. While living in polygamy and raising her children begotten by an older man, Priscilla met challenges with strength, courage, contentment, patience, and, at times, vexation.

The thread of caring woven throughout this book depicts a *bond of love* that helped mold the eighteenth surviving child from the Mountain Meadows Massacre into a worthy child of God who longed to know her true identity.

All documents, reports, letters, quotes, etc. have been transcribed from copies and original papers by me unless otherwise noted. All quotations are reproduced mostly verbatim. To the best of my ability, I have tried to preserve the original spelling, punctuation, capitalization, and grammar of the quotes used in my text.

---

[3]An army officer who helps the commanding officer by handling correspondence, distributing orders, etc. (*Webster's Dictionary*)

Through Bonds of Love

John Urie

CHAPTER 1

Stowing Away

A pretty, blue-eyed toddler, who became the eighteenth surviving orphan child of a horrifying massacre, was born in Arkansas. From the hills of the Ozarks, her parents, Alexander and Eliza Ingram Fancher, formulated their plans for a life of prosperity in California. Early on a spring morning in 1857, after all was ready, Alexander and Eliza's family gathered with relatives and friends at Beller Stand in Boone County to begin their journey.

High hopes and expectations accompanied the wagon train on its long and strenuous sojourn over plains, streams, mountains, and valleys. However, before their destination was realized, after they had spent many weeks on the trail, the lofty dreams of these unsuspecting emigrants were shattered. They met their destruction on the Mountain Meadows of Southern Utah. After the perpetrators' guns fell silent and their knives were sheathed, the victims' lifeless and bloody bodies were left lying on the rocky ground—-left to the elements of nature. Every member of the wagon train was now dead—-save a scattering of young children. Otherwise peaceful Mormon men, under military command, and a coalition of frantic Ute Indians put them there.[1]

It was through this tragic twist of fate that the young orphan was raised as a Mormon in the community of Cedar City, Iron County, Utah. Priscilla Klingensmith became her name. John Urie,[2] the man who would later help to mold Priscilla's destiny, had many adventures and trials to face before he first saw her. In time, she blossomed into the young woman who became his sweetheart.

John was a full-blooded Scotsman who spoke with a Scottish brogue. He was blue eyed and robust, standing five-feet ten-inches tall. His dry wit could be caught by anyone watching the twinkle in his eye as he spun his tales.

The hardships of pioneer days were endured and the necessities of life in Cedar City were earned by John as a blacksmith. He had known better times in his homeland, where he was the oldest son of a wealthy iron worker. John was brought up properly with the amenities of servants in a comfortable home.

Airdrie, Lanarkshire, Scotland, where John was born, April 28, 1835, was the principal town in the New Monkland Parish. In the colony the stone-built houses, with thatched or tiled roofs, had names that were indicative of their location and were on a town registry for their keeping. Small flocks of sheep could be seen with a Scottish collie at their heels, and fields of the bluebells of Scotland adorned the countryside. Shrill-toned music drifted through the air as bagpipers marched in full regalia on the holidays. A most festive mood was displayed as the bagpipers wore a sprig of beloved heather on their lapels.

Although Scotland was predominantly Catholic, "Presbyterianism had full swing. They did not forget, not only to preach that form of religion, but to fight for it."[3] John and his brothers, Thomas, George, James, and David, were raised as Presbyterians. Their only sister, Agnes, died when she was three months old. The Uries moved to nearby Glasgow in Lanarkshire before John turned two. Glasgow, the largest city and chief seaport of Scotland, was located mainly on the northern bank of the river Clyde, which empties into the Firth of Clyde on the west coast. Within the Shire were several coal mines and iron stone pits.

The Urie families attended church in the Cathcart Parish, and for ages their deceased were buried in the graveyard—-situated within a mile of the suburbs of Glasgow. The village of Old Cathcart is located on the River Cart, which runs on the west boundary between Lanarkshire and Renfrewshire.

Tomb of Polmadie Martyrs at Old Kirkyard

John heard stories that directly involved his ancestors in the six-teenth-century religious movement aimed at reforming the Roman Catholic Church, which resulted in establishing the Protestant churches. He already knew from his own experience that

Presbyterians didn't walk on the same side of the street as Catholics.

The church graveyard at Old Cathcart was a place where the Urie families visited often. While standing in front of the grave of the first known Urie to be buried there, John and his brothers were retold the stories of three Scots—John Urie, who was very well educated and wealthy, Robert Thorn, and Thomas Cook. They were reminded of the martyrdom of these covenantors who had been dragged from their cottages in the village of Little Govan by dragoons, soldiers armed with short muskets, led by Major Balfour and Captain Maithland. The three covenantors were murdered on the 11th of May 1685 for owning the *Covenanted Work of Reformation*.[4] This was an agreement, also known as the *National Covenant*, made in 1638 by Presbyterians in Scotland, who opposed being governed by bishops.

The grave before which they stood entombed in its dark interior the namesake of the Uries, named John—he was the father of the martyred covenantor. This first John Urie died December 10, 1660. His grave, which rests under a large sandstone slab, about eight feet long by three and one half feet wide and six inches thick, was always viewed by the family with reverence.

Janet Forsyth

John took great stock in the family tales and predictions he heard. The story of his parents' courtship amused him. It seems Agnes, who was about seventeen and on her way to her Grandmother Forsyth's house at Grandy Kehead, a sixty-acre farm that had been in the family for over a hundred years, had walked just beyond the New Monkland Parish in Airdrie. George Urie, whom Agnes disliked, caught up with her, and she was determined that he was not going to walk with her. While they were quarreling, two slightly tipsy farm lads came by and wanted to talk with Agnes. She retreated behind George for protection and a fight ensued between the boys. She fled to her grandfather's house and told about the whole affair. Her aunt Jean scolded her for not staying to see fair play and predicted that Agnes would someday marry George Urie. This same Aunt Jean predicted that Agnes would become a lady and be rich.

George wasted little time for education. His ambition for earning gave him ample opportunity to win the heart of Agnes—as he worked for his future father-in-law, Thomas Main, at Airdrie Toll. This family farm had, also, been maintained by succeeding families for over a hundred years.

It was after George married Agnes, who was a well-educated school teacher, that he was influenced to seek higher learning. While saving money for the university, he avoided the *ha'* penny fee for the toll bridge by wading the river on his way to work.

After starting school, George found the time he gained by fording the river with his clothes and books held on top of his head, instead of walking several miles to the toll bridge, could be used for study. This thrift and determination to further his education were rewarding.

"He became a very learned man and a mathematician of great renown in Scotland. He taught mathematics in the University and wrote the text books that many after him used for their education. He developed a mathematical formula for the strength of steel used in spanning the great bridges of Scotland and other European countries. He patented his formulas and became quite a wealthy man. . . . He was knighted by the King of England for his contribution to the British Empire, in education and mathematics."[5]

George Urie's blacksmith shop, located in Paisley, Renfrew, Scotland, was converted into a foundry. He filled large contracts for railroad companies in Great Britain and the East Indies to make steel switches, ties, and the rims for the first wooden train wheels used on locomotives. His flawless wheels were used on the *Flying Dutchman*, which ran on the main line between Scotland and England. Although a tough taskmaster, George treated his own sons and the many workers in his mill with equality—-paying the same wage for the same amount of work.

With the same undiscriminating care, George taught his sons responsibility and integrity, which influenced John for the rest of his life. The skill of swimming was taught with similar determination when George left John on the farthest bank of a river and beckoned him to swim back alone.

John's mother, Agnes, had a spiritual influence on the direction of his life. It was from her, when he was sixteen, that he first heard about The Church of Jesus Christ of Latter-day Saints. One Sunday evening John happened upon his mother and their servant girl, who had secretly joined the Church,[6] while they were studying the *Book of Mormon*. John was handed the *book* and was asked to sit with them. "He casually opened it to III Nephi chapter 11 in the old edition where it speaks of Christ's visit to the Nephites on the American continent after his resurrection. Suddenly the servant girl broke out in tongues."[7] When John's mother interpreted and testified to the truthfulness of what he had read, she also told John that he was a chosen spirit.

John became preoccupied with the Church and studied diligently with a desire to find out for himself whether the doctrine was true. With a testimony, manifest by a burning in his bosom, on December 15, 1851, John was baptized by immersion in the freezing waters of the Clyde River.[8]

Thoughts of the look on his father's face, when he returned from the river, remained in the recesses of John's mind. Such anger and ferocity had never been fraught upon him. His mother stood behind him with tears in her eyes, pleading uselessly as John was told to leave the house. His father called after him, "No need to show up at the mill, you will no longer be in my employment."

A sting of bitterness tugged at John whenever he thought about the unfairness of his father. After he had found a good job, working at his trade—-even making higher wages than paid by his father—-his new employer let him go. It was his father's influence in the business world that prevented John from finding any work at all in Scotland.

After John fled to England to pursue employment, his tenacious father went after him. The gentle persuasion of Agnes had convinced George to let their son come back home to finish his schooling. With reluctance and disdain, John submitted to his father's demands for him to return to Scotland.

It was his dear mother, who was happy to see him, that helped John succumb to staying put—-for her sake. He completed his schooling with high honors and received prizes of valuable books for his excellence.

Education furthered John's determination to pursue the life he wanted to live. There was another scene on February 28, 1853, when John rebelled against his father, who demanded that he could no longer attend the Mormon Church. John felt just in his decision to leave—-telling his father, "Never come after me again. I will never give up the Church."

While in Liverpool, England, John listened to Mormon missionaries preaching on street corners. In the congregation, Saints were talking about leaving their homeland and sailing to America. A desire was stirred in this eighteen-year-old runaway to seek freedom from his father's rule by escaping to the "New World."

With his right hand thrust deep into his trousers pocket, John fingered the whole sum of his tangible worth. He knew he had only the equivalent of twenty American dollars—-not enough to board the ship *Falcon*—-to see him through to the "Zion" these Saints were talking about. John was bent on going with them. On the departure date, March 26, 1853, he watched for a chance to board the ship without being seen by Captain Wade.

From the large and thriving seaport on the River Mersey, the ship was towed by a steamer toward deeper water in the Irish Sea, where the ship was set free and its sails were filled with the wind that carried it to the Atlantic Ocean. Three hundred twenty-four emigrating Saints were listed on the ship where John stayed hidden until it was too far out to sea for him to be put ashore.[9]

CHAPTER 2

Standing by His Convictions

John found himself becoming enmeshed with a melting pot of people from many· lands that formed a new culture—-the *Mormon pioneers*. The common motivating force of all these people was a belief in the gospel of Jesus Christ as taught in The Church of Jesus Christ of Latter-day Saints.

From America, years later, after growing from a young man to maturity, John expressed his experiences in a letter written to his parents in Scotland. He was meticulous about using proper English and grammar—-it would not do to mix in even a bit of the *Old Scotch*:

> Cedar City, Feb. 28, 1873 2 o'clock:
>
> Dear father and mother,
>
> The above date is a very suggestive one being exactly 20 years since I left the paternal roof. During this time my experience and observation of men and things has been considerable in my sphere of life. Leaving as I did, under religious influence and also a desire to see the world, and the age of eighteen, without a guardian or protector of any kind, was an undertaking of no small moment, but with fair hopes and an intuitive desire to be just and honest in all things, was and has been my inward monitor during the last twenty years of my life.

Because John was sailing with the Saints, he heard a wealth of preaching and had plenty of opportunity to ponder the Mormon religion. Time stretched into weeks as the ship sailed on smooth as well as wind-tossed seas. Small islands began to appear; and, at last, the island of Jamaica was sighted. From the starboard side, the island of Cuba could be seen until the ship entered the Gulf of Mexico.

At last, the ship, which carried John over the Atlantic Ocean, approached the mouth of the mighty Mississippi River, where it was pulled by steamer to the port of entry in New Orleans, Louisiana. The smell of the salty sea had dissipated as the aromas from the docks and city filled the air. On May 18, 1853, after inspection by the health officers, John found himself standing on American soil with joy and thanksgiving that he had arrived safely.

While walking about the streets of New Orleans, John witnessed, with dismay, the sale of black slaves, who were auctioned off as they stood in rows outside the trader's marketplace.

In his letter to Scotland, John wrote:

My voyage from Glasgow to New Orleans was a protracted one, being eleven weeks, it gave me time for reflection, the result was a shaving, of some considerable extent of my zeal and enthusiasm on religious matters and a settling down to subjects of a more material nature. Stayed there three days and came to the conclusion that I had seen better places, proceeding up the great Mississippi River to Keo Kuk—-occupying some 10 or 11 days.

The river steamer, to avoid sandbars, traveled by day and docked at night. The trees and scenery along the banks of the river were different from anything John had ever seen before. There were fine farms, large cultivated fields, and groves of orange trees. The mansions of the plantation owners were surrounded with huts of their black slaves.

At Keokuk, John met Isaac C. Haight, who became his first Cedar City comrade. As the lives of John and Isaac entwined, in due time, they would share the secret of the famed Mormon tragedy that took place in 1857—-the Mountain Meadows Massacre.

John, along with other Saints, had been encouraged to migrate to the Great Salt Lake Valley. The promise was that the "wages in this city are high, goods cheap, and meat and drink in abundance, also plenty of gold."[1]

A wagon train, organized by John's friend, Isaac C. Haight, for the overland trail to the Great Salt Lake Valley, was leaving for Council Bluff in three days. Haight, on his return from his mission in England, had the monumental responsibility of outfitting the enormous migration of Saints preparing to cross the plains during 1853.

Contracts for wagons, yokes for oxen, sets of tent poles, and tents had to be made months ahead. Thousands of pounds of bacon sides and hundreds of sacks of flour had to be bargained for. Yokes of oxen and cows had to be driven to the camp, which gathered in Mr. Potter's field on the countryside of Keokuk. All of which delighted the local merchants.

Appointing captains of the numerous companies and instructing the Saints was also under the charge of Isaac C. Haight.[2] They started out with ten to twelve Saints to a wagon, totaling 3,000 pounds, including provisions. Each wagon had two yoke of oxen and one yoke of cows, with one more yoke of cows to be added. John, traveling in the train that was led by Jacob Gates, had 1,400 miles ahead of him. On the 1st and 2nd of June, the Wheelock and Gates companies were the first to move out.

John conveyed to his parents that:

We proceeded through the state of Iowa, a distance of 350 miles with an ox train to Kanesville [Council Bluffs] occupying some four weeks, an experience, that shall never be forgotten, some of the most pious of saints got through with the religious business of their lives and dropped off on the road—-not seeing the necessity of traveling such a hard road to heaven. They were generally disagreeable, dishonest men whose firmness and grit had no foundation—-some were English and some Welsh, but honor to the character of my country, no Scotch. They were bent to see the end if there was any end.

After arriving on the banks of the Missouri River, July 2, 1853, Jacob Gates' company was supplied with provisions for the plains. The river was overflowing, and several days were spent waiting for the water to recede. Finally, on the 8th of July, Haight sent Captain Gates' company to Brown's Ferry for their crossing. John, no doubt, earned his keep by herding cattle and in various other ways. His letter gives a glimpse of his labors:

> Encamped with 136 wagons and about 150 head of oxen and cows on the banks of the Missouri opposite Omaha. Twenty years ago was quite different to what it is today. We were three weeks crossing the river on a flat boat of our own construction, landing where Omaha now stands. It was a labor of great magnitude, and your oldest son played a prominent part, being young, strong, and healthy and a good swimmer, my part of the labor was in much demand and no doubt I was imposed upon. This 3 weeks will be demanded on my old age to the extent of 2 years.

The labor John was called upon to endure was a service to the Lord and to these people while John helped them cross the challenging Missouri River. John was prepared; his father had taught him well. He carried women and children on his back while swimming the breadth of the river. He helped tow the rafts, loaded with wagons, by swimming with the attached ropes to the other side where men took hold to finish the task.

Conditions, while waiting and crossing the river during the rainy season, were just right for hatching hoards of mosquitoes that plagued the Saints and horse flies that bit the horses unmercifully.

While crossing the northern plains, the pioneers saw Indians of the Sioux Nation and the Pawnee near the Platte River in Nebraska. Peace was kept by giving the Indians bread, sugar, and coffee, which cut some of the companies short of food. Isaac C. Haight had supplied the wagons the best he could with the money he had. He was concerned the companies were not outfitted the way he wanted them to be, but he was able to secure the number of cattle he had planned on.

Haight passed the Gates company on August 4, not realizing the company was becoming low on supplies. Late in August, when the Gates train reached the Green River, John was sent in company of Richard Waddington of London, England, and an old lame horse on foot from Green River to Salt Lake City, distance 175 miles, to inform Pres. B. Young that the company was out of provisions. [They] started from Green River at 8 o'clock in the morning and arrived in Salt Lake City the 3rd day out at about 4 o'clock in the afternoon, tired and worn out, having traveled night and day with only intervals of rest of 2 or 3 hours at a time.

The wayfaring men arrived in Salt Lake City tired and hungry. After some food had been rustled up for them, and while John was sitting up for his first meal served at a Mormon table, he found himself unaccustomed to the Saints' style of serving food. When the squash was passed to him, he quite naturally placed the whole dish on his plate. He became embarrassed when everybody laughed at him, and he left the table hungry. The same thing happened at the breakfast table when they passed the bowl of mush. John had never been served family style in his whole life.[3]

Brigham Young

In John's letter to his parents, reflecting back to crossing the plains and analyzing his feelings about the Mormon people and the Church, he wrote:

> The subsequent trip to S. L. City over rivers and mountains during 11 weeks was one to me of hard service and will also be required of me in my last days. . . .
>
> Arriving at my destination on the 23rd of Sept. 1853, without friends or acquaintances, no money in pocket, and extreme youth, and disdaining to beg, I began to feel the dependence of my situation, but nothing daunted my courage. I had come here for a purpose, & to pursue that was my firm determination. I had come to a desert country, whose few inhabitants were wrestling & battling under all the circumstances attending the settlement of a new Country 1,000 miles from the confines of civilization, and such a country; there was a great lack of the necessaries & comforts of life. Everybody was poor & in no condition to help the stranger who came into their midst.
>
> Under these circumstances, I entered S. L. City, but I found friends who were strangers to me, who fed me & gave me shelter, who had love & commiseration for their co-religionists & in this I could see & feel the practical form of a religion that fed the hungry and clothed the naked. I began to understand that Mormonism was practical and material and that

long and exhaustive sermons on the God-head & on our future prospects were secondary to the object of building up a society here on earth wherein men could enjoy a little of that heaven that was always taught us to be beyond time and beyond space, ever ahead of us & never arriving there. I believe that if ever I enter heaven it will be one of my own make.

In Salt Lake City, the place for a temple had been designated by Brigham Young. When John arrived in the valley, a red sandstone wall, to be ten feet high surrounding the temple block, was underway. At Little Cottonwood, a few miles away, huge granite stones, found in the mouth of the canyon, were being chiseled into corner stones in preparation for building the temple. John's skill as a blacksmith provided him with temporary employment sharpening the wedges and chisels used by the workers.

Having worked at his trade for what he considered a fair wage--produce of the farms, he wrote in his letter to Scotland,

With varied success I was enabled to keep my head above water. . . . Work became scarce & I became idle and scorning to eat what I could not pay for, I resolved to find work on some part of God's footstool.[4]

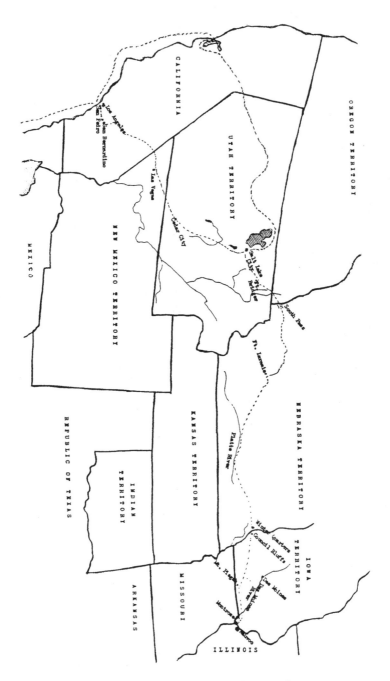

Route traveled by John Urie in America.

Map used by compliments of Eldred A. Johnson, a descendant of John Chapman and Teresa Ann Ferrell Urie Duncan, was compiled and drawn by him. Roads and highways sketched are modern.

CHAPTER 3

John's First Sweetheart

From Salt Lake City, John found work as a blacksmith with a wagon train heading north on the Humboldt trail to California. When he arrived in Sacramento on July 7, 1854, John had $40 in his pocket—-earned the hard way by shoeing horses and oxen and repairing wagon wheels. Admitting, in his letter to his parents, ". . . . this journey was a hard one, as indeed all such journeys at that time were for this character."

Finding Sacramento, California, to be a small place, John spent only a few days searching for work before making his way into the gold mines, where he worked for three or four months earning $350.

While entertaining the idea of going back to Scotland, in John's letter—-confessing his thoughts of returning home—-he concluded that, "The idea of being baffled in my pet idea of religious principles & of you my parents, & also my acquaintances having the laugh on me, turned my course toward Salt Lake City. I took shipping to San Pedro,[1] 450 miles down the coast and thence to San Bernardino, a distance of 90 miles, on foot with my budget on my back.

San Bernardino, hot and dry, was on the southern route to Deseret, which became Utah. In preparation for crossing the desert, John, while working for his board, stayed three weeks. John wrote his parents that he

bought 3 horses (2 to ride and 1 to pack) and for the first time in my life bestrode a horse, and by the bye, it was only half tamed, on a journey of 800 miles to S. L. City. You may guess my feelings, but my hopes and firm resolve bore me up under all circumstances, for 500 miles of more wretched country is not under the sun.

The forlorn, young greenhorn was desperate when his supply of food ran out. The barren desert offered little—-he was driven to eating mice.[2] At the end of thirteen days, saddle sore and weary, John arrived in Cedar City, the first settlement on the route to Salt Lake City. Continuing on with his letter, he wrote:

Met an acquaintance & resolved to push my fortune in this place.

I was hardly 20 years of age when I arrived here, in the 2 years I had passed in traveling nearly 20,000 miles, 4,000 of which was traveled by oxen and wagon and horse back. It was a great school of experience to me and has been very profitable to me since.

My experience in this place for the following eight years was extraordinary hard, often without food for 3 or 4 days at a time, at one time 4 months without bread of any kind, living on roots & weeds of different kinds. This was in consequence of the grasshoppers, bad harvests, & etc.

While contemplating going on to Salt Lake City, John was overjoyed to find an old friend in this God-forsaken place. Isaac C. Haight, who had befriended him in Keokuk, Iowa, welcomed him. Haight was now mayor of the settlement and stake president of the Iron Mission. He knew John Urie was a blacksmith and could be an asset for the cause of the *Iron Mission* in the production of iron. It didn't take much encouragement for John to decide this was where he wanted to push his small fortune.

Trees on the surrounding red clay hills and mountains were showing signs of autumn. Cedar City was in a state of commotion and poverty. The new settlement was an isolated outpost in the southern territory of Deseret. The grasshoppers had devastated the crops. The old fort, where the townspeople had finally settled, was being abandoned for a new site, designated by Brigham Young, one mile away. An influx of emigrants was arriving from the old country, furthering the hardship of the community.

Philip Klingensmith

The past September, through the Perpetual Emigration Fund, 111 Danish and Welsh emigrants were brought from Salt Lake Valley to Cedar City by Bishop Philip Klingensmith[3] and others. Klingensmith, as a representative in Iron County for the P. E. Fund, was responsible for taking care of the business and communication for bringing Saints from Europe, who were without means to finance a voyage across the ocean and plains.

It didn't take John long to find worthwhile work. The settlers of Cedar City weren't prepared with adequate implements to till their land, but John knew how to help them. He went to work making plow shares[4] from worn-out scraps of wagon tires and any other wagon iron he could find.

John enjoyed untapped talent when he became involved with the drama association that had been formed that year, 1854. The members were a lively and enthusiastic bunch, and they talked young and fairly handsome John into playing Wandering Steiny in *Forty Nights in a Bar Room*.

"The first plays were produced in the old adobe schoolhouse in the northeast corner of the Old Fort. The first scenery was designed by Wardman Holmes and painted by James Whittaker and John Chatterly." And the "first plays were brought from England by John Chatterly."[5]

Business of the territory was being taken care of in the mother colony by Brigham Young. He had been governor of the territory since his appointment in 1851 and was now seeking reappointment. A petition was sent in his behalf on December 30, 1854, to President Franklin Pierce of the United States. It was only a matter of days before Pierce declined the reappointment of Brigham Young as governor and appointed Colonel Steptoe. This appointment didn't last long, and Brigham Young maintained his power and influence in the territory.

When John became settled in the town and it became evident he was a worthy member of the Church, he received the Aaronic priesthood. On April 20, 1855, John was ordained a deacon by Bishop Philip Klingensmith.

During May of 1855, Brigham Young and other dignitaries visited Cedar City, where they delivered sermons of good will and gospel principles. As always, a visit from the heads of the Church to the Saints of this struggling settlement brought an intangible strength and spirituality that encouraged them to survive.

Success with the Iron Works became a reality, and during the fall of 1855, a number of castings of various descriptions came from their furnaces—-the most exciting of which was the new town bell that was attributed to Bishop Klingensmith for his skill in formulas and molds.[6]

When John started courting and getting ideas about marriage, he built a two-room adobe house on 83 North 100 West Street. Then, just before his twenty-first birthday, on April 5, 1856, John took Elizabeth Hutcheson[7] as his bride. She was very young, but they were sweethearts and they made a happy home together.

A typical home for the time period. This first home in Iron County was built by George Wood. It has been restored and is displayed at the Iron Mission State Park in Cedar City.

The following spring, while Elizabeth was expecting their first child, she found herself tippee-toeing on the stone threshold of their home—-waving a reluctant goodby. John was almost out of sight—-he threw her a last kiss—-while turning his team and wagon northward. He knew the trip to Salt Lake City for household and shop supplies would be lonely without his Elizabeth.[8]

Had he known the trouble she was in, he never would have left her. Upon his return to town, he was met by the doctor. Right away John knew something was wrong. Elizabeth had gone into labor early. While she was giving birth, on the sixteenth day of March, both she and their baby died. They had been buried for several days by the time he returned to Cedar City.

John fought back the tears. His chest tightened. Finally he stormed at the doctor, "Why is it ye could not save my lassie?" The doctor could see that John was blind with grief. Trying to be gentle, he answered, "I did all that I could. From her sick bed she cried for you." With this added torment John couldn't hold back his tears any longer.

The days that followed were useless. His Elizabeth was not there for him to come home to—-no baby to hold. All thoughts of his sweetheart became prisoners in his sad heart.

CHAPTER 4

Vengeance Was Theirs

In May of 1857, news of the death of the esteemed Apostle Parley P. Pratt[1] spread among the Saints. In Arkansas, difficulties over a woman and her children brought about his demise.[2] He was fired upon six times without a ball hitting him. McLean, his assailant, "then stabbed him twice with a bowie-knife under the left arm, whereupon Parley dropped from his horse, and the assassin, after thrusting his knife deeper into the wounds, seized a derringer belonging to one of his accomplices, and shot him through the breast."[3]

The following July, while the Saints were still lamenting over the loss and brutality of Pratt's death, they were thrown into another turmoil. The whole territory of Deseret was in an uproar. News had come down from the mother colony that in the East the government had refused to release the mail[4] for Utah—-a new governor, Alfred Cummings, had been appointed to the territory, and a United States army was making way for his safe arrival in the Valley. Brigham Young jumped on a bandwagon with speeches filled with determination that the army would not enter the territory.

John had missed all the upheaval of the expulsion of the Saints from Nauvoo and the very early settlement of Deseret, but he was well aware of what was happening. This new threat meant the Saints may have to leave their homes one more time. But, this time, the houses would be burned to the ground before they would be left to their enemies.

The local Nauvoo Legion in Cedar City fortified their numbers and made some revisions. John had been elected as a lieutenant in Company G, 3rd Battalion, in the 10th Regiment, on June 6, 1857; and now, on July 28, 1857, he was elected adjutant of the same company, battalion, and regiment. He wouldn't be carrying a gun, but he would be in the throes of it all.

Rumors began to fly; and after George A. Smith, general commander of the militia, had been down to the southern settlements, the fear and excitement of the Saints grew into hysteria. The militia had been made ready for war, and bullets were being made.

Word came by Indian runners that a large wagon train,[5] traveling from the area where the Saints had all their trouble in the East, was on its way through the settlements. More rumors flew, and the Saints felt they were being invaded by a hostile enemy who would, if they could get through to California, bring an army from the south to destroy them.

Among the marksmen from Arkansas, who originated from Tennessee, was a bunch of young, rough-acting wranglers,[6] who joined the train in Salt Lake

City. They were drinking loudmouths from Missouri, who made remarks about "Joe" Smith. It was all "Jack" Baker,[7] who was in command of the cattle, could do to keep them in line.

This wagon train wasn't any different than any other passing through to California. If they wanted a cow, pig, or chicken from one of the little settlements, they just took it.[8] It was a futile effort to keep a trail-driven herd of cattle out of the inviting fields of corn—-whether they belonged to a Mormon or a Gentile.[9]

After attempting to buy supplies at Cedar City, the Fancher[10] and Baker wagon train traveled on, south and west, for another forty miles to the Mountain Meadows. The deep and lush grass on the meadows and a cool mountain spring entertained the weary travelers with rest in preparation for their journey over the desert.[11] The rough bunch from Missouri, figuring they were safely through the Indian country, left the wagon train and pushed on to California.

During the interim of all that was taking place, at Cedar City, a council was held; and it was proposed that the wagon train should be destroyed. It was the Indians, who by now had become the Mormon's allies, that should do the act. Ironically, the men they most wanted to do away with would not collect their dues.[12]

In the beginning, on September 7, 1857, the white men who were on the meadows as Indian agents and interpreters painted their faces and dressed as Indians. This way, they thought, the emigrants wouldn't know any white men were involved. From behind sage-brush on the surrounding hills, the siege began. Right away seven of the emigrants were wounded—-some died before the train could get its wagons circled. Their cattle were scattered here and there. It was an ugly scene with children crying and women screaming.[13]

The Indians were enraged when three of their number were shot. They feared they couldn't uproot the encampment. It hadn't been planned for white men to be further involved. Begging for the Indians to stop was of no use. But threats to the lives of the white men did bring about the call for a militia from the surrounding settlements.

After the militia arrived, a prayer circle was held. It was manifest unto the men that they were justified in taking the lives of these heathens—-now was the time to avenge the blood of their beloved prophet, Joseph Smith, by cutting their throats. After all, some of the men from Missouri were in the mob who killed their prophet—-the ones from Arkansas may have been connected with the death of Parley P. Pratt. The babies and children under the age of eight would be the only ones saved—-they were not accountable, in the eyes of the Lord, for the sins wrought against the Saints in the East.

Several days passed—-without much success. On the 11th of September, a plan was made to talk the victims into the open. Under the guise of a white flag that was precipitated by promises of safety, the emigrants gave up their arms—-believing they were being led into safety by the militia and relieved that they would be safe from the Indians.

After much whooping, hollering, shooting, cutting of throats, and bashing of heads, the deed was finally completed. Over 120 men, women, children, and babies were slain.[14]

In the dark of night, the sorry lot of children whose lives were spared were gathered into a wagon.[15] Babies were crying for their mamas. The children were taken first to a cabin on the meadows that belonged to Jacob Hamblin. His wife, Rachel, took care of the wounded. Just before daybreak, Bishop Klingensmith took the hovering orphans to Sister Hopkins' place in Cedar City. Mormons came. Some traveled long distances to fetch a child to become their own.

John was on the meadows to help round up the cattle, horses, and mules that belonged to the wagon train. He, among others, helped corral the livestock at Iron Springs, seven miles west of Cedar City, where fifty of the cattle were seared with the unmistakable Church cross.

The feelings young John kept pent up within himself were wrenching and haunting. His disturbed mind kept remembering the sight of slaughtered bodies lying strewn on the bloody ground. Some of the lassies had fallen with their wee-un's clutched in their arms—-a sting he could hardly bear.

It was after the deed was done and time had passed, while John was looking for stray cattle, that the stench in the air permeated his nostrils. The shallow graves had not protected the naked bodies from the sun and wolves.

The horrifying sight twisted his heart—-his soul cried from within. "Why?" Pulling himself from the scene—-finding little comfort in knowing that he was not involved in their demise—-he went about his duty.

Many Indians, while licking their wounds and wondering what to do, loitered on the outskirts of Cedar City. Wagon loads of trappings from the destroyed wagon train were brought to the Bishop's Tithing Office. Several confiscated wagons were pulled into the shade of the building. The Indians had a few things; but, for the most part, the spoils were auctioned off.

A drover, Hugo Hickman, who was passing through Cedar City on January 16, 1858, had observed "poverty and rags" a year earlier. He "was greatly supprised to see the people so well dressed, In States Jeans, Silks and Satins . . . rich in clothing, cattle, wagons, julery and money was plenty with some." His friend, Sam Dukes,[16] told him that "all the property and clothing" he saw "knocking around came from the Mountain Meddows."

Dukes took Hickman to his house and showed him "a pretty little girl standing at the window who had been saved from the Massacre, Presently the Child uttered an exclamation of horrer. 'There, There, she said is the man who killed my mother.'" The only man who could be seen on the street was Isaac C. Haight. When Hickman asked the little child where she was when he killed her mother, she replied, "I was runing by her side clinging to her dress, she had the baby in her arms, he shot her with a pistol."[17]

The story about the child soon circulated through town. When the secret of her disappearance[18] finally surfaced, John's heart was wrenched—-again.

Johnston's army from the United States was on its way,[19] and all kinds of trouble was stirring in the Valley of the Mountains. The news of the massacre had hit California papers and was causing trouble for the Saints in San Bernardino. For their safety and protection, Brigham Young sent men with teams and wagons to help bring them out of California.

For the men involved in the massacre, Brigham Young had all kinds of missions and places to hide them. Some were sent to mine ore for making bullets and to find new locations for settlements. Some of the wagons from the Meadows were sent with them and had to have special care because of the dry climate of the desert. With wise instructions from Brigham Young, the wagons made in the humid climate of the Ozarks were housed at night over streams of water.

Cedar City and other communities that knew what took place on the Meadows fell into silence—-knowing the participants at Mountain Meadows had gone too far. Believing they had the right to pursue freedom of religion and the right to protect their families didn't fall in the realm of taking the lives of women and children. Broken hearted, some families left. Among the broken spirited were those who left the Church.[20]

Without mentioning the shameful Mountain Meadows Massacre in his letter to his parents, John commented:

My 20 years passed and gone has been varied in the ups and downs of life, were I particular in detail many interesting things (to Me) could be related. In the midst of all I have kept myself untainted and unspotted from the crime and degradation of the morally and physically corrupt.[21]

CHAPTER 5

They Had no Shoes

It was winter, and the youthfulness of John kept him busy in Cedar City working at his trade. On Christmas day, a wagon load of Saints from San Bernardino arrived in town. In the excitement of their arrival, John left his forge, with his blacksmith apron still tied about his waist, and helped one of the sisters down from a wagon. His troubled heart was filled with compassion for this bedraggled woman who had traveled over the same intimidating desert that tried to claim his life.

Sarah Ann,[1] with her five children, had been detained in San Bernardino for eighteen months after arriving from Australia. She felt an attraction for John as she was lifted from the wagon and decided to make her home in Cedar City. Her husband, John Heyborne, who was the father of her four oldest children, died in 1852; and she had left her estranged second husband, John Farrell, in Australia.

With mutual love and understanding of the gospel, John and Sarah Ann's courtship was like a whirlwind. In John's letter to his parents, with thanksgiving in his heart, he declared that "in 1858, Jan. 16th I was married to my present wife, and that shall ever be remembered by me as one that began my days of prosperity."

Even though John's lonely life was filled with a woman to love and the laughter of children, his monetary prosperity didn't materialize very soon. The newlyweds lived in the two-room adobe home John built for Elizabeth, where they had but little to get along on. John's scant clothing was worn; and he, along with others in town, was without shoes. John went to work and meetings without shoes. He couldn't even provide shoes for his new family.

Sarah Ann swept away the tormenting thoughts of Elizabeth that taunted John's memory. She filled his life with the needs of a man—giving him a feeling of contentment by sharing her love. John responded with tenderness and adoration—doing all that he could to please her.

John's position as patriarch of his ready-made family wasn't always smooth and easy—Sarah Ann was eight and a half years his senior. At times, while the children were working in the blacksmith shop with John, his Scotch temperament got the best of him. Also, Sarah Ann's Irish ire was sorely tempted, but she knew it was best to keep peace; and her winning disposition usually saved the day.

When word got around that Sarah Ann was a midwife and nurse, Bishop Klingensmith seized the opportunity to give her the calling as minister of the sick and afflicted within his ward. When babies were born, Sarah Ann showed up, as always, wearing "a dainty white clean apron and a spotless white collar"[2] over her dress.

During 1858, Sarah Ann became stout—-as John called it. In November, the blessed day arrived, and their first born turned out to be twins. David was born before midnight on the 3rd, and George was born after midnight on the 4th. Keeping the babies dry with four diapers that were meant for one baby was a difficult assignment. The babies' two half sisters, Teresa Ann and Agnes Eliza, who was known as "Tillie," were kept busy washing, drying, and changing diapers—-all the time.

There wasn't much chance, with the scarcity of material in the settlement, of making more diapers. Most of the families in Cedar City had one need or another, but they were using their own ingenuity and talents to make life better. Out of necessity, the industrious settlers turned their attention to home manufacture to fill their needs.

More sheep were brought in, and new lambs were born—-increasing the herders' flocks. Very few spinning wheels were in the settlement, but before long, the men learned to use iron from their furnaces to make looms, spinning machines, and carders. The talented women spun yarn from the shorn wool of the flocks and busily wove their own cloth.

Finally, the "Cotton Mission," from the southern settlements, provided the welcome cotton for homespun calico. Dying their yarns became an art as they learned from the Indians which wild flower and brush blossoms to gather for blending their hues.

In time, "tanneries, shoe shops, furniture, the making of combs, threshing machines, blacksmith wagon makers, nail machinery," and other things, according to John, were "all made here, and by as good mechanics as is to be found anywhere in the world."[3]

However, by the mid 1860s, the Iron Works was soon to fail—-it finally came to a complete standstill. All the efforts to supply the demands for machinery, with the partial success of making iron, gave way to imports.

John, who held fast to the dream of success, felt prompted to record in his journal that:

> Iron County, with the vast coal fields and an inexhaustible amount of the best iron ore in the world, is destined in the near future to be a vast business center. It needs but the magic touch of money, railroads, and business tact to develop the huge mountains of coal and iron that are here—-a deposition of the rim of the Great American Basin.[4]

Brigham Young was no longer the governor of the territory—-having been replaced by Alfred Cumming. The threat of war finally subsided, and Johnston's army was encamped south and west of Salt Lake City at Camp Floyd. Back in the states, the government was still concerned about polygamy and was set on finding the Mormons who participated in the Mountain Meadows Massacre. It was a familiar sight to see soldiers parading Cedar City in their pursuit.

Ward business became difficult with Bishop Klingensmith out of town so much of the time. Brigham Young was still president of the Church and helped keep Klingensmith out of reach of the law by sending him on mining and settlement explorations.

Because Bishop Klingensmith[5] was a participant in the Mountain Meadows Massacre, he had to keep a constant look over his shoulder. Having three wives kept the bishop busy juggling them from place to place; but, for the most part, at least two wives remained in Cedar City. Sometimes, two of his families could be found living together under the name of Smith.

John became a close friend with the bishop, whose wives kindled a friendship with Sarah Ann. The English, Swiss, Irish, German, and Scotch backgrounds of the women brought together an interesting mix of dialects and ways learned in their native lands.

Children of the Urie and Klingensmith families were playmates. Pleasurable times were spent playing with marbles made from baked clay, using slingshots fashioned with strips of rawhide, and playing cowboys with their horses, made from a limb with a few leaves on the end that swept the ground as the children galloped along. The tomboys sometimes had a rag doll; their arms were their cradles.

With only one wife, John didn't have to worry about hiding out. He was kept busy taking care of the combined family he already had. His posterity increased when on December 20, 1860, Sarah Jane was born. John now had eight children, and he was only twenty-five years old.

Work began to pick up, and John wasn't confined to his blacksmith shop. On March 4, 1862, during the excitement of the inauguration of Abraham Lincoln as president of the United States, John D. Lee engaged John to go to Washington County to work on mill irons for Lee's new mill. John worked for $3 a day and his board. On completion of his work, John delivered the irons to Harmony where he helped Lee with the mill. John was rewarded with a "Large splendid cow & calf in payment for 2 days' work,"[6] which proved to be a boon to his family.

Later that year, Sarah Ann became stout again, and milk from the cow was needed for their growing family. Christmas passed and the first of the year rolled around. Sarah Ann was right in assuming she was carrying more twins. Thomas, who was named after his uncle, and Agnes Main, who was named after her Grandmother Urie, were born January 19, 1863.

With ten children and his stock increasing, John decided to move his family to a farm. He put in crops and planned for a rosy future, but the grasshoppers continued their plague and almost wiped him out. John carried on in his faith; and, with the help of his family, he did the best he could to get along.

That same year, the 24th of July was celebrated with the whole town attending a sunrise ceremony. They gathered around the flagpole where the firing of the legion's musketry resounded, and they all thrilled at the sound of the band playing patriotic music.

The morning warmed up, and by 8:00 a.m., the grasshoppers were so bad that during the "parade, the girls muslin dresses were eaten off all around the waist." When they "got in the meetinghouse everybody was laughing and killing grasshoppers, making so much noise the program could hardly be heard."[7] Some of the Urie girls marched in the parade and were among the girls who picked up their dresses and ran home. They didn't see any humor in their predicament.

The following year, 1863, John was surprised to receive a letter from his father announcing plans to visit America. His mother was coming, too. This news gave John mixed emotions, and he worried

Agnes Main

about going to Salt Lake City to visit with them. John hadn't heard from them and didn't know what to expect. Upon John's arrival, it didn't take long for all hell to tear loose. His father, having seen the desolate surroundings they were living in and not seeing the beauty of the mountains, couldn't understand why John belonged to this strange church that brought him to such a place. In trying to make amends for his outburst, John's father offered him a good home anywhere in America, of his own choosing, if he would leave Utah and the Mormon Church.

The offer was useless. John's faith was too deep to give up for material things. George Urie stormed from John's presence; reminding his son that he was disinherited. The sputtering and pleading of John's mother was of no use. The Uries returned to Scotland without any further adieus.[8]

John watched for a letter from his father—-with no avail. One never arrived. The disappointment was eased once in awhile with a short letter from his mother and a small sum of money—-always with a mention that his father was very busy.

One year passed and just before Christmas, on December 11, 1864, the Urie home was blessed with another daughter, Eliza Ann.

George Urie

The household was busier than ever, and Christmas day was filled with a bustle of activity. Holiday or not, the chores still had to be done. They had lots of help. Sarah Ann's oldest boy, Robert Heyborne, was twenty-one; Tillie

Heyborne was nineteen; Charles Heyborne was sixteen; John James Heyborne was fourteen; and Teresa Ann Farrell, whom John adopted, was ten.

Every Sunday, the Urie family observed the day of the Sabbath--it was never taken lightly by a full-blooded Scotsman. The procession was imposing as the whole family filed into sacrament meeting. The oldest children carried the little ones as they took their places—-with the women, babies, and girls seated on one side of the meeting house and the men and boys sitting on the other. This well-behaved family was ruled by the keen eyes of their parents.

One Sunday after meeting, when John heard a young boy whistling, his Protestant upbringing surfaced. He walked up behind the boy and "with an angry Scottish brogue said, 'Lad, Lad, do ya know wot ye'r about whistlin' upon the day o' the Lord?'" The boy asked, "What's wrong with that?" And John replied, "Why Lad, d'ye know 'tis sinful to desecrate the Sabbath Day we' a loud noise. . . . Whistlin' upon the Day o' the Lord indeed. Wot'll it be next?"[9]

ELDER'S CERTIFICATE.

To all Persons to whom this Letter shall Come:---

THIS CERTIFIES that the bearer, Elder _John Elvie,_ is in full faith and fellowship with the CHURCH OF JESUS CHRIST OF LATTER DAY SAINTS, and by the General Authorities of said Church, has been duly appointed a MISSION to _Europe_ to PREACH THE GOSPEL, and administer in all the ordinances thereof pertaining to his office.

And we invite all men to give heed to his teachings, and counsels as a man of GOD, sent to open to them the door of life and salvation—and assist him in his travels, in whatsoever things he may need.

And we pray GOD the ETERNAL FATHER to bless Elder _Elvie_ and all who receive him, and minister to his comfort, with the blessings of heaven and earth, for time and for all eternity, in the name of JESUS CHRIST: Amen.

Signed at Great Salt Lake City, TERRITORY OF UTAH, _April 17th,_ 18_66_, in behalf of said Church.

Brigham Young
Heber C. Kimball } FIRST PRESIDENCY.
Daniel H. Wells

CHAPTER 6

Called on a Mission

John was twenty-nine years old; and even though he had a large family, it was time for him to start preparing for an LDS mission. Earlier, in 1857, he had been advanced in the priesthood to an elder and was worthy for a call. Men both younger and older than he had gone before him. John's emotions were torn. Their youngest child was only a baby, and John didn't want to leave Sarah Ann with so much responsibility. He knew her children were good help, but there were a lot of mouths to feed.

Finally, in 1866, after two years of waiting, the bishop came to John and told him to be ready by April conference. Arrangements were made so Sarah Ann could go to Salt Lake City with him, and John made sure she had a way back home.

During conference on Saturday, April 7, 1866, John Urie's name, along with twenty-one others, was presented, read, and sustained by George Q. Cannon as missionaries to serve in Europe. During conference, this quote from Brigham Young, as written in a letter to his son, was read: "They will go down with the teams which go after the poor."

John was assigned to be president of the Edinburgh Conference,[1] which was located in the North London Branch of the LDS Church and was within the Jewish quarters of England. It was the largest district and carried a lot of responsibility.

Endowment House

The wagons carrying the missionaries were supplied and ready for the southern route to San Pedro, California, where the teamsters were to pick up the Saints arriving from abroad. Everybody knew by now that when Brigham Young referred to the poor, he meant the Saints brought to America by the Church through the Perpetual Emigration Fund.

Before Sarah Ann bid John goodbye, they went together to the LDS Endowment House on Temple Square where she received her own endowments. John's farewell was difficult, but he looked forward to going back to his homeland. While longing to visit his parents, John wondered if his father's animosity toward him had softened to the degree that he would be allowed over the threshold of his father's home. John knew he was disinherited because his father said so, and it was Church customs that governed such things.

The missionaries embarked from San Pedro and sailed on the Pacific Ocean down the coast of California and Mexico to Central America. In the province of Colombia, the travelers enjoyed the forty-seven-mile trip across the Isthmus of Panama by traveling over green, tropical hills on a train[2] to the seaport of Colon. Settled on board ship, John was once again on the Atlantic Ocean, but this time he was going home.

James Urie

John was overwhelmed when his parents welcomed him with open arms. His brothers, Thomas and George, were married, and James was thinking about marriage. His brother David, who was only three years old when John left Glasgow, had been buried at Cathcart for four years. David was almost twelve years old when he took sick.

While Sarah Ann was in charge of the family back home, her sixteen-year-old son, John, was accidentally killed when he and his friend were playing with firearms. Being one of the first to reach him, Sarah Ann held "Johnnie," as she called him, in her arms and helped carry him home. Sarah Ann was so overcome with grief that she fainted. The weather was unbearably hot on July 24, 1866, and without ice to pack Johnnie in, it was decided to bury him before sundown. When Sarah Ann awoke and found out her son had been buried, she fainted again.

When John left for his mission, he believed Sarah Ann would be taken care of with gains from letting out their farm. Things didn't work out the way he planned—-smutty wheat was all Sarah Ann ever received. She made do with the wheat and boiled lucerne for their greens. She saved all the grease she could for making soap and went without for cooking.[3]

Sarah Ann's oldest son, Robert Heyborne, wasn't in the home any longer. He had been married to Margaret Bladen, since March 14, 1865, and was away part of the time helping bring Saints up from San Pedro. Tillie, whom Sarah Ann depended on around the house, married John M. Macfarlane during the fall, on October 9, 1866. Charles, the youngest Heyborne son, was away part of the time while driving a "six-mule team to Laramie, Wyoming to assist emigrants to Utah."[4]

After a year of service in England, on 4 March 1867—-taking the same route he left by—-John was returning to his home in America. Thoughts of seeing Sarah Ann encompassed his thoughts. Her letters were encouraging, but he knew she was having a hard time. Looking into her dancing blue eyes would erase all the loneliness and worry that was weighing on his heart.

At last, John was home; and his family was gathered about him. Some of the sting of their hardship was diminished when they saw the large wooden box[5] their father brought home from Scotland. Grandmother and Grandfather Urie had filled it with lots of wonderful things, including the fruit cakes John's family had heard so much talk about.

Jessie Tweedle

The private passion of John and Sarah Ann's union, which had thrown all precaution to the wind, brought the blessing of a sweet baby girl—-nine months later. She filled their home with the joy of Christmas on December 21, 1867. And she was called Jessie—-after her great-aunt from Scotland.

In the meantime, back in Scotland, on February 19, 1867, after John had left his mission, his brother James was baptized into the LDS Church. This was good news for John—-he felt his mission brought some good that was close to home.

James found himself a Mormon girl, Violet Swan; and they were married June 1, 1868. On the 4th of June, they sailed to America on the ship *John Bright*. James, then only twenty years old, was registered on the ship's log as a blacksmith journeyman. All of John's efforts and persuasion brought his brother close to him in Southern Utah. James and Violet settled in Beaver.

Sarah Ann was grateful to have her husband home taking charge again. Her kind and spiritual disposition had pulled her through.

It was good for John to be able to take over his farm and rally his family around him to get the crops in. John D. Lee had a broken plow, and others in town had work for John Urie to do at his forge.

When July rolled around, John was back to helping with the annual celebrations and sending news articles to the *Deseret News*. His report, written on July 5, 1869, appeared in the *Deseret Evening News* on July 14, 1869:

John Urie Esq, writing to the *Deseret News* under this date says that the national birthday was celebrated in Cedar City with great exalt in spite of the fact that the thermometer stood at 99 degrees in the shade. He adds: "We pride ourselves on having one of the prettiest settlements in the mountains. Room can be had here for a hundred more families; our facilities are excellent and inexhaustible; we feel the need of more help. Our indefatigable bishop is alive to his duties; the poor are not forgotten; our co-operative store had accomplished wonders; our sheep are in excellent condition and are managed by co-operation; other branches of industry will shortly come under this head.

John Chapman Duncan
& Teresa Ann Urie

The following new year was ushered in; and on the sixteenth day of 1870, the Urie family was blessed with a baby boy. The name John, which went on the records of the Church for him to be known by, was in memory of the son Sarah Ann lost and in honor of her husband. It seemed necessary to refer to the new baby as "Jack," to avoid confusion as to which John was who.

That same year, the exciting news came from James, John's brother, that he and Violet's firstborn was a son, whom they named George Lovett Urie.

The five children Sarah Ann brought with her from Australia were growing up fast. Her son, Robert, and his wife Maggie, had two daughters, whom she enjoyed immensely. On October 30, 1871, Sarah Ann's son, Charles, was betrothed and married to Mary Ann Leigh in the Endowment House in Salt Lake City. In 1872, on May 27, John Chapman Duncan married nineteen-year-old Teresa Ann F. Urie, and two days later he took her to Salt Lake City where they were married in the Endowment House by Daniel H. Wells. Teresa Ann was the last of Sarah Ann's children by Heyborne and Farrel to be married.

L to R back row: Agnes Eliza Heyborne; Teresa Ann Farrell.
Charles Heyborne; Sarah Ann McMillan Heyborne Farrell; Robert Heyborne.

And now, in 1873, with John's reflection of the twenty years spent since he left his home in Scotland, he expresses, in his letter to his parents, the wonderment of how times have changed:

[A]nd here I am with 8 boys and girls with their mother to look after them. My 20 years passed and gone has been varied in the ups and downs of life. . . . When I contrast the present with 20 years ago, what changes have taken place in the moral and scientific world, what changes in the government of nations, and will say that the habits and customs of men and women have changed wonderfully for the worse, in fact all things have changed, and I will ask, "Is it for the best?"

To look forward 20 years is a long time, to look behind, how short and how little done or accomplished.

John had accomplished much without realizing the depth, power, and breadth of understanding in the gospel that his posterity was yet to profit from his example and teachings.

The inheritance John felt he had been left out of, because he had chosen not to leave the Church, was dwarfed by the love and kindness of his parents. At this point in time, John wanted his parents to know of his gratitude for all they had given him in lieu of his inheritance:

The past 10 years of my life has been considerably smoothed by your kindness to me and mine—-a species of affection that is much more serviceable and also more appreciable than to be the recipient of the bequest when you have already gained a competence in the earlier years of your life.

Your loving son, John[6]

John Urie's First Family. L to R, back row: David & George (twins). Second row: Sarah Jane, Thomas, Agnes Main (twins). Front row: John Urie & Sarah Ann McMillan. John Jr. sitting on his father's lap, Jessie standing, & Eliza Ann.

CHAPTER 7

Best-kept Secret

Bishop Klingensmith hadn't been seen in Cedar for a while, but his children were still close associates of John's children. When the bishop's daughter, Priscilla, came to the Urie home, John, at times, found himself looking at her—wondering what she remembered about the horrible day her parents were killed. He knew there were whispers around town, but he hoped with all his heart that she didn't know what happened to her own parents.

Priscilla wasn't her real name. The unknown child was picked up from among the crying and terrified children found on the Mountain Meadows—-after her parents and siblings had been murdered before her very own eyes. It was September 11, 1857. Philip Klingensmith, as bishop of Cedar City, participated in the bloodshed and helped gather up the surviving babies and children. He cared for them the best he could under the terrible circumstances. It had been arranged for the motherly Sister Hopkins, who lived in town, to take care of the children until homes could be found for them.

Betsy Cattle

After delivering the children to the Hopkins home Bishop Klingensmith took particular notice of the golden-haired tyke. She was whimpering above the rest of the frightened and hungry orphans that were huddled together on the floor. His thoughts went to his wife Betsy, who he knew wanted another child desperately. His intention had been to take one infant for the Birkbecks but, now he was compelled to take this child, too.

When Philip arrived at home, where his wife, Betsy, resided, he saw horror and fear in her face. News about the massacre had preceded him. She was wiping away tears. "How could you?" she lamented. Before he could answer, the fussing of the children consumed her attention.

Philip explained to Betsy that he hoped she would nurse the baby boy for the Birkbecks until he was old enough to be weaned.

"What about the little girl?" she asked apprehensively.

"Well, I thought maybe you might keep her."

Betsy's whole countenance changed. Another child was what she dreamed of having. She had lost one baby two years earlier and was afraid she might lose Mary Alice, her only living child, who had been born in the spring of 1857. Then, while looking down at the toddler, who looked back at her with wide and pleading blue eyes, she knew this was a child she would never give up. Betsy held out her arms for her.

A sigh of fulfillment came over Philip. He could see that Betsy was anxious to keep the pitiful little thing and knew she should be kept in secret—-someday the authorities would be nosing around. It didn't take Philip long to hide Betsy in a secluded place near the Virgin River—-far away from prying eyes and probing questions that might reveal where her child came from.

Margaretha Elliker
Klingensmith

When Betsy was brought back from the Virgin, she went about her business as though she had given birth to both of her children. The Arkansan was raised believing she had been born in Cedar City and was the oldest child of the Klingensmiths. They told her stories about how she was born by the light of a burning pine knot "in the floorless room of a red adobe house heated by an open fireplace"[1] at the Old Fort.

She was given a new birthday—-March 20, 1855—-and was blessed with the name Priscilla. To further the proof of her birth, she was given a falsified patriarchal blessing.[2] Philip didn't think anybody would ever look into the Church and census records—-but he knew he couldn't do anything about that anyway.

While Priscilla was growing up in Cedar City, she noticed little differences in how she was treated by her mother and other grown-ups in town. At odd times, folks looked at her in a strange way—-when they thought she wasn't watching.

Sometimes, men came around looking for Priscilla's father. The Indians let the bishop know they were coming, and he took off to the mountains. When they questioned Priscilla's mother, Betsy, about Philip Klingensmith, she told them her last name was Smith. It was kind of confusing because Priscilla's father had three wives and several children. Sometimes, they shared a house with her father's third wife, Margaretha. To Priscilla, it seemed like her father's first wife, Hannah, and her kids were away most of the time.

Hannah was around when her twin boys, Philip and John Henry, were born on December

Hannah Creamer
Klingensmith

22, 1859. They were born just two days after Margaretha gave birth to Alfred, the first white boy born at the present site of Cedar City. Priscilla was young, but it was exciting to have all these babies born so close together.

When Priscilla was about six or seven years old, she had another full sister to claim. During the heat of the summer, on the 9th day of July 1859, Betsy Ann was born; and Priscilla adored her. She was beside her mother every moment trying to help take care of this new baby sister.

That same year, on the last day of July, while Priscilla was sitting in church, she heard lots of commotion and a long-winded talk given by someone named George A. Smith—-he was down from Salt Lake City. Her father gave a talk too—-he had tears running down his face. Philip said he wouldn't be around to take care of his church work and wasn't going to be bishop any longer.

Priscilla didn't understand why her father couldn't stay in town and be bishop. Other things were going on, too. About this time, she heard of her father's friend, Jacob Hamblin, and some officers who had been taking children away from several families and fetching them by wagon to Salt Lake City. The children never came back. When she learned later that they were sent to Arkansas, she joined the other children when they secretly made fun of the *hillbillies*.

George A. Smith

Priscilla's surviving brother, Christopher, and her sister, Tryphena Fancher, didn't see or hear about Priscilla while they were in Utah. Tryphena was too young to know her brother, but Christopher was old enough to recognize whom he believed to be Tryphena. John D. Lee took Christopher to one of his wives to care for and called him "Charlie." When the children were gathered up and returned to Arkansas, Christopher never realized he left a living sister behind.

The things Priscilla's father said in Sunday meeting were true. He wasn't around much anymore. He took "Aunt Hat," as Priscilla called her, and her kids to a new settlement named Rockville. It was lonely while he was away but good when he came home with molasses he had made and vegetables he had grown. The Indians always let Betsy know when Philip was on his way—-they liked to be there too—-to get their usual share.

The molasses and vegetables stopped coming after the big flood from the Virgin River in 1862. The home, blacksmith shop, cane mill, and every material thing that Philip had was washed away by the turbulent waters. It was hard on him when he had to start all over again—-that was when Philip relocated his family in Toquerville.

Priscilla's father had many narrow escapes with the law during this time and didn't come around for fear of being caught. Philip and his friend, John D. Lee, spent most of their time in the mountains that became known as Zion's Canyon.

Priscilla had a third sister to admire and help care for when Margaret Jane arrived. She was born in the spring of 1863, on March 5, just thirteen days before their father left on a mission to the Indians. Philip Klingensmith spoke the language of the Indians and went on several missions as an interpreter and explorer.

When Philip returned from his mission to his home in Toquerville, his feet were blistered and sore from walking so far. Most of their horses had been stolen, and they had traveled over the desert for several days at a time without water.

Philip Klingensmith was able to spend some time in Cedar City during the summer of 1863. Listening to her father's exciting and harrowing mission to the Indians in the Grand Canyon with Jacob Hamblin gave Priscilla goose bumps.

One of the breathtaking stories he told about the trip was of a trail so high on a plateau that the "stream running along its bottom appeared like a bright silver thread glittering in the sun"[3] light. The trail was on their route to the dwellings of the Moqui Indians. Some places on their descent to the floor of the canyon were too narrow to turn their pack animals and horses around on—-there was only vacant space on the outer edge of the winding trail.

Parowan, Iron, Utah, 1851-52

While on an exploration expedition in 1850, Isaac C. Haight wrote down these remarks upon leaving the Parowan Valley:

Preparing to start home tomorrow I shall leave this place with regrets. It is one of the most lovely places in the Great Basin. On the east, high towering mountains, covered evergreen forest and one of the most beautiful creeks running from them. On the west and south, a large valley of the most beautiful lands. Little Salt lake bordering the valley on the west and beyond a range of hills covered with eternal scenery. And while the clouds hang heavily on the mountains and the storms and tempests are raging, the valley enjoys a beautiful serenity.

The "Liberty Pole" was raised by Pratt January 8, 1850, in the Valley of the "Little Salt Lake."

Use of picture is by compliments of Simon K. Benson.

It was a long time after Philip left for Toquerville that Priscilla heard more stories told by her father. Friends who came by let the family know he had settled a ranch in Meadow Valley. It was quite a spread, and it was a good hideout from the law. Philip later moved his first family up to Beaver. While there, late in 1864, he led several families over the mountains east of Parowan—-a colony twenty miles north of Cedar. When Priscilla's father finally came back, she heard him talk about how beautiful the country was; and she loved hearing him describe the rivers and red-colored canyons. He said, "It was a real paradise."[4]

One time, she heard about Navaho Lake and how it got its name. Her father and other men were in pursuit of a band of renegade Indians when they found them on the banks of the beautiful lake. Priscilla's father was stopping over in Toquerville when he became angered by the Indians. Priscilla felt sad when she heard about how his prized team of mules, which he depended on for peddling, were killed by the arrows of the Indians. They couldn't steal the mules--because they were so well hobbled.

In 1865, Priscilla was to have her very own full-blooded brother, and her mother's longing for a son was to be fulfilled. A beautiful boy was born on the 16th day of April. Philip was excited about Betsy's finally giving birth to a child who could carry his name. He had been away at the time of the birth, but he showed up a few days after William Cattle Klingensmith arrived. The Indians were swift with their good news. They found Philip down on the Muddy—-a mission Brigham Young had sent families to establish before he himself had been to see the place. Besides the advantage of long growing seasons there, it was to be a rest stop for travelers going to and from California.

While Philip was home, not knowing when he would ever be back again, he decided to rebaptize Betsy and to baptize Priscilla and Mary Alice. The girls were past eight years old, but their father wasn't around long enough for them to be baptized before. Wading into the cold water at the head of the Grist Mill Flume on Coal Creek, on May 5, 1865, Philip Klingensmith baptized each of his loved ones. On the following Sunday, at the Social Hall, John M. Higbee stood in with his friend for the confirmations.

Philip, having left the Muddy Mission temporarily, returned to St. Joseph, taking Hannah and her children along with him. While Priscilla's father was home, he talked about the place—-it was on the old Spanish trail and down where it was hot. She heard about the Indians and the trouble they had with them stealing cattle. It was the darnedest place.

Through her early years, Priscilla heard many of her father's experiences that held her spellbound. Later on, when she became aware of and understood the dangers and trials he had been put through, she found a bond of love that would never be broken.[5]

CHAPTER 8

Life With The Mormons

Priscilla's mother, Betsy, had a lot of chores to do with her husband away most of the time. Priscilla wasn't very old when she was expected to help her mother with little things around the house. As Priscilla grew, her responsibilities grew. Standing over a boiler of homemade soap, while stirring with a stick, was tedious but was a necessary help to Betsy from Priscilla. After the soap was poured into trays and cut into squares, it was Priscilla who set the squares out to dry. The soap got the clothes clean, but the smell of it was horrid.

While Priscilla went into the fields with her mother, her younger sister, Mary Alice, watched their siblings, Betsy Ann, Margaret Jane, and William. Many hours were spent carefully gathering long, even straws from stacks of wheat, which were used when Priscilla's mother skillfully taught the art of how to bleach, dye, braid, sew, and block into hats.

When the girls were old enough, they helped with the outside chores and with the garden and flowers. The young family didn't always have enough food, so they, like many others, had to depend on tithing donations from the basement of the tithing house to help them along. The kindly bishop, Henry Lunt, helped watch over Betsy and her children.

Betsy enjoyed the times Philip was home. He was attentive and gentle with the children. He never raised his voice to make demands. Betsy felt his love but knew Hannah was his favorite wife. Hannah always moved to new settlements with Philip and shared most of his time.

Hannah knew she had first dubs on Philip, and when she saw him giving another wife too much attention, she fussed and showed her jealousy in unpredictable ways. One time, she threw a bucket of water on Philip and one of his wives while he was sharing a bed with her. Hannah went through all the really hard times with Philip, and she planned on keeping him close to her.

Priscilla was sensitive to the pride her father displayed when his oldest son, Moroni, was to be married. Moroni was a lot older than Priscilla, but she knew her half-brother was special. They had a big celebration, and all the families got together in Parowan. Moroni and his new wife, Cedenia Dalton, whom he married on May 16, 1867, were a happy couple.

Philip had prospects of grandsons who would preserve the lineage of the Klingensmith name. Moroni was a teamster—tall, but not very heavy, and ambitious. Just two months after his marriage, he was carrying freight between Cedar City and Parowan when he was accidentally thrown under the wheels of his heavy wagon. Priscilla saw the pain in her father's eyes on that day and for a long time after Moroni was buried.

Even though Priscilla's father couldn't be around much of the time, she was aware of how he felt and knew of his faith in a Heavenly Father. She heard him talk about it from the pulpit when she was very young. He carried a *Book of Mormon* with him; and when he wasn't working in the fields or doing something else, he spent time reading. He always asked her if she was attending her meetings and saying her prayers.

When it came time for schooling, Priscilla walked to the Social Hall where she was taught under the tutelage of John Macfarland. Priscilla was proud of the award of merit she earned—-Macfarland was an excellent teacher, but his main interest was music. After about six weeks, Priscilla attended a "Mrs. Spiken's school, but she taught sewing, crocheting and but very little out of books."[1] Priscilla's mother, and sometimes her father, taught her reading, writing, and spelling—-mostly by studying the scriptures.

While Priscilla was still young, she used the skills, learned from her mother, of spinning wool into yarn and knitting, by making a scarf—-long enough to go around her neck and for one end to be thrown over her shoulder. Her uncle, George Bennett, admired the scarf and paid Priscilla cash for it. The beautiful, flowered silk belt she bought with the money she earned was highly prized by her.

One warm summer day, Priscilla and her chums went for a walk up Cedar Canyon. On their way back, they were playfully running down through the brush when Priscilla noticed her belt was lost. They had gone so many directions Priscilla thought she would never see her beautiful belt again. She was discouraged, but she kept an earnest prayer in her mind as she tried to retrace her steps. To Priscilla's grateful surprise, she found her belt. She always believed "it was a direct answer to faith and prayer."[2]

When Aunt Alice Randall came over from England, she was around a lot. She didn't have a husband with her, and she didn't have children; she taught school. After their own mother died, when Betsy was seven years old, it was Alice who raised her. When Betsy turned sixteen, she sailed to America with their sister Mary, who traveled with her husband, Thomas Bladen, and their five daughters.

Going to visit Aunt Mary Bladen was fun for Priscilla and her sisters—-there were two boy cousins to play with. The girls were too old to play and helped their mother most of the time. The home was "a dugout, one big room, about three feet down in the ground, and built up above the ground about three feet with adobe wall and a roof made of poles being put on top and covered with mud and dirt. One window in the east gable end, and the door in the west and a big fireplace over which [they] cooked all [their] meals."[3]

Mary Bladden

Priscilla's Aunt Mary had her hands full after her husband was called on a mission to England. For some unexplained reason, someone wrote to Thomas and told him their house had caught on fire and his whole family burned to death. He was devastated and couldn't bring himself to return to Cedar City.

It was Priscilla's aunts who tried to help her mother when William became so very ill. The summer and the weather were unbearably hot, and Philip was gone. Betsy did all she could to try to comfort her little son. His sobbing cries worried her. He was burning with fever. She looked into his mouth and didn't know what to do for his swollen gums. Sixteen-month-old William gave out and died on August 3, 1868. Priscilla wrote in her diary, "I thot my heart would break for we all loved him so dearly. He was a fine big boy with white hair and large blue eyes."

The strain for Betsy of the loss of her little William went unnoticed by Priscilla—-life seemed to be going along the same as usual. But Priscilla was only thirteen years old, and she was having a time of her own adjusting to being more grown up now. Priscilla brushed and took extra good care of her beautiful hair and tried to look nice—-but it didn't help much. She liked the boys, but they didn't give her any attention—-only to make taunting remarks that bothered her. Mostly, she was too busy to fret about it.

That same year, the law was bearing down so hard on Philip Klingensmith that he knew he had to leave for good. Betsy and Margaretha were to be left behind with their children to shift for themselves. It was an upsetting day when he said goodbye. Priscilla followed her father to the gate and watched him go down the road—-she thought she would never see him again. Panaca, Nevada, to her, was a long way away.

The feeling of abandonment welled up in Betsy until she would not have received Philip even if he had come back. The years of his coming and going wore her down. Finally, the burden of full responsibility of her four children and all she had to contend with was too much. When Betsy became too weak to go on, her sister, Alice, took her and her children in. Alice fussed and hovered over Betsy for a year, trying all she could to make her strong.

During this time, Priscilla watched over her sisters and helped her Aunt Alice in every way she could. The moments Priscilla spent with her mother were comforting for both of them. Two evenings after Priscilla had gently combed and braided her mother's dark, waist-long hair, for what turned out to be the last time, she was called to her bedside. Betsy quietly slipped away. The pining for her son and the anguish of Philip's leaving came to an end for Betsy on the blustery 16th day of March in 1870.

The funeral was well attended—-but Philip couldn't be there. Priscilla knew all the good things that were said about her mother were true. Betsy was a faithful Latter-day Saint. She was honest and always told the truth—-she did suffer wrongs rather than do wrong to others. She was a good mother to her children and taught them all the attributes and skills that would help them throughout their lives. Priscilla was filled with pride for all the good things that were said. When it was all over, the girls weren't left with money and couldn't buy a headstone for their mother's grave.

Priscilla was cheered up when the Indians brought a letter from her father. The letter, written on the 28th of March 1870, was sent from the ranch Philip called Smith Ville. Priscilla wrote back to him and waited a long time for an answer. She finally heard that he had to leave Nevada in a hurry and had set out alone for California. She knew her father meant well especially because of the things he promised. Priscilla treasured her letter and almost wore it out from reading it so much. She read over and over the words:

Dear Daughter,
    It is with a very sad heart I take my pen in hand to write you a few lines. I have heard the dreadful news about your mother's death. I am very sorry that I was not there with her but I count not. It was impossible. I do not want my children scattered. I expect to come in and fetch them out here. I will pay all expenses of your mother's burial when I come in. Write to me as soon as you receive this letter. Say to your aunt, I expect she has had a very hard time but I will pay her for her trouble and expense.

                    No more at present from your
                    Affectionate Father
                    P. K. Smith.[4]

The four girls were still living with their Aunt Alice three months after their mother died. Aunt Alice died too. She had taken good care of the girls, and now they were on their own.

On June 26, 1870, in reply to a letter from Sister Mary A. Wimmer, a good friend of the family, Priscilla reveals her lonely life and expresses her belief in a life after death:

Dear Mary,
    I sit to write a few lines to let you know how we are getting along. We are all well and I hope you all are the same. You say be comforted. We try to be but you know how lonesome it is, though I have plenty of work and care on my mind at present.
    Mary Alice is working at John Chatterly, Betsy Ann, I think will go back to Alice Bullock's to live then Janey and I will be alone. Aunt Mary stays with us at night for a few weeks.
    We think she has gone to a better world to rest with the hope of a glorious resurrection. As you say it is a comfort and a satisfaction to us all. She went to the city and got sealed to a man of God.
    Aunt talked to us before she died. She willed all her property to us four girls except that what belongs to the Co-operative Institutions which

she wished to give as a token of respect to your father though she wished us to draw the dividend for a year to pay expences.

We do not feel hard that some of you did not come down. We know how it is where [there is] sickness. As you say you would like me to come and see you. I will as soon as possible.

Priscilla[5]

Very little was left over from the inherited dividends after burial expenses were paid. Their concerned Aunt Mary Bladen worried about Priscilla and her responsibility at her young age, and so it was finally decided that six-year-old Janey should go to live with her. Although Mary Alice continued to work for John Chatterly, she decided to keep Priscilla company in the house that was left to them. Priscilla was fifteen, and Mary Alice was thirteen. They were determined to make their own way without any help from the Church.

The unfinished cloth their Aunt Alice had on the loom was completed by Priscilla—-it was for the Relief Society. Sister Sarah Ann Urie, the Relief Society president, was reluctant to take the cloth, knowing the girls needed help.

Priscilla and Mary Alice "arose while the stars were still shinning and went to the wheat fields to glean wheat for their pigs and chickens. They looked carefully for fine, even straws and took them home."[6] After the straws were cleaned and dyed black, they used the skills learned from their mother and aunts, who had been ribbon weavers in England, and made very good-looking hats.

They were beautifully trimmed with bits of silk ribbon and feathers fashioned into flowers. They had a good market for selling their hats to women in town, and plain ones were sold to men and boys. When the annual county fairs were held, the girls entered their hats and won first prize, against strong competition, for three years running.

Bargaining with the Indians for many buckskins, which Priscilla tanned and made into gloves to sell, added to the girls' income. In the evenings, Priscilla knitted socks in exchange for firewood. Priscilla was good at embroidery and had already learned to make temple aprons to earn a little money. When she and her sister became desperate for something to wear, they went about making their own. They began by washing clothes and scrubbing floors all day long for one yard of calico per day. They knew how to spin and weave their own linsey.[7] They cut patterns from an old dress, or from one they borrowed from a friend, to make their first dresses.

In time, Priscilla and Mary Alice became good enough at sewing to make clothing for neighbors and friends who wanted to help them out. Their stitching was all done neatly by hand until Mary Alice earned enough credit from sewing to own a sewing machine.

While trying to meet their own needs, they joined a community spinning club and donated time to weaving wool for the Relief Society. Minutes for the organization when the girls were accepted as members show:

> Dec. 2, 1869-Aug. 11, 1870. It was moved and seconded and unanimously [voted] that the following sisters become members of the R. Society: Elizabeth Perry, Teresa Urie, Jane Parry, Arrabella Coombs, Annie Macklesprang, Rachel Corry, Elvira Coombs Birkbeck, Sarah Jane Leigh, Ellen Hunter, Mary Alice Smith, Martha Amelia Connell, Mary Alice Melling, and Priscilla K. Smith.[8]

Priscilla and Mary Alice, "along with many other Relief Society women made a practice of having sewing bees, going into the homes of women with large families, or motherless families, to lend a helping hand. Spending the whole day, cutting out and sewing the clothing for the family, to get them ready for school. They had carpet rag bees, and quilting bees."[9] When Priscilla was sixteen and Mary Alice was only fourteen, their service was also given when they were called to lay out the dead and sew their clothing.

The girls were following in their mother's footsteps. Back in November of 1856, before Betsy Cattle married Philip Klingensmith, they became members of the first organization of the Relief Society formed in Cedar City. John's first wife, Elizabeth Hutcheson, was also a member, and Betsy's sister, Alice Randall, was treasurer. Later on, Sarah Ann, John's second wife, became president and was serving in that capacity when Priscilla and Mary Alice became members.[10]

CHAPTER 9

No Beaux For Priscilla

Priscilla thought and thought about her father and wondered where he could be. No word came, and she waited. When rumors started flying—-saying he had been murdered—-she didn't know. She comforted her sisters by telling them they would see him again some day.

In the fall of 1872, Philip Klingensmith surfaced in Pioche, Nevada. Priscilla and her sisters were filled with happiness to finally know their father was alive. Priscilla heard he had made some kind of confession or other. Lots of people were talking about it. Some of them were angry. They said he should have kept his mouth shut—-saying he was trying to save his own skin. Priscilla talked with people closest to her, and they consoled her—-saying he had been the best bishop they ever had; and they were talking about how good he was to the Indians.

Keziah K. Simmons

Priscilla didn't hear any more about her father for a long time. Finally, in a newspaper article, Priscilla read that her Aunt Keziah and Uncle Daniel Simmons, through the help of John Eley, had found her father. He was hiding away in the canyons; and, after feeding and clothing him, they helped him get out of the state. Priscilla's Aunt Keziah was furious about the newspaper articles, written by the tyrannous Salt Lake *Daily Tribune*,[1] about her brother and was trying to set them straight. Priscilla understood better now why her father didn't come back to Cedar City. But, oh, how she wished he could.

Some of the newspaper clippings were brought to Priscilla. She read them intently. This Mountain Meadows Massacre was a terrible affair. Her father's confession claimed he took care of the children. She was glad for that, and she knew he didn't have anything to do with the killing of any of those people in the wagon train.

Priscilla was seventeen, and she thought the boys didn't come around because of her father's reputation. Lots of girls her age were already married and had a child or two by now. It puzzled her some when

Daniel H. Simmons

she saw the boys buzzing around her sisters. Well, she guessed, she just wasn't pretty enough to attract a beau.

John had been watching her. He thought she was a bonnie lass. While she was growing up, he saw her often. Knowing she probably came from Arkansas, and remembering the circumstance of her being in Cedar City, furthered his compassion for her.

When John first saw Priscilla, he was only twenty-two years old; now he was thirty-seven. How would it be for him to take such a young bride? What about the mysterious stigma that still hung over the town? Priscilla was, after all, from *Gentile* people.

John was healthy and was still considered on the handsome side. Sarah Ann was beyond bearing years. His children were quite well grown, and he wanted a greater posterity. John had been on one mission, and he would probably go again. He guessed he should think about it for a while longer.

The government was still determined to wipe out polygamy. Now wasn't a good time to take another wife. Brigham Young was preparing everybody to move to the mountains again. John was trying to prepare his family in case they had to flee.

While Abraham Lincoln was president of the United States, the Mormons were pretty well left alone as far as military advancement went. After Lincoln's assassination in 1865, Vice President Andrew Johnson succeeded him with renewed vigor against the Mormons. But when Ulysses S. Grant, a military man, became president in 1869, he was even more bent on ousting the practice of polygamy—-even if it meant war.

In John's letter to his parents in Scotland, he finally got to the real intent of his letter. By the time he got to this point, he was, to say the least, angry:

> I cannot help but contrast 20 years ago with the present time, in my life and fortunes, I was then young and inexperienced and hardly knew what was ahead of me.
>
> Today how is it? It seems that the power of the nation is about to be brought to bear on us as a people, by reason of incessant industry and patience we have become a power in the land and we dare ask for our inalienable rights, political, capital and religious bigotry have made our rulers mad and they swear "By-God, they will uproot us." Perhaps they will.
>
> I scarcely know what is ahead to-day, but my faith and hopes and stern will bids me say, "I will conquer as I have done and I care not for their threats, nor all they can do." I have seen hard times before. I can go through them again.
>
> When they bid me change my principles, they talk to a dumb idol that has no tongue to talk or answer. To be warned is to be fore armed and this is what I am doing now, to have family in safety, something to eat and to wear and having the means of travel. Grant and Parson Newman[2] can kiss my foot and from that along on up. . . .

This was February of 1873, and John had sent two previous letters to Scotland with instructions for funds and some supplies. The mail had been irregular of late, and he wasn't sure his parents had received his letters. He asked his parents to send a box by Wells Fargo and Company by fast freight to Salt Lake City. They were to send it payable in Salt Lake City and to send enough money to pay for it. He let his parents know:

> I have some money, but when I put myself in a position of safety by buying wagons and teams, I will be swamped, but plenty of sheep and cattle and those I will not sell as I may need them. Notwithstanding the threatening attitude of the United States against the Mormons, you must not take alarm for me. I will take care of myself and family.

Before signing off, John went on to tell his parents about the disease, which was of epizootic proportion and which spread among his animals. One of his fine, large mares died from it. The severity of the winter, with much snow and hard frost, weakened his cattle on the range. In conclusion to his letter, he wrote:

> Mining is dull, not began farming yet, freighting of course is stopped—-times on the whole are rather tight.
> My wife is in excellent health and also my children and they rejoice in the prospect of a home in the mountains. They, of course, know little of hardships, attending such a state of things.

John purchased wagons and supplies and took his families to the mountains—-just in case. His sons and sons-in-law helped him build a log cabin. A little house was built over a cold mountain spring where cheese was aged and where milk and butter were kept cool. The families took weaner pigs and raised their pork. A

Going up Shirts Canyon

neighbor built a cabin near an ice cave; and the children all delighted in making and eating ice cream. The Urie cousins, George and Martha (Agnes was yet too young), came to visit and shared with all the fun.

The families enjoyed being away from the heat of Cedar City on these hot summer days—-to the children, it seemed more like a holiday than a refuge. The unyielding meddling of the government, in regard to polygamy and other issues, was a constant wrinkle in the peace of the Mormon settlements. However, it didn't reach the point of abandoning their homes for a permanent refuge in the mountains.

The year 1873 was busy in all sorts of ways. John's stepson, Robert Heyborne, who was only seven years younger than John, was called on a mission to England. Robert's wife, Margaret "Maggie" Bladen,[3] lived in the house Robert built, on 200 East, where she took care of their children: five-year-old Mary Ann Eliza, three-year-old Sarah, and John James, who was born during January. She contented herself the best she could—-knowing Robert would be gone for two years. [4]

CHAPTER 10

For The Last Time

Priscilla Klingensmith

In 1873, John, bringing himself to the present, claimed, "Indeed, now at the age of 38, I begin to feel the effects of my intemperance in youth caused by hard fare, hard labor, and exposure."[1] But he still felt virile enough to take another wife.

Priscilla hardly knew what to think when John Urie started acting like a beau. She had little experience, and she had thought of him more like a father. John was a good friend of her own father, and she had always admired him. She enjoyed hearing his Scottish brogue and was pleased when he called her his bonnie lass. She couldn't exactly say she loved him, but she said yes when he asked her for her hand in marriage.

John knew it was proper to ask the father of his intended bride for her hand, but he didn't know where to reach Philip Klingensmith. He had, of course, talked it over with Sarah Ann before he approached Priscilla. But, most importantly he had the sanction and encouragement of the brethren of the Church. John was a member in good standing and was worthy to be the head of two households.

The more Priscilla thought about it, the more she liked the idea of marrying John Urie. Her sisters and their Aunt Mary didn't seem to be concerned that John was so old. In the Mormon Church, it was common practice for older men to take young wives. John's wife, Sarah Ann, had given her blessing to the union and wanted to help Priscilla prepare for her marriage. She showered "the same love and helpfulness upon Priscilla that she had upon her own family."[2]

The thoughts of going to Salt Lake City to be married were exciting for Priscilla—-the farthest north she had ever gone, that she could remember, was Parowan. It took a lot of preparation for a three-week trip by covered wagon and oxen. Her sister Mary Alice helped her prepare plenty of food, and they rounded up lots of quilts to keep them warm. John and Priscilla, and of course their chaperon, waved goodby and arrived in the city before Thanksgiving.

On November 24, 1873, John and Priscilla entered the Endowment House where Daniel H. Wells, counselor to the president of the Church, pronounced them man and wife for all time and eternity. Their wedding day was celebrated with a gift from John. Priscilla was delighted with the full set of china dishes—-beautifully adorned with bluebirds and sprigs of apple blossoms. In remembrance of their special day, they had their pictures taken by a professional photographer. John was a romantic after all. Thanksgiving dinner with friends was the crowning touch for their special excursion to Salt Lake City.

John and his young bride, Priscilla, made their way to her home in Cedar City—-Mary Alice moved in with the Chatterlys. The beautiful, fair lass with the golden hair, whom John had watched grow into womanhood, was his to cherish and love forever. He was filled with joy and had a new zest for life. For the first while, he stayed with Priscilla and shut everybody out. They were alone—-John was consumed with passion, and Priscilla's shyness gave in to an eagerness to be loved.

Nine months later, during the lingering heat of summer , on August 27, 1874, Priscilla gave birth to Kathleen. The excitement in John's first family was high. Jack,[3] John and Sarah Ann's youngest child, was seven years old. This beautiful new baby tugged at all their heart strings. Sarah Ann hovered over Priscilla as though she were her own child.

Before Priscilla gave birth to Kathleen, it had been important for her to attend her meetings. Until she started showing, Priscilla was able to go to church without being detected by the marshal as a plural wife. After she was showing, Priscilla stayed away from church but continued to attend Relief Society. All the sisters knew Priscilla was John Urie's wife. The men knew too, but the marshal wasn't quite sure.

Priscilla stayed home now that the baby was born, and for a month they all watched and worried over Kathleen. She didn't seem to be gaining and was listless. On September 27, 1874, their concerns were manifest—-Kathleen was too weak to survive. The pang of sorrow was with Priscilla, who blamed herself—-she was sure her milk was not good enough for her baby.

Priscilla finally consoled herself, with the help of John, that she had been blessed with a baby whose mission on earth had been accomplished when she received her body. Kathleen's spirit was perfect, and she had been returned to her father in heaven. Priscilla resolved to be a happy wife for John and a helpful companion to Sarah Ann. Little time was spared for the longing to hold

Kathleen and to remember.

September turned into December. The crops were in, the fruit was bottled and dried, and thoughts were turned to the Christmas holidays. Priscilla became involved with helping Sarah Ann sew a few special things for the children. John was proud that his two wives were so helpful to each other.

No contention existed between the wives—-but Priscilla sometimes wished she could have more private time with John. Time passed slowly, but Priscilla finally got her wish. During the short days and long nights of January and February 1875, Priscilla noticed John found his way to her bedroom more often. She was thinking he must be anxious for her to have another child. This pleased her, and she welcomed his visits with anticipation.

The summer of 1875 saw John about his business helping the town prepare for the 24th of July celebration. Horses had to be curried and their manes and tails combed free of burrs. Handcarts and covered wagons were adorned while costumes for the parade were being sewn. The band was practicing the most patriotic numbers and marching in step—-it was an exciting time of year.

Amidst all the activities, a hubbub came over the town. The trial of John D. Lee was already anticipated. Philip Klingensmith, the leading witness, whom the penal system was sure could implicate the Church in the Mountain Meadows Massacre, was nearing Cedar City. The Indian runners carried the news, and the town bell brought attention to his arrival. Priscilla carefully made her way toward the commotion—-she was heavy with child, but she tried to keep herself covered.

Many who knew and loved Philip were there. All they could do was stand and watch—-no conversation, just watching the horses with two men astride go by. Priscilla's father looked pale, weary and forlorn--the marshall was puffed up. The captor pulled on the reins of his notorious ward and held them tight while they made their way north and out of town. After they were gone, a few disgruntled participants of the massacre couldn't resist making a few piercing remarks among themselves. They were afraid they would be implicated, by Philip, for the crime of the massacre.

Alfred Klingonsmith

A message came over the telegraph wires about the trial to be held in Beaver beginning on July 23, 1875. The wind was taken out of the sails for the 24th of July celebration. All anybody could talk about was the trial. They knew it was coming when the marshall came looking for witnesses. Joel White and others were summoned to go to Beaver. Wagons were loaded with supplies, and many of the townspeople headed for Beaver. Priscilla thought it best to stay close to home—-with her condition and all.

News about the trial filled Priscilla's thoughts about her father. Mary Alice,

Betsy Ann, Janey, and Priscilla worried and wondered if their father would be indicted for murder. Their half brother, Alfred, gave them moral support. Word came down that Philip was ill and hardly able to stand trial. None of the siblings knew what to do.

Privately, John and Priscilla discussed all that was going on. John had nosed around and found that a record had been made when Philip adopted Priscilla. Now that John was her husband, he thought it best to tell her about it. Priscilla wasn't very surprised. But the proven knowledge of her parents being murdered and her brothers and sisters gone too was heartbreaking. She had been raised as a Mormon, and now the conflict of loyalties was almost more than she could bear.

Mary Aice & Betsy Klingensmith

It was now that Priscilla fully understood the odd glances and whispers and why there were no beaux. Mary Alice, after all, was the oldest child; and this was the reason why Mary Alice had her picture taken with their mother. Priscilla was left out—-she wondered why but now she knew. She was only an adopted orphan from Arkansas. Oh how Priscilla hoped her sisters would never find out—-they may stop loving her and claim she didn't belong.

Priscilla was distraught—-what was going to happen to her if the courts got wind of her circumstance? She remembered hearing about the children who were gathered up and never brought back. Priscilla was one of those hillbillies, made fun of so long ago—-but it wasn't funny at all. She was afraid she might be gathered up too—-even though all these years had gone by. Cedar City was her home, and this was all the life she knew. Priscilla had no way of knowing which family she came from and could not think of going back to the unknown Ozarks. John vowed to keep her secret and somehow—-someday—-get hold of the papers and destroy them.

The trial finally ended. John D. Lee was held over for another hearing. During the trial, Mr. Spicer, John D. Lee's attorney,

asked that Philip K. Smith whose name is upon the "omnibus" indictment and who is present in court, be also put upon trial, to which the United States Marshal said, "that there is no such person known as Philip K. Smith." This required a word of explanation. Among the score or so of persons indicted for participation in the Mountain Meadow Massacre appears the name of Philip K. Smith. This is an error in the presentment. Philip Klingensmith being the person intended, and he is here present as a witness.[4]

It turned out that John D. Lee was the only participant of the Mountain Meadows Massacre who was put on trial. The other participants were exonerated because the judge ruled they hadn't participated by their own free will.

This meant that Philip Klingensmith would be released, supposedly a free man to go his own way. He had asked for protection, but when it came time for his return, to wherever he decided to go, he chose to travel alone.

Priscilla knew her father would stop by on his way through town—-he just had to see his children. Word that Philip was on his way preceded his arrival in Cedar City. Priscilla's sisters rallied around to help prepare a good meal for him. They wanted him to stay and rest for a few days, but he explained that he could not—-his life was in danger. His eyes looked at Priscilla with a distant and haunting fear—-he had been dragged through hell and back.

Philip was happy the girls were situated as well as they were. He lamented about the past and how he wished he could have come after them when their mother died. He told them about the posse that was always after him and about certain men who were bent on taking his life. Hannah wasn't agreeable to taking the girls in, so he just didn't know what to do. All he could think about was trying to keep ahead of all the men who were pursuing him.

John was cordial with Philip and tried to lift Philip's spirits. They discussed a few of the unjust things that had gone on with the government and the taunting marshals who constantly appeared from out of nowhere. John gave Philip a gentleman's embrace and assured him he was always welcome under their roof. As Philip turned to leave, his shoulders were slumped; and he seemed reluctant to move on. Priscilla was shy and dared not hug him, but her eyes told him that she loved him. He was the only father she knew. Telling him that she learned the truth about where she came from was the furthest from her mind.

Philip's horse, given to him by the officials after the trial, was spirited but obedient to his rider. After a roll in the dust, a long drink at the watering trough, and a meal of oats, the horse was well rested and ready for the road. The saddle, also given to Philip, was well worn and comfortable and was thrown over the horse's back and cinched just right. A bedroll was tied to the back of the saddle; and the leather pouches, hanging on each side, were filled with necessities to see Philip through his long journey. The family all bid him goodbye. Philip put his foot in the stirrup and slowly lifted himself to mount his horse. With a click of his tongue, he pulled his reins toward the south, and he was on his way. Priscilla wondered, as she watched him disappear down the dusty road, "Will this be the last time I'll see him?"[5]

CHAPTER 11

Could Priscilla Dare to Dream?

During September of 1876, while John D. Lee's second trial was taking place in Beaver, Cedar City was in a hubbub again. Lee had been held over for this second trial, and now the court was intent on putting all the blame on him. Priscilla wanted to stay clear of any attention to herself—-John remained with her.

The court got its way, and John D. Lee was sentenced to be shot on March 23, 1877. The night before the verdict came in, Lee's friends "made an effort to dissuade the prosecuting witnesses . . . from appearing by classing such as the *Tribune* supporters, whose testimony would verify the prediction of that paper, that the Church had sacrificed the defendant." His friends didn't succeed; they found "It would not work."[1]

For the ones who understood Lee was following orders from those who presided over him, it was heart rending—-but maybe now, they thought, if one man could pay the debt, the whole Mountain Meadows affair would be put to rest.

After the sentence, a month rolled by, and Halloween was just around the corner. The first pumpkin pies were made, and jack-o-lanterns were carved. It was October 29, 1875. Sarah Ann was summoned to attend Priscilla, who gave birth to a blond, blue-eyed baby boy.

Most of the Urie family names had been given to Sarah Ann's boys, but landmarks of Scotland, which were familiar to John, were yet to be honored. When the blessing circle was formed by Bishop Henry Lunt, John's oldest boys, and John's sons-in-law, and John, who gave the new son a name, Priscilla had to be content with Donald Clyde. Clyde, of course, was for the river Clyde, in Glasgow, Scotland, where John was baptized a member of the Church.

Now that Priscilla had her little son, Donald, it became harder to fool the marshal—-and since the trial, things were all stirred up. None knew when the marshal would be lurking around the church to see who showed up with more than one wife. The marshal noticed Priscilla was carrying a baby into church, and when he snooped inside, he saw her sitting in the same pew as John Urie's wife, Sarah Ann. It was difficult to tell if she had a separate husband. The men, of course, were sitting on the opposite side of the room. When the families left the church the marshal was still scratching his head. He couldn't tell who belonged to whom, because of John's older sons, David and George, who were attentive to Priscilla.

After keeping an eye on John, the marshal finally figured it out—-that John had two wives. The marshal warned John that he could pick him up for polygamy. The Church still sanctioned and encouraged men to have plural wives, so John just kept out of the marshal's way.

Letters to and from Scotland were fairly regular. John's mother kept in touch. As always, she encouraged her son, John, to come home. She offered to pay his way. John talked about going—-he was weary of dodging the law. He was very interested in searching the parish records for his ancestors.

Could Priscilla dare to dream of going to Scotland with her husband? John's brother, James, had taken his wife, Violet, and two children to Scotland; and in 1872—-they stayed for four years. Surely she and Sarah Ann would get to go, too. Priscilla was only two years old when she was brought across the plains and hadn't traveled much since. She guessed it was unthinkable, as she was the plural wife. John's parents were not yet reconciled to the idea that their son should have two wives; and, in the eyes of the law, Priscilla was still a spinster.

Priscilla knew about John's father, George, who added a provision to his will that "specified that if at any time any of his sons should engage in polygamy the children of the plural marriages should be disinherited."[2] Priscilla still thought about going to Scotland, hoping the polygamy thing would all blow over, but she tried to put it out of her mind. Well, if she couldn't go, she was going to be happy about Sarah Ann having a wonderful trip across the ocean.

Don was almost a year and a half old when Priscilla was beginning to have morning sickness and suspected she might be carrying another baby. Thoughts of bobbing up and down in a boat headed for Scotland took care of any fanciful ideas of a trip for herself. It was just as well because John was going to be set apart as a missionary, and wives didn't get to go on missions with their husbands. Being sent to Europe as a missionary and spending time on genealogy justified a trip to Scotland.

It was difficult for the families to keep their minds on John's departure with the talk and gloom among the townspeople. The time was near for John D. Lee's execution. Hordes of people, spectators, that is, were arriving and wanting places to stay. John never turned anybody away, so his homes were full. The women were kept busy with making beds and preparing meals. The execution was going to take place at the Mountain Meadows. To Priscilla, it seemed appropriate—-but horrid to think about. The ones who witnessed the execution described how brave John D. Lee had been.[3] At the last minute, Lee tried to put the blame where it belonged—-but it didn't do any good.

Just two days after John D. Lee was shot on the Meadow, now March 27, 1877, John Urie was set apart to become a member of the Sixty-Third Quorum of Seventies of the Church. On this same day, he left alone for a second mission, but this time to Scotland. Although John wouldn't be doing much proselyting, he carried his Seventies certificate with him to verify his authority:

Seventies Certificate
To whom it may concern!! = This certifies that John Urie is a

member of the 63rd quorum of Seventies of the Church of Jesus Christ of Latter-day Saints in good standing and is hereby authorized to officiate in all the duties and callings of his office.

And we pray God the eternal father to bless Elder Urie and all who receive him and minister to his comfort with the blessings of heaven and earth for time and for all eternity in the name of Jesus.

Richard R. Birkbeck President

Cedar City March 27th, 1877   Jos H. Smith

Geo Perry

Councilors Robert W. Heyborne[4]

While John was on his mission, Priscilla's sister, Betsy Ann, was married to John Creighton Hamilton, on June 26, 1877, in the St. George Temple. John Hamilton was from Hamilton's Fort, located a few miles south of Cedar City, where he took Betsy Ann to live.

THE CEDAR CITY AREA

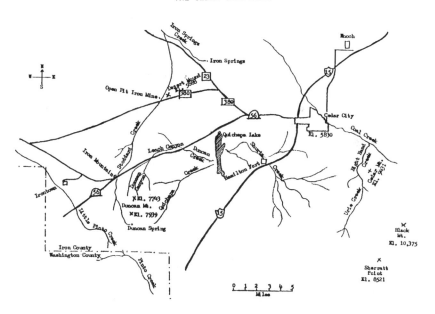

Cedar City Area
By compliments of Eldred Johnsom

Upon John's return to Cedar City, on August 9, 1877, he felt his journey to Scotland was rewarding indeed. Two small record books were filled with 4,000 to 5,000 names of relatives found in the parish archives of Edinburgh. He had spent over four months, with the aid of a professionally trained genealogist, searching records. He preached the gospel as opportunities to do so came to him.

John's father, George, had been cordial and glad to have his son home but repeatedly begged him to give up one of his wives so his children could share in the inheritance of his fortune. John had tried but was unable to bring his father to an understanding of how he felt about the principles he lived by and the practice of polygamy in the Church.

John's mother tried to persuade him to stay longer—-but could not. John was anxious to get back to his families. His wives and children welcomed him with anticipation of what the wooden boxes from Scotland obtained. They weren't disappointed—-it was so exciting. And John, of course, this time brought a gift for their gardens—-tubers of his beloved bluebells of Scotland.

Everything at home went well while John was gone, and life went on much as usual—-notwithstanding life of late was a little harder for John's young wife. Priscilla had been right—-she was carrying another child.

When November 24, 1877, arrived, Thanksgiving was going to be celebrated in a very special way. It was hectic—-Sarah Ann and the children helped out. A festive dinner was prepared during the commotion of the birth of John and Priscilla's first daughter, Betsy, who was named after Betsy Cattle Klingensmith, Priscilla's mother.

Charlette Emerson Main

The winter was windy and cold with lots of snow and frost. John took advantage of the long, dark evenings sorting out names he collected from the parishes of Scotland. He put names on lined sheets with parents and children as family groups. By carefully sorting the sheets, he put them in a descending order. Tracing a direct blood line, for John, was exciting! It wasn't only for himself and his children. Now he could have his ancestors' names ready for their work to be done in the newly completed St. George Temple.

In the temple, both living and dead, parents would be sealed to each other and their children would be sealed to them for all time and eternity. The links that tied them to their Heavenly Father, in an eternal progression for the Urie family, were coming together—-one by one.

The St. George Temple was completed without interference from the outside world and was a beautiful sight to see. The dedication of the newly completed temple took place on April 6, 1877. Brigham Young and many leading brethren of the Church were there. The occasion was wonderful for all the Saints. Brigham Young, who had weathered many storms and had seen the completion of this great edifice, succumbed on August 29, 1877, after returning to Salt Lake City and after a brief illness.

The Uries joined the mourning of the Saints. They had seen Brigham Young for the last time. For the residents of Cedar City, there would be no more dressing in their best clothes and lining the streets, waving and paying their respect while Brigham Young passed through their town. No more bands playing and flowers to gather for strewing in his path. No more fussing or dinners to prepare in preparation for his stays. Their prophet was no more.

After Brigham Young's death, speculation about the strength of the Church was sweeping the country. Threats against the Saints' peace and safety were rampant. One of the reverends of a Protestant church in Brooklyn, New York, T. DeWitt Talmage, unleashed his hatred toward the Mormons before his congregation, declaring:

> Now my friends—-now, at the death of the Mormon Chieftain, is the time for the United States government to strike. They are less organized than they have been, and less than they will be. If these Mormons will not submit to authority, let so much of their rich lands be confiscated for the wants of the government as will be sufficient for their subjugation. If the government of the United States cannot stand the expense, let Salt Lake City pay for it. (Applause.)
>
> Turn their vast temple into an arsenal. Set Phil Sheridan after them. (Immense applause.) Give him enough troops and he will teach all Utah that forty wives is thirty-nine too many. I call upon the Church of Jesus Christ to pray for the overthrow of this iniquity.[5]

In spite of all the speculation and threats, the Church held strong. It never faltered under the direction of the Twelve Apostles—-with John Taylor, who had been with Joseph Smith and who had taken a bullet during Joseph's martyrdom, as president of the Council of the Twelve.[6]

John Urie's Cabin

Janey Moves in With Priscilla

With the death of the Mormons' prophet, Brigham Young, life went on as usual in Cedar City; but the men with more than one wife had to be even more careful than before. The ones who were known to be polygamists had to keep a close lookout for the marshal most of the time. Usually, someone warned John that the marshal was approaching town.

It was convenient for the Urie families to have their getaway in the mountains, and it had become an annual event to go there. The place became a ranch where love and unity tied the families together. It wasn't unusual for the Urie cousins, Martha, Agnes, and George, to come down from Salt Lake City to join them.[1]

In the spring of 1878, the Urie families looked forward to another summer's stay on the mountain. John and his oldest boys mounted their horses and prepared for departure. "The cows and riding horses were started well ahead of the wagons, usually arriving before the wagons and families."[2]

When the women and children appeared at the ranch, everybody pitched in—-supplies were unloaded and everything was put in order.

Putting Up Hay

With prospects of good crops, John and the older boys left and were down from the mountain a good share of the time taking care of farming. Priscilla was left with the beauty surrounding the cabin, which brought her contentment and inner peace—-while knowing she was tucked away in a safe place high above a deep ravine.

Priscilla kept busy most of the time with her children and chores. She paused at times to observe the variety of birds and listen to their songs. Sometimes, when Priscilla wasn't helping with the butter and cheese, she took Don by the hand and carried Betsy in her other arm while searching for mushrooms—-she had been well taught by the Indians and knew which ones to gather.

At summer's end, after Priscilla had come off the mountain, her sister,

Janey, who was living with their Aunt Mary Bladen and was all grown up now, wanted to begin making her own way through the world. When Janey let her sister know about her plans, Priscilla, good naturally, said, "Well, come on over and stay with me."[3] When Janey took her up on her offer, Priscilla welcomed her company to help fill long, lonely days. John could come to the house only when the coast was clear.

Seventeen-year-old Janey went out doing housework for women who were confined and took in sewing until she had all she could do. The two women and two children had a busy household. In the evenings, after the children were in bed, Priscilla and Janey reminisced their childhood. They were still speculating on the whereabouts of their father—-they hadn't heard from him. They guessed he had gone back to California, and the Indians seemed to think he was okay. The men who came around asking about Bishop P. K. Smith, as they called him, worried them. It was bad enough that their father was chased down because of the massacre but, the fact that he had more than one wife added to the pursuit.

With the holidays over the girls were anxiously waiting for a meeting coming up on January 15, 1879--for women only. Back in 1856 President Isaac C. Haight organized the women of the Cedar City Ward into a society for benevolent purposes. Thus, it was known as the Female Benevolent Society.[4] Since then women of the town held a close bond in support of each other.

Priscilla was surprised when John showed up to tend the children. She assured him that she and Janey would hurry home soon. The day was cold and windy. No January thaw, yet. There was a cozy fire burning in the stove at the meeting house where the women were busily greeting each other. Sarah Ann stood and brought the meeting to order. After a song and prayer, Ellen Lunt was appointed to preside over the meeting. Proudly she announced, "It now becomes my duty to state the object of this meeting, viz; To defend our views and religious convictions and to protest against the anti-polygamy movement and petition."

After the petition was read by the Secretary, Sarah Chatterley, a committee of five women were appointed to draft the resolutions. While the women were absent, Lunt presented her views on plurality. Ending her comments with, "I was one of the pioneers to this place 27 years ago, and have helped make the place what it is, and all I ask of the outsiders is to mind their own business, and let the Latter-day Saints mind theirs. May the Lord bless and maintain our cause. Amen."

The committee returned the following:

> Resolved—-that we, the women of the Church of Jesus Christ of Latter-day Saints of Cedar City, in mass meeting assembled fully endorse the Preamble and Resolutions passed by the women of the Latter-day Saints in mass meeting assembled, in Salt Lake City, Nov. 16th 1878.

After the Preamble and Resolutions were read by the secretary and adopted by the congregation, one by one, women stood on their feet to express their feelings about living in polygamy.

Sarah Ann was the first to stand. She was humble and sincere when she said, "I believe in polygamy and feel blessed and proud to say I love every member of my husband's family, and would not have our family relations interfered with. I desire that we be let alone to worship God according to the dictates of our own consciences."

Nodding in agreement, Priscilla brushed away a tear. For Sarah Ann to publicly announce her love for Priscilla's family made her feel all the more welcome. Priscilla could hardly wait for the meeting to end so that she could tell John all about it.[5]

Priscilla noticed that, even though Sarah Ann was a busy grandmother, she treated Don and Betsy the same as she did her own grandchildren. She enjoyed them just the same as she did Robert's five children, Charles's one son, and Teresa Ann's four children, who lived nearby. Tillie's four children were frequent visitors until she and her husband, John Macfarlane, moved to St. George. They had a son born there, who died young. Sarah Ann's happy disposition made them all welcome.

Priscilla didn't always know what was going on over at Sarah Ann's house, but she was always interested. Sarah Ann liked to see Priscilla's youngsters, so she happened over quite often. The children were growing up fast, and it was getting time for Priscilla to have another baby.

Sometimes, Janey went out dancing with a beau—-that's when John slipped in and spent some alone time with Priscilla. He missed her so much and hated the straps of the law that kept him away from her. Priscilla was still his bonnie lass, and he loved her dearly. John enjoyed hearing about the children and peeked in at them while they slept.

Priscilla's love for John had deepened, and she didn't have any trouble conceiving his children. Even though she hadn't been told how many he wanted, Priscilla knew he would be happy to know she was carrying another of his posterity. John was happy, and he did all he could to make her comfortable. He saw to it that the wood was chopped and stacked for the winter fires. When the weather became cold enough, a side of beef, a mutton, a smoked ham, and a hunk of fresh bacon were hung in the shed for the two women's use. The pig's head and hooves were brought for them to make head cheese.

The home of John's first family was filled with anticipation that the oldest Urie son, David, would soon be going on a mission. In preparation for his mission, David, now that he was twenty-one years old, was making plans for going to the St. George Temple, on January 29, 1879, where he would receive his endowments.

Priscilla knew she was going to miss David. He and his twin brother, George, who were only two years younger than she, were the ones who were there when she needed help. Priscilla thought George should have a little more gumption about going to the temple and planning a mission. She had noticed, though, that he had his eye on a special girl, and she guessed his mind was more on courting. Their sister, Sarah Jane, who was two years younger than the twins, was all excited about her betrothal to David Hunter.

That fall, Priscilla helped Sarah Ann with the wedding festivities for Sarah Jane and David Hunter.[6] On October 8, the young couple were married by John F. D. Macallister in the St. George Temple, and then Priscilla was able to settle down to prepare for the arrival of her new baby.

White cotton cloths were always saved by Priscilla, for some cause or other, and a piece of white wool was tucked away for making mustard plasters. From the stash of bleached flour sacks, the women got busy preparing for the upcoming blessed event. While Janey spent time stitching at the sewing machine, Priscilla contented herself with embroidering everything, except diapers and belly bands, of course, that her infant might wear. Janey helped hem diapers and made Priscilla new T-straps, which would be used to hold the cloths the women had folded for sanitary use. A large white cloth was saved to be used as a "belly binder" for Priscilla after the baby was born.

When the time came, on December 10, 1879, Janey was there to help John's faithful wife, Sarah Ann, with the birth. The baby was healthy and perfect. Priscilla was flattered when John chose to name their new baby girl Priscilla. For four-year-old Donald, whom Betsy called "Don," Priscilla was more than he could say, and Zillie became her name. It didn't seem fair to Don that now he had two sisters and no brothers.

The families hardly had time to enjoy Priscilla's new baby and get Christmas over when arrangements were on the way for another marriage of the Urie children. Agnes, Thomas' twin, became Peter Albert Nelson's wife on January 21, 1880.[7]

CHAPTER 13

"Bonny Scotland"

John was a little surprised when, during July of 1880, he received a letter from the First Council of Seventy. In part, it read: "I am directed to notify you to communicate to said Council your condition as to your ability to pay your expenses and support your family in your absence; as to how long it is since you have been on a mission, and what your feelings are in responding to this call."

It seemed to forty-five-year-old John that he had more than enough to worry about. Finally, after wrestling with the knowledge that his oldest son, David, at long last had received his call on the same day, John's negative thoughts were soothed—-he was filled with pride at the prospect of serving a mission with his son. John, of course, had to let his parents know. Agnes and George would be happy and eager to help their son come to Scotland. His wives gave him moral support—-it was an honor to have a husband who was chosen to serve more than one mission.

The necessary letters went back and forth, and the First Council of Seventy was satisfied that John Urie and his son, David, were worthy and able to serve missions. They were going to Great Britain and would be traveling elders in the Glasgow Conference, to labor under the direction of Elder D. C. Dunbar.

When all was ready, both families bid John and David goodbye. It was a long procession of handshakes and hugs. Priscilla said her goodbyes in private so she didn't

David Urie

have to put on a display in front of the others. She wasn't about to let on that she wanted John to stay home. Janey comforted her and promised that she would continue to stay with her—-for this, Priscilla was grateful.

It was the 15th day of September 1880 on a cloudy and drizzly day. The roads were good, and John's wagon was loaded with ample supplies for camping and lunch for the train. George and their brother, Thomas, who was now seventeen and was called "Tom," were with their father and David. After traveling all day, going through Beaver and heading westward toward Milford, John could no longer see the road in the dark—-it was eight o'clock at night. The tired travelers made camp on the ridge of Minersville Mountain.

After prayers were said and all was ready for a night's rest, John lay awake thinking about his wives and children. He missed them already. He missed them before he left, but he couldn't say so. He was resolute in his commitment to a mission. He had spent the last winter writing long sermons on the Godhead, Deity, Adam and Eve, eternal life, and man's opportunity to work for his own salvation. John sent a copy to Scotland, in a letter to his brother George. At the end of many pages, with just a wee bit of his wry humor, which he knew George would catch, he wrote,

> You may read this letter to anybody you think proper. Suppose you read it to the Master of your Lodge. I have not written this in the spirit of religious controversy but simply to have you understand my ideas of Deity. I am myself a Mason but not of your order.
>
>   I remain your brother, John Urie.
>   Write soon George

On the third day out, at three o'clock in the afternoon, the wagon creaked into Milford. Train tickets were bought, and camp was made where the men prepared to get as much sleep as possible before departure time, 3:40 a.m. While boarding the train, John gave instructions to George and Tom to watch over his wives. He knew Janey was with Priscilla, but he wanted to make sure the boys didn't neglect her.

The long ride on the train ended at 6:25 p.m. in Salt Lake City. Ironically, John spent his long ride musing over the mystery of how the farmers along the way lived and kept their heads above water while farming desert land.

After spending a long day in the city and retiring to Gremgas, an adequate and private hotel, John wrote in his diary about his busy day:

John Taylor

Sept. 18. Went to President Taylor's office, had a social encouraging chat. Was set apart by Apostle Carrington—-blessing very good. Did some trifling business during the balance of the day. Subscribed for the S. L. City *Weekly News* to be sent to Glasgow for one year, also contribution to be sent home. . . . Walked through the city in the early part of the evening and then returned to my hotel to prepare for my long journey to Great Britain. Wrote home to my family encouragingly and retired to rest.

The local Utah Central delivered John and David Urie to the Union Pacific station in Ogden, where tickets were bought for

Omaha—-from there on to Chicago and New York. The trains traveled slowly and were always behind schedule, which eliminated most meal stops. The nuisance of driving cattle off the tracks furthered their delay—-at one point a litter of pigs was lying in the way.

The click-clack of the rails lulled John into thinking of his first trip across the plains. Traveling by a steam-powered train was a far cry from a covered wagon pulled by oxen. And now, even though he was hungry—-after the last of their two day's provisions were long gone, he felt blessed for this modern convenience of the railways.

After a tedious, six-day ride on the rails, John and David arrived in New York at 8:00 a.m.—-weary, dirty, and hungry. They beckoned to the driver of a horse-drawn coach to fetch them to the Stevens House. It was "a fine place and good enough for any ordinary man who is careful of his money . . . no grandness or empty show to pay for." It was "sort of a first class second rate house . . . for $1.00 per night."[1]

They "washed up and dressed," John "had a dram of whiskey which was very refreshing," they "ate very heartily—-rested a bit and at 11 o'clock A.M. went in search of a vessel sailing to Liverpool." John was pleased with himself at finding cabin tickets for $10 under the regular price.

September was cool and pleasant for traveling. A cab delivered them to Pier 37. John and David were on board at 8:30 a.m. and were "glad to be out of the way of busses, cabs, horses and carts, [and] tramway cars." From the deck of the S. S. City of Berlin, John amused himself by watching the boarding passengers. In his mind, he thought: "They represent every variety of intellectual and physical capacity—-the ways of men are curious."

John took on a cosmopolitan air—-this was after all his sixth crossing of the Atlantic Ocean. He had his bout with the usual seasickness but recovered fairly well. Poor David had a difficult time adjusting to all the travel. John knew that David was feeling far from home and lonely among strangers, which indeed he was. John knew that David's mountain life was "far different to traveling as a first-class passenger by sea or land," and he was "unused to upper tin society." And John thought, with an amusing and keen perception, "He feels like the speckled bird."

David remained a faithful tenant of his bed, and John whiled his time with reading, chatting, and strolling the decks. On Sunday, John attended an English worship meeting, after which he reported to David,

What comfort can be derived from what I heard is inconceivable to me. Cost me a schilling, the irrepressible hat being the wind off [of] the service. I suppose what money is gathered on such occasions is given to the poor or some charitable institution. With this end in view, I gave the schilling hoping that in my own case the people to whom I am sent to preach the gospel to, may administer to my wants and necessities and that

I may be inspired to speak the truth as it is in Christ Jesus bringing comfort and happiness to the weary and the poor of the earth.

On the evening of Monday, September 25, while longing for a bowl of bread and milk for supper, John ended his diary entry by writing:

> Lunch at 1 P.M. Good enough for dinner. Dinner at 6 P.M., a rather strange time of day to eat dinner—-foods from the real solids down to every delicacy that depraved tastes and strong stomachs can get away with. I thank my Heavenly Father that I was not born and brought up in polite society—-one of many reasons being obliged to eat food that nothing but an ostrich can properly digest.

Thereafter, when lunch was served at 10:00 a.m., John made dinner out of it; and, at 6:00 p.m., when dinner was served, he simply took light food and not much of it. During one of John's conversations with David, he commented, "How the so called Americans hide away so much rich food is astonishing to me. Were I held deserving to deeds done in the body and my punishment was to eat like those fellows, I could consider my case hard indeed."

The ship passed the banks of Newfoundland on September 28. After sailing the open sea for five days, the passengers watched the coast of Ireland appear on the horizon. It was early morning, and John's heart was warmed with the thoughts of nearing the isles of Great Britain. David was feeling better, and the two of them spent the day watching the coastline of the *dear ould isle* of Ireland.

The ship sailed around the southern tip of Ireland and approached Cork Harbor where Queenstown,[2] the first port of call, was located. John was anxious to point out to David the St. Colman's Cathedral, which could be seen from the distance, rising above the shore with a majestic three-hundred-foot spire and a carillon of forty-two bells. At the dock, John

Thomas & Mary Cowan Urie & family

and David stayed on board while the ship let off passengers and took on English tourists.

While sailing up the St. George's Channel, which spilled into the Irish Sea, John pointed out many more points of interest to David. John had prayed that the blessings of the Lord would be with the ship, its crew, and the passengers and that the trip would be successful, and it was. The ship, all intact, docked at the seaport of Liverpool, England, on Monday, October 4, 1880.[3]

John was pleased that his telegraph message had gotten to Scotland. His parents and his brothers, Thomas and George, with their families were on the pier waiting for their arrival. They were duly impressed with John's handsome son David. David was happy to finally meet his grandparents, uncles, aunts, and cousins and felt their acceptance of him. It was good to put his feet on solid ground again.

John Benson

John's and David's missions were going well. Letters from loved ones were sent to and from Cedar City and Scotland. John expected more letters, and Priscilla watched eagerly for the mail. Priscilla knew she hadn't sent a letter lately, but she would get one off soon. Priscilla had been busy helping her sister, Mary Alice, prepare for her wedding. She married John Benson from Parowan during the busy time of Thanksgiving preparations. Priscilla just couldn't find time to write.

When Priscilla got letters going again, they were regular for a spell. But Priscilla got bogged down again; and, for some unknown reason, she hadn't heard from John either. Priscilla worried and wondered when John would be coming home. In her last letter, Priscilla came right out and asked John to come home. Maybe he was thinking about it.

"Priscilla, it's here! Priscilla!" Janey came running with a letter in her hand—-the bishop had stopped by on his way into town with the mail. Priscilla didn't wait for anything; she just sat down and read her letter—-while Janey quietly left the room to take care of the children.

Dear Priscilla   Glasgow June 10th 1881
    I hope your eyes will not be deceived when you behold this venerable looking likeness of mine.

    I am not like you women who cannot get anything of this sort to please you. I rather pride myself on the success of the artist who took my picture, he has taken it to the life—-I feel pleased & well paid for my five shillings. In comparing this picture with the one of four years ago, I perceive a marked difference.

    To relate to you the beauties of the present one would be superfluous. It is wrong for me to say that I do not look young—-grave and gray is the prevailing characteristic of this beautiful work of art.

You will pardon my opinion of the ruler of your destinies—-the patriarch of a rising family. You can pass your opinion of course, I hope it will be good, and although not equal to the original you must in the meantime rest satisfied.

Priscilla paused momentarily and smiled a little at John's going on about his looks. She snatched the picture from the envelope and, while admiring the "beautiful work of art," noticed that the "ruler of her destiny" did look a little older. With both hands, she held John's picture close to her heart and yearned to have him near her. As she wiped away a tear, she read on—-eager to see if he might come home soon.

I think you owe me a letter, but of this I will find no fault.

I was thankful to hear from you that you and children were well. Your pluck I must say is commendable, your affection for my character as a preacher of the gospel is grand & smacks of the true spirit of the wife of a Seventy. I will not, I cannot leave for home until I have fulfilled an honorable mission.

Priscilla's hopes were dashed! She knew John hadn't been out a full year yet, but she thought with the children and all that he might come home ahead of David. Now she knew she would not see him until September. Through blinking tears Priscilla finished reading John's letter—-

I think of you and the "bairns" often & wonder how you get along. I left you in the hands of God—-I put my trust in him, firmly believing that you are a ward in His care. I am preaching, counselling and advising all the time & take great pleasure in it. I enjoy my calling under every circumstance, & I believe the result is good to those among whom I administer & to myself. God is true to his promises, while laboring in the ministry He is my friend and supporter. I think often of Donald and Betsy, bless their souls I wish I could see them. I have here in Glasgow near my fathers house a little girl just about like Betsy, she jumps into my arms every time I see her & I give her pennies & candy, it makes me look at home & long for a meeting with my family. I dare not indulge too much on the thoughts of home. And little Priscilla I can scarce think of her, I can hardly imagine what she is like, I will come home to her a stranger, I shall have to cultivate her acquaintance.

Well Priscilla, God bless you, God bless the children, kiss them for me & keep them in remembrance of their father, I think I see them while I write—-& hear their prattle. Take care of them, teach them to be good.

The weather here at present is delightful, crops are splendid & the whole country is "Bonny Scotland" clad in flowers & greens of spring. Give my love to Jane, Betsy & the kid, that is the other kid . . . everybody & take my blessing yourself. Father & Mother are well & so is David.   Your affectionate

John

Priscilla was flooded with emotion when she read how much John missed the children.

"That 'Bonny Scotland.' Why, oh why?"

"Well," Priscilla whispered, "I will go there someday and see for myself."[4]

Agnes & Janet
Urie

George & Elizabeth
McLellan Urie

CHAPTER 14

Missions Accomplished

Priscilla K. Urie

It was a hot August day in 1881. Priscilla was downhearted. Her sadness was almost unbearable—-John was gone clear across the ocean when she needed him the most. It was in all the news. It must be true, Priscilla thought. She sorted through the papers again and picked one up to read aloud: "The 'Destroying Angels' Accomplish a Mission they are sent to do."[1]

The article told all about how her father, Philip Klingensmith, had been found murdered in a prospector's hole in the state of Sonora, Mexico.[2] "He was right," she thought. "He expected to be murdered."

Priscilla reached out to grasp Janey's hand while the two of them concluded that it must be true—-their father was dead. He had been such an outstanding man of the community; and now, after being driven into exile, the thing they dreaded most of all had finally happened.

Their sisters and their half brother, Alfred, came to call often. The siblings were distressed with the hashing up of all the bad things that could be said about their father. Friends reminded them that he had been the best bishop they ever had and he had been a good and kind man. The Indians didn't believe the stories they heard—-to them Philip Klingensmith had been a "heap good bishop."

A sad part of Philip Klingensmith's death was that there would be no last words to be said before a congregation in his behalf—-no grave to visit. Not knowing just where he was buried was the worst of all and haunted Priscilla's soul. It was the same for Philip as it was for Priscilla's real parents—-buried in unmarked graves where no words had been said to comfort the ones who mourned for them.

At times, in the still of the night, Priscilla's thoughts turned to the massacre. She couldn't help but think Philip Klingensmith held some key that may have helped her know for sure who her parents were and if any of her brothers and sisters survived—-if, indeed, she had any at all. When she last saw Philip, she deliberately kept it from her mind. He had been through so much, and she just didn't want to harrow up feelings that would add to his grief. Anyway, now, she would never be able to ask him.

It was best to let things lie and hope nobody found out about her secret—-for sure, that is. Priscilla worried so much about being a plural wife, and she felt the business of where she came from must be kept still. Her sisters never asked about anything, so she guessed they didn't know.

It was nearing September and baby Zill (Priscilla) was able to walk and talk. She joined Don and Betsy in asking, "When will *Father* be home?" Zill didn't remember him, but she heard a lot about this stranger and was eager to see him.

September finally came, and John with David was ready to board ship on the 2nd day of the month. The voyage back to America, to say the least, was very different from the trip over. At the dock, all was in an uproar and confusion with the 607 Saints, including twenty-two returning elders, and about 400 Gentile passengers, both cabin and steerage, trying to fit into the protocol of boarding the ship.

Gratefully, the weather was good. It was 7:00 p.m. before the passengers and mounds of luggage were on board. John and David found their way to their cabin. In steerage, there weren't enough berths; but Scandinavians, Germans, and those from Great Britain made the best of an uncomfortable night. Next morning was still unorganized, but by 3:00 p.m., the ship, *S. S. Wyoming,* finally pulled anchor.

At 4:30 p.m., the returning missionaries organized themselves for the benefit of the Saints. "Finlayson Pres., Olsen and Funk Counsellors, Jackson and Stohl Chaplains, Maycock and Adder guards, Urie Clerk." It was decided to "place some discreet person over every room (each containing from 16 to 30) as a ward and to take general oversight." Carpenters made more berths, and the missionaries went about to help make everyone as comfortable as possible. The ship's officers were "gentlemanly and kind." By nightfall, there remained some "confusion, sea sickness, and a little grumbling."[3]

Good weather prevailed, and the Irish Sea was smooth. On Sunday, the 4th of September, the ship took on a hundred more passengers at Queenstown, which caused another shortage of berths. After two hours at the docks, the ship left the inlet and headed around the south end of Ireland into a rough and rolling open sea. John, who already had his sea legs, and two other elders were kept busy helping the sick passengers.

During this voyage John made the acquaintance of Sarah Robertson Matheson from Scotland. The trip was difficult for her while traveling alone with a young son and nearing her time for another child to be born. Her husband, David, had gone to America ahead of her and was working on the temple at Manti with his father while he made a home for her. Sarah became very seasick and was thankful when John helped her to the upper deck for fresh air and tied her son to her so he wouldn't become lost.[4]

Determination and long-suffering helped the Saints in steerage to endure the voyage. Encouragement and instructions from the elders were "to care for each other and to hang by one another" and "to keep the spirit of religion."[5] Bearing up under the present inconveniences, now and on through their lives, was the price they had to pay for their salvation on earth and the hereafter.

It was a misty morning on Monday, September 12, 1881, and the "big horn" was blowing. The ship had made its run in nine days. At 10:30 a.m., the pilot was on board to steer the ship into the New York harbor. To expedite the transportation of the Saints to the West, the missionaries had spent many hours getting train tickets ready. A meeting was held to instruct "the Saints how to act on landing and during the railroad passage." Elders Urie, Maycock, and Hanson were in charge of the commissary, and Elder Hart was in charge of forwarding the Saints West. Young David Urie was glad to be back in America and heading home.

The anxious George and Tom were waiting at Milford for the two travel-wise men whose missions had been accomplished. The boys were all ears and wanted to know all about their father's and brother's experiences. They rattled off question upon question—-among which they quipped, "What treasures shall we find in these boxes from Scotland?"

Paisley Shawl

John was quick to bring them about to answer his questions. "I dinna want to an-swer anymore now until I hear about my Sarah Ann, and Priscilla. What about my wee ones—-and ye Tom, what about ye?" John had heard all about Tom's accident early that spring. He had been kicked in the head by a horse, which broke his lower jaw and knocked five of his teeth out. John was thinking Tom looked pretty good for all his troubles. The conversation swung to every-thing pertaining to John's loved ones and occupied their remaining journey home.

When Priscilla flung open the door to greet John, she stood all aghast. When John could see she was startled at the change in his "countenance," he was quick to humor her. "I am very stout as you can see." With his hands on his waist—-stepping to the side with his right foot, he stood in a familiar stance and added, "Weighing over 200 lbs." Don, Betsy, and toddling Zill came running, and it was a merry reunion.

John could see that God had watched over Priscilla and her household, and he was eager to show her the "splendid" shawl his mother had bought for her. It was a red and gold wool paisley with fringed borders on each end. A jeweled anchor pin was sent to enhance its beauty. Priscilla was pleased, and this endeared her to John's mother. The shawl was spread, covering the entire top of Priscilla's bed, for everybody to admire.[6]

While the things brought home for the children occupied their time, John was free to visit with Priscilla. He could see that she was troubled. Priscilla was happy that she finally had John to lean on and was anxious to talk about her father. She wanted to know what John thought about all the newspaper reports and gathered the papers for him to read. With discerning interest, in part, he read:

August 4, 1881   **Deseret Evening News**

"Klingensmith, He is Supposed to Have Been Murdered by Mormons, Salt Lake *Daily Tribune***."**

News has reached Pioche, says the *Record*, that bishop Philip Klingensmith, at one time a man of high standing and great influence in the Mormon Church, and the exposer of the Mountain Meadows massacre, and the names of the men who participated in the bloody deed, is dead. His body was found in a prospect hole, in the State of Sonora, Mexico, and a letter from there, which was received in the vicinity of Pioche, states that the mystery surrounding the body indicates that Klingensmith had been murdered. Klingensmith died just as he expected.

John was reluctant to believe all he read in the papers and advised Priscilla they would just have to wait for some proof. This advice helped Priscilla to go about her own life with a little more contentment. Priscilla knew that John had a lot of wisdom, and she was willing to wait patiently to see if Philip Klingensmith showed up alive.[1]

CHAPTER 15

No Other Choice

Spring in Cedar City was an important time of the year. There were always lots of seasonable tasks to be done. Lambing kept even the children busy. Some of the sheep had twins or a weak lamb and it was a challenge to raise the bummers until they could survive on their own. Priscilla, with help from the children, found time to raise a few of these lambs. She also had a gentle way with honey bees and liked her hives to be placed where the bees could find sweet-clover blossoms to gather their pollen.

Priscilla watched over her flower beds and admired the bluebells of Scotland that John planted for her. They were pretty while they bloomed; but they, she thought, were more like weeds when they died down, and they took over everything around them. John loved them, and Priscilla always thought of him and his "Bonnie Scotland" while they were blooming in the spring and wondered if she would ever see the lowlands where they came from.

Priscilla smiled when she heard George was going to get married in the fall. The young girl, Alice Jane Perry, whom George had had his eye on, and he tied the knot on October 16, 1881. John's first family was growing up, and this was the third child of his to be married. Between Sarah Ann's children and theirs, he was getting quite a few grandchildren, and he was only forty-six years old.

John wasn't finished having children. Priscilla had conceived her fifth child. Her first child was born in August, and this child was due in August, too. Priscilla's last months with her three living children were in the cold months of the year, and she dreaded the last months of this pregnancy to be during the heat.

Don was almost seven years old, Betsy was four and a half, and Zill was two and a half. They were eager for a baby brother. Finally, at the end of the hottest days of the year, August 23, 1882, their brother was born. He had trouble with his lungs and had a difficult time breathing. For two days, he struggled; and just moments before he succumbed, his father, John, gave him a blessing and a name. James was the name that he would be remembered by. John's brother, James, was proud the baby was named after him and worried about his own mortality as he was, it seemed of late, sickly himself.

Don, Betsy, and Zill had a difficult time understanding why their baby brother couldn't live. Priscilla tried to take her baby's death as a matter of course—-knowing that she would see him again someday. Her recovery was slow, and she again blamed herself for having bad milk. John tried to talk her out of this notion but could not change her mind.

The aging and wealthy parents of John and James still kept in touch and wrote about their vacation on the coast of Scotland and about the purchase of their new home. They boasted of having five rooms, a bathroom, and hot and cold running water. It was a flat on 32 Leven Street, Pollokshield, Scotland. James hoped to get well enough to see his parents' new place but never regained health and died January 30, 1883, in Salt Lake City. He left his wife, Violet, and three children, George, Martha and Agnes.

That same day, John had just returned from witnessing the marriage of his daughter, Eliza Ann, who was married to John J. G. Webster, when he heard about his brother's sudden death. He would have to scramble to get to the funeral—-which was to be held a few days later in Salt Lake City. Before the day was up, the weather turned bad; and the snow stacked up until it was too deep to travel through to the train station in Milford. John felt down and sorrowful when he couldn't go, but he sent his regards on to Violet and the children.

Priscilla was perking up and trying to do the best she could with all that was going on around her. She wasn't very happy when Janey, who preferred to be called Jane now that she was all grown up, moved to Parowan to live with a friend.

Jane, who was trying to make good on her decision to make her own way through the world, spent several months working in different homes. When Jane became dissatisfied with the amount she was earning, she decided to go to Salt Lake City with her friend to become a dressmaker. Jane was all packed and ready to leave when her sister, Betsy Ann, took sick; and she was needed at Hamilton's Fort to help care for her.

One day, about the time Betsy Ann was able to take care of herself, Jane was at the ditch, where she was dipping a bucket of water, when a dream she had had three months earlier came rushing back to her. A man walked up to her and made his acquaintance. He smiled knowingly at her and said, "You are the girl I have been looking for." In her dream, Jane had been impressed to remember that she would marry this man—-it was all so romantic, and it was coming true. Now Jane knew his name was Alma Platte Spilsbury.

Alma Spillsbury

On the day of the wedding, March 2, 1883, which took place in the St. George Temple, Jane not only became a wife but also became the mother of Alma's two orphaned children. Jane's happy union separated the Klingensmith sisters when, on the day after the ceremony, Alma took his family to Arizona. Jane had never been farther away from home than Parowan, and now she was traveling in a covered wagon and learning to cook over a campfire.

Weddings were in the air, on April 20, a quiet marriage took place for David Urie and his sweetheart, Zelpha Wood. Nobody knew for sure whether Zelpha was in the family way, but they surmised as much when John's son David, who had been on a mission, wasn't married in the temple.

Six months and one week later, on November 6, David and Zelpha's son was born. It was kept kind of hush, hush, because of the embarrassment and all. At the young couple's home, on December 12, 1883, the baby's uncle, Robert Heyborne, blessed him with the name David Claude. Following the special blessing, Robert, as counselor to Bishop Lunt, was asked to stand in with the latter and his other counselor, Francis Webster, to cut both David and Zelpha off from the Church. The reason named was "lacurous [lecherous] cohabitation previous to marriage." The couple "acknowledged & voted the justice of the act."[1] Sarah Ann was sorry that it was her son who had to stand in for the excommunication—-but, she thought, he did well with the blessing.

For John, the hustle between wives and children was never ending. Two days after the excommunication, John and Sarah Ann were called to Priscilla's home. She was in labor, and at six o'clock in the evening, Priscilla gave birth to a daughter. The baby was a weak little thing, and John thought it best to bless her that night. John gave her the name Janet Forsyth, in honor of his grandmother.

Janet was fussed and hovered over until she was finally strong enough to be out in public. Almost three months later, on March 6, 1884, the family gathered at Church, and Janet was blessed before the congregation by her father. Betsy and Zill were happy about their sister, but Don was still wishing he had a brother. Most of the time, Don's new sister was called "Net," but sometimes she was called "Nettie."

In the meantime John and Sarah Ann's oldest son, Tom, had taken a fancy to Catherine Keturah Tidwell Gower, whom Tom called "Kate," and had asked her to marry him. His father was excited about the marriage and wanted to perform the ceremony. Authority was given to John Urie by bishop Henry Lunt, and on April 19, 1884, the nuptials took place in the home of the bride's mother in Cedar City.

Another family gathering took place during the same month. John was so proud that his son, David, and his wife, Zelpha, had stayed close to the gospel and were able to renew their memberships in the Church. This meant they were worthy for their temple marriage in the St. George Temple. It was a beautiful ceremony, Priscilla thought, which was performed on, April 30, 1884, by the temple ordinance worker Elder J. T. D. Macallister. Tears of joy were spilt when, after the ceremony, David Claude was united with his parents to be sealed to them for all time and eternity. The occasion was a momentous one for John, who beamed with pride.

John was becoming more concerned about his position with two wives. His relationship with his children formed an inseparable bond of love—-they were of him and they filled his life. The unity in his homes, and their love for one another, made this way of life a matter of importance and was as natural for

John as anything could be.

Because of stronger laws—-the antipolygamy laws of the U.S. Congress that were passed in 1884—-the life John had created for himself was crashing down around him. Mormon men were, by law, to choose one wife and divorce the others. Many of John's friends and other Mormons were caught up with "fines and imprisonments [that] were of constant occurrence, and hundreds of heads of families gave themselves up, and stood their trial."[2]

John's two wives were dear to his heart—-he loved them both, and it was unthinkable for him to choose one wife over the other. For him to live by this new law, he would have to do just that or go to jail.

John had been warned before about his wives, but now he had no other choice but to go into hiding. Most often he was out in Hamilton's Fort where Priscilla's sister, Betsy Ann, and her husband, John Hamilton, hid him from the law. It was boring and distasteful to John, who would rather be working the land and attending to his cattle. He longed to be with his wives and children. John wanted to walk around free and uninhibited by threats of the law. The desire to fulfill his stewardship as the father of his many children intensified with each passing day.

A letter had arrived from Scotland on July 12, 1884, and found its way to John. His mother talked about his father, who had been ill and seemed to be improving. He wasn't strong enough to "walk out in the street yet," but they took a "drive in an open machine every other day." The Glasgow fair was coming up on the first of the month—-a celebration that brought fond memories back to John. Being unable to attend, his mother planned, if George was able, "to go to some country place for 2 or 3 weeks."

Letters arrived on a regular basis, and John was kept abreast of his father's condition. He lingered for a year, and then word came to John that his seventy-five-year-old father, George Urie, had passed away on June 30, 1885. John made arrangements as soon as he could to be appointed to labor in the Glasgow Conference of the Church as a missionary. He was going to go anyway, and he felt that serving a mission furthered his work in the Kingdom of God.

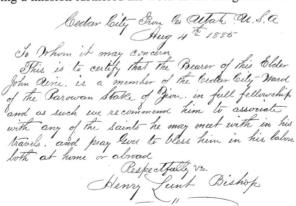

John worked diligently as a missionary under the direction of Elder Burt. He revisited members he had baptized, who were glad to see him, and chastised some who had become complacent about their conversions. He most of all searched for new members of the Church and found success.

Agnes, John's mother, was grateful to have her oldest son home to help console her and give financial advice. John found that the polygamy clause had not been removed from his father's will and that his mother was distraught about it. The $200,000 estate had been left "under the management of a board of trustees."

John made an appeal to the Court of Session and "instituted a claim for his share of the estate, on the ground that a father could not, under the laws of Great Britain, disinherit his eldest son. He found the money had been invested chiefly in bank stocks in such a manner as to be proof against his claim."[3]

John's claim, however, won him a percentage of his share of the estate; but because his children, under the law, were not viewed as "legitime," they were not given a share. Now that the money wasn't going to be awarded in a lump sum, John was dependent on his mother to send him his allotments and to send Sarah Ann and Priscilla a divided portion of their share.

The feelings John had felt so many years ago about being cut from his inheritance had changed considerably now that he had a growing family and so many mouths to feed and backs to clothe.

At the end of John's four-month mission, Agnes tried to keep her son in Scotland for a longer stay, but to no avail. John loved his mother and wanted to please her, knowing she needed his attention; but his families needed him at home. Before John left, Agnes promised him she would send the money as the dividends came in.

When John arrived in Cedar City, he found his families in good keeping. They flocked around him and welcomed him home. Priscilla had been alone with her children so much before John left on his mission that his four months' absence was almost more than she could stand. When they finally found time alone, although John was fifty years old, he still had plenty of passion in him; and he wooed Priscilla into another conception.

John's mother was good for her word and faithfully sent money each month to John's two wives. In a letter sent to Priscilla, with her first remittance, Agnes explained the amount she was to receive:

> 32 Berlin Terrace
> Pollokshield,
> May 18th, 1886

Dear Priscilla

I have enclosed a bank of England five pound note. Also 1-10 dollar bill which makes seven pounds . . . Sarah will give you ten shillings, as I enclosed eight pounds . . . each.

Priscilla was pleased with the letter and money—she would save it for a rainy day. Knowing John's mother had remained faithful to the Mormon Church, Priscilla had invited her to come to Utah for a visit—suggesting how nice it would be for her to go through the St. George Temple for her own endowments. She was disappointed when the letter informed her that she couldn't come:

> I have wrote to my son John telling him how I am situated in my bodyly health, I am not able to come to Utah at this time the doctor examined my body, he told me that I was not able to travel so far distance, perhaps I may be able yet, to come to Utah to do my own work, which I desire very much to do, but if I am never able John will see it done for me.

From reading the remainder of Agnes' letter, Priscilla could see that John had informed his mother about his hiding and running from the law:

> Priscilla I hope you are enjoying good health. Also the children I pray God to bless you all with health & strength and that John may be protected from all enemys. I need not say any more you will see the letter that I sent to John. Perhaps I may be able to come to Utah by & by. Please to acknowledge the receipt of this letter as I will be anxious to know if you have got it all right.
>
> Your Mother-in-law

Priscilla got busy and answered the letter, wanting to ease the worry for John's mother about receiving the money.

Nine months after John arrived home from his mission, on July 30, 1886, the passionate conception brought forth another daughter into the Urie family. She was a sweet little baby, and everybody enjoyed her but Don—he still wished for a brother. On her blessing day, she was given the name Mary, after her Aunt Mary, and the middle name was Main—her Grandmother Urie's maiden name.

Priscilla had given birth to Mary during the heat of the summer, and this worried her. As time passed, Priscilla could see that Mary was healthy and strong—she was going to live. Priscilla's heart sang, and she went about taking care of her five living children with happiness and contentment.[4]

CHAPTER 16

News About Philip Klingensmith

It was almost time for the 4th of July celebration, and the weather was hot. John sat near an open window—-the buzzing fly went unnoticed. With sadness in his eyes, he was remembering his last trip to Scotland and the good visit he had had with his brother Thomas. A telegraph message was in his hand; his brother was dead. He had turned fifty years old on April 28, and just one month later, on June 30, 1887, he was taken away suddenly by the silent reaper. John shook his head, muttering, "My dear old mother, George, and I are the only ones left."

John's sister, who lived only a few months, hadn't become a part of his life. John's brothers, David and James, were twelve and fifteen years younger than he; and even though James came to America, John never was as close to him as he was to Thomas. John's relationship with his brother George was strained at times. Since their father died, they hadn't seen eye to eye on financial matters and such. John had been dependent on George in the past to send him books he needed for history references, which he reciprocated with old coins and current coins of different countries to add to his brother's collection.

Because John was now in hiding, nobody close was around to console him. Aloneness crept into his soul, and he mourned without the comfort and doting of his families.

Priscilla missed John more than ever before. Not only did she long for his companionship but also their five children were a handful, and she needed his guidance and help. Sarah Ann was feeling her age, and although Priscilla was active, Sarah Ann was slowing down. The sons who used to be so much help were married and not around as much as they used to be. John's letters helped cheer Priscilla—-but she needed him near her.

Cedar City wasn't such a big place that strangers from other parts of the territory could be there and not be noticed. One day, when Alfred Klingon-smith,[1] Priscilla's half-brother, was in town, he observed a man he had met before. The man named Gibbs was kind of excited when he saw Alfred walking along the street. He had been down on the Colorado while nosing around for documentation on characters whom he was writing about in a book. Alfred was drawn in by Gibbs and eagerly listened to his tale about his father, who he thought was dead. As soon as he could break away, Alfred hightailed it over to Priscilla's house.

Priscilla exclaimed, "My lands Alfred, sit down and catch your breath." Alfred was still breathing hard when he exclaimed, "Joshia Gibbs says father is alive." Priscilla was anxious to hear what he had to say and asked, "What did he say?" "Well, he was talking about father and he said, 'Klingensmith had taken refuge with a band of Indians in Arizona at a place on the south side of the Colorado river, opposite Eldorado Canyon, in southern Nevada, where he took unto himself a squaw as his fourth or fifth wife.'"[2]

"Do you really think father would go to bed with a squaw?" Priscilla exclaimed. Alfred wasn't so sure about that, and they had a long discussion while pondering such an idea. Priscilla was happy to believe her father was alive, and she didn't want to consider that it might be a fabrication. Now that Alfred had a lead on where their father might be, he decided to set out to find him on his own.

Priscilla bid Alfred well and told him to take care of himself. She was concerned about his going down into that primitive and foreboding country. It was a desert, Priscilla heard, that had deep ravines and crevices where coyotes, rattle snakes, lizards and scorpions were the most abundant inhabitants. Priscilla was sure it would be a long time before she would be seeing Alfred again, so she went about her business—-trying not to worry about him.

Days went into weeks, and the few times John was able to slip in during the nighttime didn't fill much of Priscilla's time. Her father's twin boys, John and Philip, came into town once in a while and stopped by. The boys told Priscilla that their mom, Hannah, knew their father, Philip Klingensmith, was still alive after stories were splashed in all the newspapers about his being found in a prospector's hole in Senora, Mexico.

Priscilla's hopes were up now, and when Alfred finally returned, he told her about his visit with their father on the Colorado. The journey had been long and strenuous, and he was glad to be back home.

"The country down there," Alfred explained, "looks hot and dry, but its kind of sultry—-the nights are pretty chilly." Using his hands to help draw a picture, Alfred continued with, "lots of cactus—-some ten to fifteen feet high with arms on—-lots of stickers. The trail to where the Indians led me to father was narrow and steep—-I hardly recognized him."

Alfred talked with Priscilla about all the good advice his father had given him while he was working with him in his blacksmith shop before he ever left Cedar City.

That was years ago, and now Philip had some new advice. Alfred said, "You know Priscilla, I can hardly believe the words father spoke to me about." "What were they?" Priscilla asked. "Well, you know how religious our father was when he left?" Without waiting for Priscilla's reply, he exclaimed, "He told me not to get too religious, and that 'all the religion a person really needed was to live by the Golden Rule.'"[3]

Priscilla was understanding, and she asked, "You mean the scripture that says, *'Therefore all things whatsoever ye would that men should do to you, do ye even so to them?'*"[4] "Yes," Alfred replied. They talked about it for awhile and realized their father had been chased from pillar to post and not treated very well most of the time. The years Philip Klingensmith put in as a good bishop didn't count for anything.

Their father had been good to people, especially the Indians, and the wrong he had done was in the name of the Church. It was easy to see why he felt religion was less important than how a person should be treated. Alfred and Priscilla figured he should have held to the idea that the "Golden Rule" was part of living his religion. But then it was the so-called religious people who turned against him.

Alfred told Priscilla that their father was haunted and tormented by what happened to those people in the wagon train. It was hard to watch him weep as he talked about it. The mixed emotions rose up in Priscilla, and she fought back the dark feelings she herself was haunted by. Her compassion for Philip Klingensmith was stronger than any hate she could ever feel for him. Priscilla pushed aside all the thoughts that were racing through her head, lest she should give in and tell Alfred all that she knew about where she came from.

In the ensuing months, Priscilla thought about the words Alfred brought back from their father. She knew it was good to be kind to others, and she had always tried to be thoughtful. She wished she could get on a horse and go find her father, too. That was out of the question. Priscilla was very stout, and it wasn't long before her due time to give birth—-for the eighth time. Priscilla finally pushed the thoughts of her father and all that concerned him into the deep recesses of her mind while she attended to the immediate future.

William Cattle

John's wife, Sarah Ann, was called to care for Priscilla on this joyful and blessed day, September 10, 1888. Priscilla had done herself proud—-finally giving John another son. When John blessed their new baby, he wanted his name to represent Priscilla's side of the family. William Cattle was decided upon—-William was his Grandmother Klingensmith's brother's name, and Cattle was in honor of his Grandmother Klingensmith's maiden name.

Thirteen-year-old Don was elated—-he finally got his brother. He teased his sisters, Betsy, Zill, Net, and Mary, saying his brother was cuter than they ever were. Don wanted to hold his brother all the time and had to fight his sisters for the chance. The fuss the grown-ups made over his very own brother didn't bend his nose out of shape—-Don knew they would be great friends; and he decided to call his brother "Will."

The five oldest children were getting old enough to be a lot of help to Priscilla, and Mary was just a toddler. It seemed to Priscilla that little boys wet their diapers more often than girls, but she didn't mind. She had swollen John's posterity by quite a bit, and she was happy she was able to bear his children—-

she sometimes wondered how many more special spirits she would bring into the world.

The following spring, Priscilla took her family up on the mountain for the summer, where she made cheese and butter. Don seemed so grown up and dependable. He was, in his mind, the man of the house and was his mother's helping hand. Don felt he was old enough to have his own horse and asked his father about it every time he saw him. The pigs and lambs fattened up and did well under Don's care. Betsy, Zill, and Net helped with the butter and cheese. Mary and Will made their presence known often enough to keep everybody busy.

John & Philip Klingensmith

Not long after Priscilla came down off the mountain, her half-brothers, John and Philip, came for a visit. They had gathered up supplies they couldn't get in Panaca and then met up with Alfred, their half brother, at the photo studio, where they had their pictures taken together. Their birthdays came just before Christmas, and the pictures were to be a surprise for their mothers. Priscilla hoped they would bring her one too—-they were such a handsome "Klingensmith" trio. Alfred looked a lot like the twins. She remembered when they were born—-just one day apart. It was hard to believe that it had been so long ago.

Priscilla inquired about their wives, Clara and Elizabeth, and then hastened to ask about their father. Philip and John didn't believe he was still alive. Their mom, Hannah, after not hearing from Philip for such a long time, had sent them south to search for him. The twins said they came back with stories that claimed Philip Klingensmith "moved to Arizona, where he located a rich mine,[5] but he took sick and the Indians took him to their camp and cared for him until he passed away and was buried by them."[6]

The twin, Philip, didn't take much stock in this story, and he told Priscilla he believed "His father was killed by Mormons and buried in a dry wash just south of Caliente."[7] He didn't have much regard for the Mormons and didn't mind saying so.

Priscilla was sorry Philip had such an attitude about the Mormons, and she argued that her father was still alive. She told them how Alfred had visited with him down near the Colorado River. But, if her father was dead now, she figured the Indians buried him and not the Mormons.

At any rate, after John and Philip's visit, Priscilla didn't want the world to know that her father had taken a squaw for a wife, and she planned on letting everybody believe the newspaper stories about his being found dead in Mexico. She had been working on her genealogy; and on the line that asked where her father died, she wrote: Senora Mexico.[8]

CHAPTER 17

John Moves Priscilla to Panaca

Wilford Woodruff

In 1889, a lot of to-do was made over the rumor of continued plural marriages performed in the Endowment House in Salt Lake City. Because of the "Edmunds Law," which had been enacted by Congress in 1884 to forbid plural marriages, President Wilford Woodruff, the newly appointed president of the Mormon Church, ordered the Endowment House to be torn down.

All of this stirring around of the government caused increased trouble for the men who chose to keep all their wives. In Iron County, the U.S. deputy marshals, "Armstrong and McGeary," seemed to appear from out of nowhere while searching for the wives of men who were in hiding. "Wives were not imprisoned for the 'usual charges,' but they were subpoenaed, like the children of polygamous brethren, to go to Beaver and testify against their husbands."[1]

John and Sarah Ann Urie's daughter, Tillie, who married John M. Macfarlane, put the family in stitches when they gathered for her daughter's wedding. She could hardly keep from laughing and crying at the same time, when with the remains of soot and dough clinging to her hair, the story was told:

> While she was cooking the wedding feast . . . It happened that at a crucial point in the preparation of the dinner, the stove pipe became loose and fell down. Tillie was mixing dough at the moment, and her hands were covered. Smoke was pouring out of the stove; without waiting to get the dough off her hands, she jumped onto a chair and was guiding the black, soot-covered pipe back into the flue when one of the children came running into the kitchen, crying out, "Run and hide quick, the marshals are coming!" Tillie let go of the stove pipe and clapped her hands to her face, exclaiming, "Oh, my God!" She hesitated for a moment, then jumped down from the chair and ran for the barn, her face streaked with white dough and black soot. She dived into a manger and the children covered her up with hay. The marshals came and looked all around for her, returning several times in hopes of surprising her, but she was wise enough to stay hidden in the manger until they had finally headed east out of town.[2]

Although the family got a laugh over how Tillie escaped the marshals, it was getting too hot for John. Right away, he decided to move Priscilla and the children to Panaca, Lincoln County, Nevada.

Priscilla wasn't looking forward to the prospects of living so far away from the rest of the family. But pack she did, and they loaded all they could onto a wagon and headed west. It was early spring and she had been looking forward to a summer on the mountain. It had been raining. The road to Panaca was bumpy and, in some places, muddy. Along the way, the piñon and cedar trees adorning the rolling hills were fresh and clean; and the scent of the wild sage mingled with their bouquet to fill the air. The red soil, into which the evergreens set their roots, completed a beautiful setting against the misty sky.

The children enjoyed the new experience. Don, Betsy, Zill, and Net sang songs and kept themselves entertained. Mary and Will kept Priscilla occupied most of the way. Making camp on the desert was worth the whole trip. Sitting around the campfire at night and listening to the coyotes howl—-even though coyotes weren't unusual--seemed like a vacation.

When the family finally approached Panaca, they found the scenery to be different. The valley was generally flat with a white butte cast with a tint of green, called courthouse rock, jutting above the quiet settlement nestled on its south side.

Priscilla wouldn't be a total stranger. She had lots of Klingensmith relatives living near and around Panaca, including Philip's wife Hannah, who, after Philip left, married Adolphe Londrush; young Hannah, who married Thomas Mathews; Helen Amelia, who married Charles Mathews, and Ellen Adelia, who married Martin Mathews. Eliza Ann "Lizzie," who married Louis Sharp, had a young family living nearby in Cherry Creek.

John looked up the bishop, who happened to be Milton L. Lee,[3] to see if Lee could help them find some of Priscilla's kin and a place to stay. They found a little house that would do. The house had a fireplace but not a stove—-and the house needed quite a bit of fixing up.

Because of the time of year, John would soon be heading back to Cedar City. He helped unpack and set Priscilla up as comfortably as he could. The youngest children clung to their father and wanted him to stay. It was difficult for John to pull away, but he knew he could depend on Don, Betsy, Zill, and Net to help their mother. On his way out of town, John stopped by the bishop's home and asked Brother Lee to keep a watchful eye over Priscilla.

The slow and undependable mail made it difficult for John to keep track of Priscilla through letters. John had his birthday in April and was still in hiding when a letter from Priscilla finally found its way to him. In reply, he wrote:

Dear Priscilla,   May 15, 1889

Your letter after being through the whole Southern Country arrived here safe at last, 11 days is a long time to come 100 miles. My birthday was like all the rest that have come and gone, I am now in my 55th year, hale and hearty with nothing to complain of in particular.

Your letter gave me comfort in that you were all in good health and spirits, I am still sitting in the corner.

Alma Platte Spilsbury and Margaret Jane Smith and children. L to R, back row: Carmelita S., Estella May S., Josephine S. Back row: Donald Grant S., Alma Spilsbury, Jane K. Spilsbury, Hortensa

In continuing his letter, John included his visit with Priscilla's sister, Jane, who had been left in Cedar City by her husband, Alma, while he was away juggling with the law and making preparations for moving her to Old Mexico. John wrote: "I saw Janey, she looks well, better I think than she feels, our Alma don't send much to her, $10.00 I think since he was here. . . .[4] I read Betsy's letter to Janey, it was a good one, well written and full of news. I felt a little proud of it. Zillie she is a rattler, but she did very well & no doubt will improve."

John wanted to convey to Don that his half-brother, Jack, was in need of a letter. The two boys had spent a lot of time together, and Jack was lonesome for Don. Priscilla was always happy when John made mention of all their children. She smiled as she read: "Donald you are getting behind I think. Why don't you write to John [Jack]. All the little girls enquire after Nettie & wish they could see them all. Mary and Will, God bless them, will loom up after a while, kiss the whole family for me."

John liked to include news about the relatives, and he knew Priscilla would want to hear about her Aunt Mary Bladen. After all these years, her husband had returned to Cedar City from England. Priscilla got a chuckle out of John's writing: "I saw Grandma Bladen she is the same old sixpence, she takes but little stock in Bladen, of course she asked a hundred questions about you and the children. Bladen is a wreck of his former self, I did not know the man, he is company for nobody, the family are disappointed in him, & I think little wonder."

The courts in Beaver were kept quite busy with all the polygamy indictments. Thomas Jones, who became second counselor to Bishop Henry Lunt after Philip Klingensmith was released as bishop, had somehow held on to some papers about Priscilla's adoption. John finally had the news he wanted to give to her. It seems Jones was sweeping the house for all kinds of reasons. John slipped the bit about Priscilla among the rest of the news knowing she would understand what he meant:

> T. J. Jones has come home from Beaver. I had a chat with him today, his case is not settled & is put off till September, he gave me the assurance that your Bond with others are burned.[5] There is no indictment against Bp. Lee, his papers are also all gone up in smoke, you can tell him so and to rest easy. C. J. Arthur went up to Beaver to-day to get his dose.

Priscilla could hardly believe the news. She had been so worried, and for so long, that she would somehow be sent back to Arkansas and be separated from her husband and children. She could barely contain herself to read the remainder of the letter. She found it to have news about lots of things. She was sorry about John's wife, Sarah Ann, and was glad to hear that John was coming to Panaca.

> The weather here has been cold and very stormy, rain, snow & hail wetting the ground a foot deep, finest storm in years. Fruit all safe yet, crops look excellent. Sarah is up and down, on the whole not in the best of health, but feels first rate. Jess, John and all the rest of them are O.K. . . Coal and Iron excitement here runs high, but no purchases are made, no money stirring. Cattle and Sheep buyers are in here, prices are reasonable. Money is scarce, so is flour and everything else eatable. The stores have shut down on credit.
>
> I will leave here about the last of this month & bring those things you sent for. I am waiting on some money transactions & cannot get away before that time.
>
> I am afraid I had better buy a cow in Panaca, be looking out for one.
>
> Well God bless you Priscilla and the children. God bless them. Take good care of them. By the by Donald will have to come in & stay all summer. Donald see the garden is all planted before I come out. I think I have given you all the news. I will bring flour & meat & cheese. God bless you all   Yours
> "The Smith"

The end of the month found Priscilla and the children watching the road in anticipation of John's arrival. At last, a strange wagon pulled up in front of the house. When John swung down to greet them, they were happy that it was he. While unloading the things he brought, John introduced his family to the folks who were kind enough to bring him along on their trip to Panaca.

John was pleased with the fresh cow Priscilla had taken him to see. He soon had the cow in a pasture nearby, and he and Don built a shed for her. They made a tee out of two short boards to serve as a milking stool for Priscilla. John wanted their new cow to have a calf in the spring, so he told Priscilla he would be back in a month or so to see about having a bull brought in.

Don had the garden in, and he and his father completed the first hoeing. John advised Betsy and Zill that before they finished milking the cow to be sure she was stripped. Don had stacked plenty of kindling, and John was glad to see Don had taken that responsibility.

Priscilla always had to have a few chickens around and had accepted a setting hen from Lizzie. She came off with a dozen chicks, and John decided he had better attach a run to the old coop that was on the place. He hoped the chicks weren't all roosters so Priscilla could have plenty of eggs for her cooking.

The outhouse needed moving and a new hole dug—-so John took care of that and made a box for ashes to be used to cover the stink once in a while. When John felt like he had taken care of all he could, he started making preparations to leave. He dreaded leaving Priscilla without a man in the house, but he knew he had to get back to Cedar City. Sarah Ann was sixty-four years old now and was needing a lot of attention—-what little he could give her while trying to keep out of the way of the persistent U.S. deputy marshals.

Priscilla didn't want to give Don up to his father, but she knew he was needed and would return for the winter and his schooling. Don was told about the colt his father had for him, and he was eager to get on the road. Also, Don hadn't stayed with Sarah Ann, whom he called "Grandma Urie," before; and he knew he would be bunking in with Jack. It didn't take John long to find a ride for the two of them to Cedar City.

The next spring rolled around, and Priscilla started looking forward to the wedding of John and Sarah Ann's youngest daughter, Jessie. She was betrothed to Richard Williams, and it was going to be a swell affair on April 22, 1890. Things hadn't settled down on the indictments, so Priscilla had to miss the wedding.

Several of Priscilla's chicks turned out to be hens, and most of them wanted to set. She knew just how to build nesting boxes low to the ground and separate the hens so there would be no ruckus among them. All but one rooster had gone into the frying pan and they were long gone. The cow was getting ready to calf and Priscilla was watching her closely.

The days seemed long to Priscilla, and she was feeling down. John hadn't been able to get out to be with her during the winter months. When Priscilla wrote to John, she felt that her news was stale and that she was a grumbler—-she signed her name that way.

John replied, in part, to one of these letters on July 3, 1890, with:

Dear Priscilla

Your letter was not stale news. I was surprised but thankful they did not get Terry. I cannot understand how they come to shoot at Barnham, how was it?

The three worthies[6] were gone from Cedar just ten days. In St. George they got McArthur, Jarvis & Woodberry. They left Cedar last Monday. I cannot hear of any other arrests, I think that was all. They went south & west blowing that they would make a big haul, they were cunning & very quiet, they made the usual enquiries for your beloved, all of which came to my ears in good time so that I could keep out of the way, which I did & I am safe yet. I am housed close which is damned hard on me—-I have seen but few people. I have not been on the mountain yet. The folks have just started up, that is Dave & Tom. Eliza, Agnes, Robert, & George have not gone yet. . . .

All the folks are well, but I am only a pest to them here, they are always in dread and fear lest I am caught. I do not blame them. . . .

Donald put in your best licks & you too Betsy & Zilla & Nettie. Kiss Mary & Will for me. . . . Hoping you are all well, I ask the Lord to bless you.

Your Beloved John

P.S. When you write don't sign your name as Grumbler.   John[7]

Cedar City Choir. Back row, L to R: Annie Wood, Eliza Hunter, Margaret Heyborne, Mary Ann Corlett, Tillie Heyborne, Lizzie Corry, Ellen Lunt. Front row: Alice Bullock, Sarah Chatterley, William Unthank, Daniel Macfarlane, John M. Macfarlane, John Chatterley, Joseph Smith, John Lee Jones.

CHAPTER 18

Priscilla Did Dare to Dream

Just a few days before the 1890 4th of July celebration, the wind was cold and blowing hard night and day. The weather warmed up in time for the holiday when beef, replacing the scarce mutton, was wrapped in heavy wet cloths and buried in deep pits lined with rocks and surrounded with hot coals, then covered with dirt, and cooked to a mouth-watering goodness.

Betsy Ann and Jane were disappointed when their sister couldn't get in for the celebration. John had hoped Priscilla could find a ride in, too. He was rather lonely now that Sarah Ann had gone with Aunt Mary Bladen and Sage Jones to Logan to do temple work. This was a long way for Sarah Ann to travel for this purpose, but it was a good opportunity for her to see the new temple she had been wanting to see—which had been dedicated six years earlier.

John was making plans to visit Priscilla and their children for the 24th of July. After waiting, with no avail, for the letter and allotment money from his mother, which he expected by the middle of the month, John made plans to leave without it.

There had been quite a fracas over the allotment money, and John's brother George was right in the middle of it. John had written to his mother inquiring about what she had done with the money that should have come to him and his wives.

Agnes had sent Sarah Ann's and Priscilla's allotments but suspected, after not receiving acknowledgements from them, that George, who had been handling her affairs, hadn't sent the last payments. Agnes claimed, in her letter to John, that when it came to money, "I cannot depend on your Brother George much, he is so fond of money that he would sell himself to the evil one."[1]

With John's report back to Scotland about his wives not getting their allotments, her suspicions were confirmed. To say the least, this caused feelings between the Urie brothers.

There was another hang-up because of money matters with Thomas' widow. Since Thomas' death, Agnes had given his wife, Mary, more than she should have. After John's letter of inquiry about the money, his angry mother wrote back to him with these biting remarks:

> I had a letter from you. . . . It did not improve me, enquiring what I had done with my money. Well I will tell you what I did with a good bit of it, which I aught not to have done, but I could not help doing so. I have been too liberal to Aunt Mary in her time of need when her husband, your brother, died. . . . Your Brother promised to give her

some help. I was to put ten pounds down. He said that he would give her the same, and when the time came he did not do it, but told me to give his ten pounds, also which I did. More than that I had to give her, but I have stopped giving her any more money now. I have got very little thanks for it all. I hope our heavenly Father will spare me in good health & strength a little longer on the earth so that I can help you more.

Agnes went on to explain to John why she was short on money, and it was becoming obvious that the lawyers were eating up a lion's share of the money.

You are aware when you was in Scotland that I was in debt to the fund, one hundred & ninety five pounds which I had to pay the lawyers. I have about 200 pounds in the house at present, which I will have to live on until I get more at Martimas[2] on 11th of November.

The money matters were a burden for John's mother. She was a kind-hearted soul, and she tried to do right by everybody. In her letter, she talked about the Mormon elders.

The Elders which visit me, I give them a mail of food perhaps a very few shillings, they never ask anything from me. I sometimes go to the Conference House to get the ordnance performed on me when I feel that I need it.

Your loving Mother[3]

John couldn't wait any longer for the expected letter from his mother——he was eager to show Priscilla his new rig. For some time now, John had endured great discomfort from "piles," and riding a horse was painful for him. All of the remedies he tried, which the doctor and others recommended as well as the ones his mother had sent to him, did little good.

So he could come and go when he pleased and travel in comfort, John purchased a fine, one-seated, two-horse buggy. Because ready cash was scarce and was needed to provide for his families, John paid with beef, in exchange to the Sheep Co-op, which amounted to $115.00.

Priscilla couldn't believe her eyes when she saw John sporting such a nice buggy. Her "beloved" arrived in time for the 24th of July celebration. The kids were excited and eagerly waited for their turns to ride in the buggy. Of course, Don wanted to take over and be the driver, his father surrendered the reins.

After all the excitement settled down, John was able to tell Don about his colt. He had grown and weighed about 1,100 lbs.——Tom was breaking him in. John quipped, "He is a beauty, but fractious." Don knew he was high spirited but figured he could handle his horse.

Priscilla, while being glad to see meat and cheese in the house again, got busy with the girls preparing a picnic for the holiday. Panaca wasn't a large town, and there weren't a lot of people to participate in a parade, but everybody had fun. It seemed appropriate to have a family picture taken to complete the day. John warned, "Now I dinna want to see any smiles."

John, Priscilla, & Family. L to R, back row: Betsy, John Urie, Donald, Priscilla K., Priscilla. Front row: Mary, Janet & William (sitting on his mother's lap).

Later, after the picture had been set aside for hanging, the whole family was dismayed to find Betsy's face had been scratched out. Betsy, herself, in secret, while believing she was as ugly as anybody could be, did the terrible deed. She was scolded and told not to believe such a thing, but the damage was done. Priscilla couldn't imagine Betsy behaving this way.

In the evenings, after all the chores were done and the house was quiet, John and Priscilla enjoyed a stroll in the moonlight. They talked about this and that and wondered what they could say to change Betsy's ideas about her looks. She was rather plain looking, but they figured she would grow up into a beauty.

At the end of one of their strolls, the subject of Scotland came up. John was making plans to get out of the country—-it was getting harder all the time for him to hide from the law. He hadn't heard from his mother lately, but he was hoping, well, he knew, she wanted him to come home.

Right away, while John was talking about Scotland, Priscilla envisioned her dream of going to Scotland with him. She longed to see the places he talked about and, listening to the bagpipers. He was such a part of her, and she held all that he was close to her heart. His endearing Scottish brogue was always pleasing to her ears.

When Priscilla more than hinted she would like to go to Scotland with him, John replied, "Maybe my lass, maybe it will work out."

Before John left Panaca, they consummated their love and vowed that neither the law nor anything could ever tear away what they felt for each other.

When John arrived back in Cedar City, he went to see Sarah Ann. She was doing fine. He had lots of news to catch up on. Sarah Ann enjoyed her trip to Logan but was a bit weary from the travel. She had been resting for quite some time. Before John left the house, Sarah Ann handed him two letters from his mother.

John found it best to go back into hiding; he didn't dare go up on the mountains to join the rest of the family. It was late, and John Hamilton had gone to bed. But Betsy Ann was quite sure it was John Urie knocking, and he was welcomed in.

Before retiring, even though it had been a long hard day, John read his letters. One envelope contained the remittance of his allotment money and a letter conveying that he was his mother's "best friend on this earth" and that she relied on him. The other letter was in reply to his last letter. He had asked about pictures of his ancestors and his brothers' families—along with an apology, to his mother, for his last letter. He was pleased with the tone of kindness he received in return.

John didn't have to ask if he could come to Scotland. His mother felt she was nearing death's door and wanted to see him before her time came. She promised that

George Urie II

George would be on his best behavior. George had been taking good care of her, and Agnes wanted her sons to be on good terms before she left this earth.

John sat in his corner and read:

My dear son John   7th August 1890.
    I received your last letter to me from Panaca, Lincoln County,

Nevada, and was glad to learn that your health was good.

I wrote to you on the 16th July, enclosing one hundred pounds. I do hope that you received it all right. I except of your apology with grace. You have a right to enquire what I did with all my money. I think I told you in my last letter to you that Aunt Mary got more than she should have got, but I could not help myself. . . .

Your Brother George has advised me to invite you to come to Scotland for a little while, it will do you good. Your sons will do your business while you are in Scotland. He says that he will make you very welcome and I believe that he will. George is very kind to me. . . .

John if you make up your mind to come to Scotland on a visit, I will pay your expenses to Scotland & home again. I would like to see you face to face before that I pass away into my next abode. I have only 2 sons alive now. Yourself & George, may our heavenly father bless you with health & strength is the prayer, also your 2 wives . . . . Please to write me in return if you can come in safety to Scotland. Please to come by yourself.

Yours ever affectionately
Your Old Mother

P.S. About the pictures if you come to Scotland you will get the pictures and something more besides.

Your Mother

John read again the words, "Please to come by yourself." And again he read the words, wondering how his mother could do this to him. He was pleased about the pictures he had asked for and all the rest of her generosity, but how could she ask him to come alone?

Leaving Priscilla behind smacked him as a sting in his heart. This, in all probability, would be his last trip to Scotland—-he knew Priscilla's dreams would all be dashed to pieces.

Priscilla had dared to dream of going to Scotland with John. He had crossed the Atlantic Ocean many times and sailed on the shore of the Pacific three times. Priscilla's trip across the plains couldn't be recalled. John knew that this was Priscilla's last chance to go and to see beyond the world he had created for her.[4]

CHAPTER 19

Manifesto Taken Advantage of

Priscilla worried about John, wondering if his enemies had caught up with him. When his letter finally came, she knew why it had taken him so long to write. As she read his words, her disappointment brought her to a standstill. Priscilla didn't move for several moments—-and then she plopped into her favorite chair, where the reality of what John wrote to her was clear. She wasn't ever going to Scotland. Never. Never ever.

Oh, he had been gentle and tried to explain all right; but the truth still remained, and she read between all the lines. When he was with her last, they were so close, and she could still feel his arms around her. Priscilla was having a difficult time thinking about John going to Scotland again—-and without her.

October came and Priscilla was sure now that a "wee one," as John would call it, was kicking inside her womb. She was having some hard thoughts about John's leaving and the doting of his mother. Telling him about the baby seemed like the thing to do, but she wasn't of a mind to tell him anything right now. She guessed that rather than write a letter, she would wait until he came out to Panaca with his goodbyes to spring the news.

"Zill" Elizabeth

Priscilla was worried about the law catching up with John all right, and she knew he needed to get away for a while. It went over and over in her mind that it didn't seem fair that neither she nor Sarah Ann ever got to go to Scotland. John was so well educated, worldly, and well traveled—-she guessed she didn't count for anything and was looked down upon.

Priscilla watched for John to arrive, but he never showed up. So many things had to be done to get ready for winter. Zill had gone in to Cedar City to live with Sarah Ann while she attended school. Betsy, being the oldest girl, stayed to help her mother, and Don, now a teenager, took care of the outside chores.

Don was starting to buddy with the riffraff coming in from Silver Reef and the other local mining towns. Don was a good boy, but he seemed to be more difficult to handle lately. Don was gone on his horse often—-sometimes so late that it was a relief when he came home. This troubled Priscilla, and she wanted to ask John about Don's going to Cedar City for the winter.

The gossip going around the little town of Panaca, about Priscilla's being John Urie's wife and who knew what else, was getting her down. What more would these whispering know-it-alls say when they found out she was pregnant and left by John to make it on her own?

The worry about John was getting to Priscilla when a letter arrived. She was taken back a little to see that it came from New York and had been written on October 21, 1890. Priscilla understood now why she hadn't heard from John when she read:

Dear Priscilla

Left Cedar Thursday Oct 16 in a big hurry. Depose were on the way to Cedar & I slipped out to Milford, left Milford same night—-at 7:30 got to Provo next day, Friday, at 8 in the morning. Left Provo same day at 1 o'clock for New York & here I am all well . . . Will leave here tomorrow at 12 o'clock noon by steamship "Bothnia" that is Wednesday Oct 22. Will be in Glasgow by the time you get this.

God bless you all I am off to bed & so good night

John[1]

Well, Priscilla could tell from this letter that John was a little disgruntled, she supposed, at not hearing from her lately. He would just have to get over it all on his own—-or maybe with the help of his mother.

Sitting on the train for five days with his hemorrhoid condition, constipated, without warm water to wash himself, and no medicine was a bit hard on John's disposition. Landing in New York, miserable and tired, put him in no frame of mind to care much about anything but sleep to ease away his pain.

Traveling on the steamer, first class, helped eradicate John's problems. Finding himself the only passenger traveling in a cabin was lonely for a day or two, until he "got alongside the Captain, Purser and Doctor."[2] Considering that the four of them were Scots, they had, as may be expected, a good time together.

The passage to Liverpool took eleven days. "A long trip," John thought, "for this modern age of fast steamers."[3] When John stepped from the ramp onto England's shore, November 3, 1890, he was surprised to find his brother George waiting for him.

After a little over six hours of travel, the two men arrived at their mother's home in Glasgow, where she had breakfast waiting for them—-porridge, thick slices of day-old Scottish bread, and milk.

The wet, windy weather kept John inside where he listened to "a thousand and forty things." He answered questions from the old "Queen"[4] as well as he could—-she was eager to hear all about her son's wives and weans.

The 3rd of November rolled around, and John hadn't heard from either of his wives. He figured they hadn't had time to reply yet. John sat down and wrote Priscilla a letter starting with:

Dear Priscilla

I hope you got my New York letter. . . . Not withstanding I am in the midst of a hearty welcome, I cast my eye homewards & I am wondering how you all are. . . . How long I will stay here I do not know. I am pressed to stay till spring, but—-then I'll see. Home with all its troubles and inconveniences is dear to me. Be patient Priscilla & God bless you.

Your monthly will come along in due time to yourself in Panaca, say about Dec 1st.[5]

Before signing off, John asked for God's blessing on the children, asking them to mind their mother, and made his plea for Priscilla to write—-giving his promise to write every week.

His faithful letters were filled with news about the weather and the welcome response he was receiving from nieces and nephews, who called him "Uncle John." In one letter, he wrote, "I am here & the very best care is taken of me, but then it is not home. Mother was anxious about me as when I was a baby, airs my shirts, puts on my collar & neck tie & puts the blankets round me when I go to bed, oh my, what it is to have a good kind old mother."[6]

And another letter read, "Mother is in fine condition & is as much a fussy mother of a family as she was 50 years ago, to see her about her two babies is indeed laughable, she talks often about you & the children & sends her kind love to you all." [7]

When Priscilla read these letters, she thought, "Well, old girl you have your babies right where you want them, and I'm back here wondering when John will ever come home."

It was going to be a while before December 1, and supplies for Priscilla were getting short, so she prayed to her Heavenly Father for guidance to help her to be patient. John had mentioned in one of his letters that Jack was to bring some supplies out.

Priscilla was going about her daily chores when a knock came to the door—-as it pushed wide open. She smiled and gave the young man a hug. Jack was eager to tell Priscilla about his father's frantic hurry to get out of town. He explained, "Papa was getting ready to come here to Panaca when he got word about the deputies. He hurried so fast he forgot his medicine. On his way out the door, he told me to come out and see that you was okay and to bring you the beef, flour and butter."

When Priscilla asked if the deputies got there and if they asked about John Urie, Jack replied, "Yeah, they were pretty upset when they couldn't find him."

Priscilla could see now that John had made an effort to get out to take care of her, and she was relieved that he was able to leave ahead of the deputies. It didn't seem to matter after all that she hadn't gotten to go to Scotland.

Among all of Priscilla's thoughts and resolutions, she was now eager to write to John. She missed him so very much, and his letters warmed her heart. Priscilla's thoughts and worries spilled onto the pages in rapid succession—-it felt good to finally give in. She wondered how many letters she would receive from John before his first letter from her arrived.

Time for Priscilla was slow, but "Lou" and Lizzie were good to her. Sometimes, when they came into town, they invited all the Uries to go along to visit Hannah. Priscilla liked going all right, but the visits were often upsetting to her.

The last time they went over, Hannah was sitting on the back porch smoking her pipe. She was getting quite old now, but her memory was keen; and she, as usual, cursed John D. Lee for talking Philip into joining in that Mountain Meadows Massacre. Hannah hadn't heard anything about Philip for a long time—-she supposed he was dead.

Priscilla always felt gloomy and sorrowful after visiting with Hannah. It seemed like that feisty old woman always wanted to talk about the massacre, and it started Priscilla wondering about what life would have been like if the massacre hadn't happened. To keep from blurting out that she knew she wasn't really a Klingensmith was about all Priscilla could handle. She needed John home to help ease her mind.

John, in the meantime, concerned himself with thinking his wives had deserted him. "Perhaps," he thought, "they are paying me off for my neglect in the past."[8] He finally consoled himself in thinking, "Well, 'the Atlantic is very stormy, so much so that almost every vessel that crosses comes home disabled, also loss of life frequently occurs,'[9] perhaps my letters aren't getting through."

John wrote three more letters to Priscilla before he ever received a letter from her. In his last letter, he wrote:

> I am still without any letters from you or Sarah. I get no *Deseret News*, neither *Herald*, never was so short of news in all my life. Why don't you write Priscilla, this is the fifth time I have asked you. I am still a husband and a father & as such very anxious to hear from home. You are not sick or I would have heard of it as ill news come's quick and unbidden, I comfort myself with the idea that you are all well. It is humiliating to me to <u>ask</u> you to write, you ought to be only too glad to do so. . . .
>
> How are you getting on anyway, you might let a fellow know . . . Donald I hope looks after you, tell him I won't forget him if he is good to you, as also Betsy, is Zillie with you & how is Nettie, Mary, God bless her, is she as old fashioned as ever & that blessed Will, does he talk yet. . . .

I never retire to bed at night without asking God to bless my wives & weans. Priscilla Lass take good care of yourself, do the best you can until I come home . . . Good night my lass while I remain your, Beloved John[10]

When the *Deseret News* and the *Herald* began arriving, John caught up on the news from Utah. John knew before he left Cedar City that the Mormons, in order to submit to the laws of the land, had given an official statement to the press declaring, according to President Wilford Woodruff, that "We are not teaching polygamy or plural marriage, nor permitting any person to enter into its practice."[11]

In John's letters to Priscilla, he wrote: "I am pretty well posted in relation to Utah affairs from Cedar & Beaver." Her heart wretched when she read, "My heart is sore for some polygamists. I boast not, but rather fear for myself & ask the God of Jacob to keep me firm in the truth." She was relieved when he added, "I have been to meeting of course & preached as I thought a very good sermon, at least my hearers were very well pleased."[12]

Priscilla wished this nightmare could be over so she and John could live in peace from the law. The feeling of being forsaken by the Church was demeaning for Priscilla, and she hated being looked upon as an unlawful wife. She knew John was right when he wrote, "I see by *Des. News* that some are taking advantage of Pres. Woodruff's Manifesto, it is as I expected . . . that many would throw aside their families, it is another sieve through which such as I am must pass in order that our integrity may be proven."[13]

Having read of his fears and anxieties, Priscilla prayed that her letters would reach John swiftly.

The overwhelming elation for John, when he finally received his first letter from Priscilla, was romantically described when he wrote: "Dear Priscilla, Your most welcome letter came to hand a day or two ago, could you have been in my skin, you would have felt so good, so much so, that you could not have contained yourself."

John's expression of love thrilled Priscilla to the tips of her toes. She understood this deep kind of love. In times past, when they embraced as closely as they possibly could, she wished his whole being could be inside of hers. If she ever wondered, she knew now why she loved John so much. He had deep feelings that were rarely expressed, but now she knew they were really there.

Priscilla smiled, and her spirit perked up when she read, "Well Priscilla lass keep up your heart, look on the bright side of things, shake off the feeling that you are looked down upon because you are John Uries wife—ignorance and unfaithfulness is the part of many of our people [and] cannot be helped."[14]

The rapture of reading this letter accelerated to a new height when she read:

Priscilla, I recollected Nov. 24 & on that day bought you a

handsome gold watch & chain for a wedding present, I think you will be pleased with it. . . .[15] long may you live to wear it.

Yes, 17 years have passed & gone since we two were made one, ups and downs have of course been our lot, this was to be expected & is it not the lot of all, the next 17 years will also have its ups & downs, but I hope we will be the more able to philosophically bear it & have it to say we have done the best we could. Yes, we have had a good deal of comfort & happiness, it will be so again, providing as you say we stick to the truth, which may God grant. . . .

Your Affectionate

John[16]

CHAPTER 20

Priscilla Speaks Up

Chubby little Will was prattling in his own language when, while holding his stick up high, he motioned his mama to see his picture drawn in the red earth. Winter had come and was gone, and Priscilla made it through. She was hanging diapers—-her wee one was born.[1]

Priscilla looked across the untamed landscape and remembered the words of her beloved, "I will be home as soon as possible, in the midst of my family is my place notwithstanding our troubles and vexations, I would rather smell the sagebrush of Iron County & Nevada than my native heather."[2]

Priscilla turned to look at John, who was sitting on the porch holding little Elizabeth Hutcheson Urie in his arms. She was glad they had named her after John's first wife. John hadn't made it home in time for the blessing, but at the moment Bishop Lee pronounced her name, Priscilla felt a closeness and understanding of the tender love John held for Elizabeth.

John knew he wouldn't be home for the event and had written:

> In a previous letter you say you expect to be bedfast about Feb. first, I cannot be in Panaca in body, in spirit I will be there. My anxiety will be intense, keep up your spirits & all will be well. . . .
>
> Take good care of yourself & have everything prepared for the interesting event. . . .
>
> You done right to make yourself as comfortable as possible, nothing pleases me better, want for nothing in reason Priscilla. . . . Get you a stove & somebody to put it up for you . . . .
>
> Should I not be in time to bless my child, if a girl, name it "Elizabeth Hutcheson Urie." My hopes & feelings are that it will be a boy, in that event call it "Philip Smith Urie."[3]

A warmth and good feeling came over Priscilla as she watched John happily rock the baby. She remembered how sad she felt for John when he was so far away on New Year's Day. His letter revealed his deep feelings and regret for not being home:

> A good New Year to you & God bless you lass, not forgetting the children.
>
> I am in very good health, but not in spirits, New Year to me in this far away Country has no charms for me. I have been shedding tears all morning, I know not why, I could not help it. Your expectations of my

arrival will certainly be disappointed as you already know by my previous letters. Stormy weather & the wish of Mother has induced me to stay a little longer, it is all for the best Priscilla.[4]

With apprehension, Priscilla accepted John's decision "to stay a little longer" and wrote back with some of her fears. Half jokingly, she cautioned him to keep his eyes off other lassies while he was in Scotland—-and he firmly replied: "No doubt you will be full of anxieties about me, I have hitherto kept straight on all my visits here—-I will do so again. I am aware of being watched like a cat watching a mouse, nothing would please some of them better than to find me in fault, they will be disappointed."[5]

Priscilla was glad to have John home at last—-safe and sound. As it turned out, the voyage home was a perilous venture. When John left Scotland during February of the new year 1891, the wind-swept sea was still a danger to ships—-so much so that the captain gave orders for everybody to put on life jackets. When John was noticed walking about the decks without a life jacket, the captain asked, "Why aren't you wearing your life jacket?" John was emphatic when he replied, "Because I'm going to land." The captain decided that if this man was going to land, he would too; and he took his own life jacket off.[6]

It was the example of John's faith and steadfastness that carried Priscilla through. John was home now, and all her loneliness was behind her—-he had finally had enough of Scotland! Priscilla was smitten with John's love. His desire to be with her had been so strong that the deep snow of the late winter storm had not kept him from making his way to Panaca.

Priscilla enjoyed musing over John but had important concerns to discuss with him. It wasn't easy to always come right out and ask him things—-it was usually John who brought subjects up. Her work was done for a few moments, and she sidled her chair as close to John as she could. She didn't want the children to hear them talking.

Priscilla wanted to move out of Panaca. It wasn't the same place now that Hannah and Lizzie were gone. Most of all, she didn't think it was a very good place to raise their children—-so close to the mining towns and not having enough work to keep Don occupied. John could see Priscilla was right and replied, "I am tired of running back and forth to Panaca and also having nothing to do for Donald just as bad as you are."[7]

John had written from Scotland asking Priscilla to keep Don with her in Panaca because he felt she needed him. But, now that John was home, he could see what Priscilla had been up against. He was glad she had used her own judgment by sending Don to Cedar City to live with Sarah Ann and to be in Mayhew Dalley's school.

While agreeing that it would be good to purchase a farm near Cedar City to give Don and the girls something to do, John hastened to remind Priscilla that he would not be free to go between his wives anymore now than before. He was a little defensive when he explained, "I don't go much out of the house, it is very few people that I see. It will be worse for me, but I can stand what you can't. I will have to take the best care I can of myself—-if I can only get the families established it won't matter so much about me, will it?"[8]

Priscilla felt a little vexed and confused. She wanted to be back in Cedar, but she didn't want things to be worse for John. Priscilla wondered if it was a good idea after all. John, feeling her frustration and wanting to close the subject, emphasized his last statement by saying, "I will be pleased at least to see my children and wives permanently provided for."[9]

They sat in silence, admiring their sleeping baby, knowing nothing more could be gained on the subject. At last, with concern and compassion, John broke the silence by asking about the recent deaths in the Klingensmith family.

Priscilla was sad about Hannah's passing and worried about Lizzie's kids. It was just a horrid thing to have happen. The contagious viral disease going around, which everybody called grip,[10] took them both. The look of an old woman had crept onto Hannah's face. Priscilla guessed that after the hard life Hannah had endured, she just couldn't weather any more adversity. Lizzie was young, but, while she was trying to take care of herself and her family, the disease took her down.

Sixty-five-year-old Hannah died on the tenth day of March; and two days later, she was buried. The crowd hadn't been so big because of all the sickness, and there wasn't much of a sermon--Church wise, that is. Lizzie was buried soon after—-Lou and the kids were terribly upset.

John and Priscilla's visiting ended. Little Elizabeth, whom they already nicknamed "Libby," aroused from her nap with a cry—-bringing the whole family to attend her.

Having stayed a few weeks with Priscilla, John felt he had better get back to Cedar City. Wee Mary seemed to be better from her sickness, and with all the disease going around, John was concerned about Sarah Ann's health. Priscilla dreaded seeing John leave for Cedar City again. She enjoyed their time together and hoped he could get back soon. John was ready to leave when Priscilla asked, "What about Don?"

"I am satisfied that he will not go far astray. God bless the lad,"[11] was his reply. He then counseled her: "Have patience with the boy, he is just the age to be foolish and needs looking strictly after."[12]

Priscilla, however, wondered how he and Jack were getting along now since their last go-around. John assured her that, "Cedar is a better place than Panaca, and I think John and him agree better than formerly."[13]

At the last moment, Priscilla spoke up and asked: "What about my moving out of Panaca?"

John, who was now looking down into her eyes, ready for his goodbye, was surprised that she would bring it up again so soon. Wanting to assure her he replied: "I think it is under the circumstances the wisest course I can pursue, I also think you will be pleased and better satisfied."[14]

As Priscilla pushed back from their embrace, she nodded in agreement and quietly answered, "Thank you John."[15]

CHAPTER 21

John Keeps His Word

When John arrived in Cedar City, he found that Sarah Ann had come down with the grip. Don sent word, but his letter passed his father on the road. Sarah Ann was feeling a little better after spending a couple of days in bed.

Almost everybody in town was being affected with either the grip or the mumps. School had been closed down for the week because of so much sickness. The Uries' neighbor, "Old man Chapin," had died, and his wife was near to it.

After Priscilla read Don's letter, she was relieved that John had left for Cedar City. She was worried about Sarah Ann, too—-her health hadn't been so good lately.

Priscilla rested easy after judging from Don's letter that the miserable weather had cleared up for the last three days and that John therefore had traveled in good stead. She was glad, too, that John was in Cedar City to see about Don's needs.

The boy was without any money and had written, "I wish you would send me a couple of dollars to get me a new hat and put another dollar to it and make it three so I can get a pair of overalls because I have to wear them very fine clothes that father got for me and I am afraid I will spoil them."

Don bid his mother to "Tell Willie he might see me some of these short days coming on a horse—-tell Mary she must eat lots of that Panaca beef to make her fat again—-tell Net to learn all she can—-Betsey and Zilley must write to us once and awhile."

Because his father had been suffering with pain in his arm, Don concluded with, "God bless you all . . . father must take a good share of it his self because it is good for the neuralgy. . . . I would like to have seen father in the house for a week without being out, I guess it is a new thing for him. Well I will hav [to] stop for this time. Your loving boy. . . ."

As an afterthought, he continued by saying: "Well it is too bad about Hannah and Lizzie—-who will he have to take care of his kids now." Priscilla accepted his words of condolence but was flabbergasted when he added, "It makes me sigh to think I am your first boy so when you die I will come to the head of the family."

Your Dear boy
Don Urie[1]

Priscilla felt bad about her fourteen-year-old boy troubling his mind with such thoughts. Seeing how Don was affected by all the deaths that were happening, Priscilla anxiously wrote back—-conveying to Don that she "just wished he wouldn't worry about his own folks dying too."

Before she knew it, the month of May whirled around the corner; and Priscilla was still wondering when John was going to stand by his word and move her out of Panaca.

When John's letter, written on May 12, arrived, it was full of news. Priscilla was most interested when she read:

> I was at Hamiltons last Friday and had a good time at Betsy's, was there all day, it was then that Hamilton boned[2] me about buying his place. If I get the place you will have to occupy it, as it will be deeded to you, so there is not only a chance of you coming in to stay for good, but also employment for Don & the girls.[3]

After reading the letter, Priscilla thought, "It looks like I will be getting out of this darn place after all."

While John was preparing for a trip out to Panaca, money matters concerning his inheritance loomed up again. His brother George had found a new trick.

Elizabeth, sitting on the right, & her son, William, standing.

On the second day of June, John took his pen in hand and wrote these facts to Scotland:

Dear mother,

Enclosed find registered envelope containing three blank half sheets of paper received by me a few days ago. The address is I suppose in the hand writing of George's clerk and mailed in the Strathburgs Post Office on May 26/91. It is no use to me and hence I return it to you to give to George with my compliments.

There is no sign of the letter being tampered with, the post officials here are satisfied that it never contained anything else than the three blank half sheets of paper when registered. I address this letter to George III for the reason that I think you are perhaps sick & probably your correspondence with me together with my answers or letters is obtained by George to cover up what I think his dishonesty.

Will you answer this letter immediately, if you are not able to write yourself let George the 3rd do it for you as I have no confidence in my brother George. . . . I will write you a long letter when I feel satisfied that you get my letters.

All well. Your Son John

While John waited anxiously for a letter back, he pursued his transactions on purchasing the farm.

Because Priscilla was always concerned that she might lead the law to John's whereabouts, she tucked a letter to John in with her letters to Don. Her last letter was delayed several days, when Tom mistakenly took the letter with him to the mountain and gave it to Don.

Priscilla had all kinds of trouble to report. Her ham spoiled and the gopher holes and weeds were taking over the garden. John, concerned about her welfare, made a hasty reply:

Dear Priscilla   Cedar City July 8/91

In the first place I will say that I am only too glad that you are all well & very sorry to think that you lost your ham. You must not stunt[4] yourself because of that, get something to eat, send to Pioche for meat if you cannot get it in Panaca.

Gopher holes & weeds are no doubt troublesome, but then what can we do about it. Do the best you can in raising the cabbage anyhow & also the beans.

I have got possession of Hamiltons farm . . . I have not seen Donald since the first day I came in, he is on the mountain at Tom's, he did not come down on the 4th. Tom will send him in with some butter to be in Panaca by the 24th, in all likelihood I will come with him. Donald is well & I hear a good account of him. . . .

I have had a doctor after my piles, but I stood him off, like that Indian he is a beast. . . . My old hat on a bet that he has (the Indian) not made one cure in Panaca. The Mormons are the easiest of all people made fools of.

I am on the street sometimes, but am cautious all the same. McGarry has said that he would not come after me anymore, but I take no stock in this.

Be good to yourself & the kids. Betsy & Zillie, Mary, Will & the baby, God bless them & I bless you all.

Write soon.   Your John[5]

Don had been out to see Hamilton's farm, and even though he figured the farm had the best grain in the field, he didn't think much of the house. So, while writing a long letter to his mother, he included, "I don't soppos you will move in until next fall—-if you knew how this old house looked you would not move in it."[6]

Hamilton's

After seeing that the crops would be cared for and attending to some business, John headed for Panaca with Don—-where he found a little trouble had been stirred up. Priscilla saw him coming with his fancy buggy and met him at the gate. John hardly had time to greet the weans before Priscilla started asking questions about the house.

John was taken back a little and wondered what had gotten into Priscilla. He defended himself by saying, "I examined the house from top to bottom and am well pleased with it, the upper rooms are finished and are neat and clean. One of the large rooms is papered, the other is not."[7]

While glancing at Don, wondering if he had told Priscilla about the old part of the house, John continued: "The stove room and kitchen of course is the original old house and is dobie. But," he quickly added, "there is a fine rock cellar under the dining room. Besides," he said, "the crops, that is wheat, barley, oats, and potatoes, as well as the lucerne, look well. Jack is cutting the lucerne now."[8]

Priscilla, wanting to know about fruit trees, had John admitting: "Not much of an orchard—-but I am pleased and everybody seems to think I have made a good bargain and I think I have."

John hesitated a moment, while Priscilla handed him the baby, and then added: "Your mind in relation to making that place your home need not be disturbed—-I think it is a good move for both you and me." He added a clincher by saying, "Betsy is quite tickled at me buying Hamilton."[9]

John knew this would mellow Priscilla. It meant a lot to her to know Betsy Ann was glad about the place, and Priscilla wanted to live near her. It would be good to live near her other sister Mary Alice, too—-even though she was in Parowan. Priscilla learned from John that Mary Alice was having trouble with nerves since her last baby, and Priscilla was eager to see her.

All seemed to be smoothed out, and Priscilla was now looking forward to her move to Hamilton's. Don knew he was off the hook when he saw his father smile with contentment—-knowing all was well.

The letter that finally arrived from John's mother was indeed a disappointment. Nobody seemed to know what happened to the money, and George for sure wasn't going to own up to anything. Agnes, not wanting to cause trouble with George, her precious boy, supplemented the money and assured John that come November 11 she would see that he got his fair share of the money.[10]

Mary Alice, Betsy & Priscilla

GLASGOW
RAILWAY
SWITCH &
CROSSING
WORKS.

381. Pollokshaws Road,
Glasgow, 18

or agreeable .... what he
means .... the best
thin .... completely
i .... ame, keep
.... le.
.... ll over
.... is
n .... e for
a f ....
are ....
Others ....
but wh ....
give them ....
possibly ab ....
predomina ....
country. Tax .... gher
every year. So .... lism
and scoundrel .... ing the
constitution to p .... m fairly
well off for work but very little

Envelope:

John Phie Cory?
Hamilton
Soar Cedar City
Iron County
Utah U.S.A.

GLASGOW
6.45 PM
AP 11

CHAPTER 22

Heaven Can Wait

To Priscilla, the new attire John was wearing seemed extra nice for all the work she had cut out for him to do. "My lands a gracious, restraining one's self," Priscilla thought, "would have been better than gaining so much weight that it took new clothes to cover his 204 pounds." She guessed that if his mother hadn't fed him so well and if he could have had some wood to chop, he wouldn't have been in such a fix.

Having John home for a while was just what Priscilla needed. He was so knowledgeable on so many subjects, and he always brought a breath of the outside world with him. Priscilla, however, had a hard time keeping up with all the controversy of 1892. John's conversations were filled with political talk. He had all the Salt Lake newspapers, including the *Herald*, sent to him in Cedar City.

On December 19, 1891, a petition to the United States Government for a "proclamation of amnesty to polygamists for past offenses, limited to those who entered into the relation before November 1, 1890"[1] had been made by the First Presidency and apostles of the Church. It had not been passed by the Senate yet, but the prospects of its approval relaxed the reins on the U.S. marshals.

Nonetheless, Priscilla still worried about John taking the risk of being out in public. The news that John delayed this last trip to Panaca just so he could attend stake conference was upsetting for Priscilla. Brigham H. Roberts was the principal speaker, and he drew quite a crowd.

John's reply to Priscilla's concern was, "Well Priscilla it makes me feel quite funny to be about the streets in Cedar. Perhaps I am a little too venture-some, but it makes me feel good—-everybody seems to be glad to see me as well as me them. To be from under restraint for a while is indeed a Gods blessing that I appreciate."[2]

Newspaper articles airing views from Roberts, Moses Thatcher, and C. W. Penrose, all Democrats, and articles concerning Frank J. Cannon, running on the Republican ticket, were clipped by John and brought to Priscilla for her to read. One article delved back in time, just ten days before Joseph Smith's martyrdom, showing the prophet died as he lived—-a "Jeffersonian Democrat."[3]

With Priscilla, John expressed his ideas about all the talk going on about political control of the Church. Supporting his own resolve on the subject, he read an excerpt from B. H. Roberts' talk given at a political convention in Provo, Utah:

In December, 1889, the charges that the Mormon church claimed the right to dictate its members in their political affiliations and actions being reviewed, the first presidency of the church and the twelve apostles over their signatures said: "Church government and civil government are distinct and separate in our theory and practice, and we regard it as our destiny to aid in the maintenance and perpetuity of the institutions of our country."[4]

While the family gathered around the table in the kitchen, by the warmth of their new stove, Priscilla enjoyed, most of all, the many poems and stories John found in the papers sent to him from Scotland. He entertained them all with his Scottish brogue—-bringing forth giggles and laughter.

While John was in Panaca this time, he told Priscilla about seeing his mother's "will." John felt the need to assure Priscilla that she was just as important as Sarah Ann, and he said to her, "You are a wife as much as Grandma in the eyes of George as well as Mother. None are omitted, and I must thank my brother George for this, he is more liberal than many polygamists that I know of. Fathers will was narrow, Mothers is broad and liberal."[5]

Little time was spent by Priscilla wondering if she would be rich or not. While she and John were visiting on the porch one evening, John had been telling Priscilla that Grandma Bladen didn't look like she would last long, and in the course of their conversation, he said, "Caleb and Nell are of course married, I intended being there, but the damned marshalls came in about 2 o'clock that day, it was a grand affair and took place in the furniture store. Justice Chatterly performing the ceremony—-about 200 persons were present."[6]

It didn't seem fair to Priscilla that John had to be so careful of the marshals all the time. Sarah Ann was hardly ever seen in public anymore. Priscilla hated herself for thinking about John being all her own, but she had to be honest with herself. She knew Sarah Ann was ailing so much that she was coming close to giving up this life and leaving John to her.

The final agreement on Priscilla's place at Hamilton's had been made in June, but delays seemed to keep popping up. When John left Panaca during the last of August, he assured Priscilla that he would set a fire under John Hamilton to see if he could get him moved out.

John Hamilton

Priscilla felt a little guilty about her previous feelings when a letter written on September 7 was received from John telling her about Sarah Ann. She had been sick for about three days when John reached Cedar City.

Another outbreak of sickness had taken hold in Cedar City. In regard to Sarah Ann, according to John's letter, "Diarrhea of a very severe type, together with her old complaint—-has brought her down very low, to all appearance she is now mending, but not by any means out of danger. I fear the result, yet I am in hopes of the old lass getting round again, should a relapse occur her days will be short."[7]

John let Priscilla know that Betsy Ann and her family were all right, but Mary Alice was still suffering from melancholy. His newsy letter also conveyed that:

> The weather is warm and sultry, sometimes it rains a little, just enough to keep the farmers from hauling their grain and lucerne. The thresher is going and doing good work. I now own 4/5 of it, that is 4 shares out of 5, but not yet hauled. I ought to have Donald out there, but Tom is on the machine & so are John & David, all are as busy as bees.
>
> I saw Donald the other day. I hardly knew him, he grows so much he is nearly as tall as I am. He is in splendid health, he came down on his fancy horse, he is a beauty.

It seemed to Priscilla that her sister, Betsy Ann, and John Hamilton had had long enough to move out of the house she was waiting to move into, when John wrote: "Hamilton has begged for a few days more to stay in the house."

According to John's letter, the worry of being caught and arrested was finally going to come to an end. Tears were already brimming, after Priscilla read about Sarah Ann, and now they were flowing freely as Priscilla read: "Jas. Low called on me the other day & stayed all night, he gave me very encouraging news of the Marshalls, they will not come after me or bother me any more, yet my eyes are all over me & I cease not to be careful."

John concluded his letter with:

> I hope you and the kids are all well, be careful of your own & the childrens health. Kiss them for me & God bless you all & I bless you. I hope things will turn out all right here.
>
> I am bothered Priscilla & have no jokes, neither do I feel jolly just now. God bless you. John[8]

The weather was changing—-frost was on the ground. The crops had to be brought in soon. John sent Tom to bring Don off the mountain. It was important for the boys, after spending a bit of time with Sarah Ann, to get out to Hamilton's to help haul the grain and lucerne as soon as possible.

John fussed and stewed for most of a week. He was worried about Priscilla, too, and wrote to her saying: "Priscilla watch the kids, nip sickness in the bud, should any appear. . . . Should anything serious occur I will telegraph."

Three weeks passed since Sarah Ann was brought down by her sickness. Her condition wasn't improving. Sending for all the children, John was "thinking that perhaps they could raise her spirits and also that it may be the last sight of her alive."[9]

The eleven children who gathered around Sarah Ann's bedside were quiet and sad. Her last hours, after slipping into unconsciousness, were calm and peaceful. Tender loving care had been given to Sarah Ann by Sisters Berkbeck,[10] Unthank,[11] and others.

On Tuesday morning, September 14, Priscilla received the news about Sarah Ann. Right away she sent Zillie with friends in to Cedar City to be with her father. Having arrived too late for the funeral, Don, who was the same as all the other children—-overwhelmed with grief—-represented the family.

A crowd packed the meeting house where the funeral was held on Thursday the 16th. Brothers T. J. Jones and C. J. Arthur and Bishop Corry, speakers for the occasion, gave an impressive tribute to Sarah Ann.

On Saturday, when John had gotten a semblance of peace, he wrote Priscilla a letter. While pleading for Priscilla's understanding he wrote:

"Priscilla, I have lost, for the present at least, a good wife and an excellent mother, notwithstanding her bits of faults & failings, and God knows we all have them. I am overwhelmed with grief & hardly know what to think."[12]

For Priscilla, what to think came easily. Saddened by the loss of her dear friend, Priscilla mourned and wished she had always had good thoughts, but she soon began thinking about brighter days.

Priscilla's eighteen years of hiding had ended, and she was free to be seen with John Urie as his soon-to-be lawfully wedded wife. He was going to be hers on this earth and only hers—-now, heaven could wait.[13]

CHAPTER 23

Nuptials in Order

John Urie

Fifty-six-year-old John was bent on traveling the long bumpy road to Panaca as fast as he could. He had told Priscilla that if all was well, he would be there by the end of the month. John's business was in order, and the crops were in. The cart was loaded with cheese and butter to sell for Tom, and John had some extra for his family.

John told Priscilla weeks ago that Dan Mac was to leave Cedar City with Tom's cheese and butter. Knowing Priscilla was dependent on supplies and having heard from their daughter Zillie that Libby had been fretful in her teething, John was anxious to see how they were.

It was the last of September. Priscilla was thinking, "Should my dress be white, or what on earth should I wear?" She was as nervous as any young bride could ever be. Thirty-six-year-old Priscilla had seven children. She couldn't let the neighbors know what was going on. It would be another tidbit for them—-all they had to know was, she was going to move.

Priscilla, after having bottled her preserves, gathered together the bags of dried fruit, corn, and beans. She was ready to start packing. John wrote, saying, "Do the best you can till I come. Sell your things that we don't care about bringing in. . . . We cannot move in before the middle of Oct or thereabouts. I do not know whether Don will be out before I will or not."[1]

Feeling shy seemed a little foolish, but when John pulled up front in his loaded cart, Priscilla felt strangely different. John wasn't young and dashing, but he had that way about him.

While hugging the weans and helping them unload the cart, John, looking up at Priscilla, smiled as only he could. The glint in his eyes melted away all her concerns.

When he could get to Priscilla, while observing that everything was all right, John, as he drew Priscilla to him whispered, "Thank God for his blessings to you and the children."[2]

Right away they started making plans for the wedding. Should it be private? "Yes, yes," Priscilla exclaimed.

Priscilla finally settled on what to wear. The white dress Priscilla wore on the day John took her to the Endowment House was a bit tight, but it was what she wanted to wear. The beautiful dress brought from Scotland would do for some other special occasion.

John and Priscilla, wanting all the children to be there, waited for Don to come in. By the time Don arrived, the house was spruced up as best could be—-with the moving and all.

When the appointed day arrived, Priscilla and the girls prepared a nice meal and some refreshments to be ready to enjoy after the ceremony. The family crowded into the two-seated wagon brought out by Don and went to see the county clerk, N. P. Dooley, at his office. It seemed like it took forever for the license to be carefully drawn up.

Although the residence of Panaca frowned on polygamy and harbored very few such families, the laws in regard to marriage were much more lenient in Nevada than in the Territory of Utah.

When the document, written in beautiful script, was finally ready, the bishop asked the family to stand while the civil and legal binding of their parents in matrimony was performed. Betsy was holding Libby, and Will was tugging at his brother's sleeve, while Zillie, Net, and Mary tried to stand still.

At day's end, when the excitement was over, Priscilla, after combing her long, golden hair, sat by the light of the lamp—-reading the marriage license again and again. In part, it read:

> Panaca, Nev, Oct 7th A.D. 1891
> I do hereby certify, That John Urie and, Priscilla Smith were joined in marriage by me in Panaca, on the 7th day of October A D 1891
> Witness my hand on this the 7th day of October A.D 1891
> (sgd) Geo A. Wadsworth ⎤ (sgd) Milton L. Lee,
> (") Chas C. Romour   ⎦ Witnesses   a Minister of the Gospel

John was standing beside Priscilla when he placed his hand gently on her shoulder, saying, "Yes my lass we are, on this earth at least, legally married."

When Priscilla pleaded, "But John, I want to have you for all time and eternity," he assured her, "You will my lass, you will."

As the loaded cart and wagon rolled into Cedar City, the sight of the town brought back happy and distasteful memories for Priscilla. To be seen on the streets, sitting beside John Urie and holding their new baby, for Priscilla, was a proud moment. She held her head high—-but not so much that she appeared haughty.

The Urie family stopped by Sarah Ann's house. John had kept the house so Jack and his sister, Jessie, as well as her husband, Richard Williams, would have a roof over their heads. John knew Priscilla felt strange—-being in the house without Sarah Ann to greet her.

After refreshing themselves a bit, the happy Uries traveled a few miles further to the south where the settlement of Hamilton's Fort was located on the main thoroughfare. John prepared Priscilla to not expect very many neighbors—- the place had but a scattering of farmhouses.

When the two-story house finally came into sight, it was framed with the silhouette of leafless trees against a background of rolling hills and mountains in the distance. The wagons rumbled over the bridge covering Shirts Creek, which ran in front of the house.

The leaves crackled under the young children's feet as they scampered around the yard. John, Priscilla, and the older children started taking care of the business of moving in. Browns from across the street came to help—-bringing a large pot of soup and some hot biscuits. Betsy Ann and John Hamilton came up from their new house around the corner and pitched in, too. Betsy was famous for apple dumplings—-she was sure Priscilla would be happy when she showed up with a dripper full.

When Priscilla stepped into the house, she could see John had been busy. In the kitchen was a drop-leaf table[3] that had been painted by the Indians—- plenty of side tables and chairs, too.

John could hardly wait for Priscilla to see the parlor. John knew it needed her touch, but his library of over three hundred books was there. A nice rag carpet, padded with straw, covered the floor. Best of all were the two plush rocking chairs,[4] both covered with red velvet—-one for John and the other for Priscilla.

While Priscilla was standing in the parlor admiring their brass bed, John was quick to tell her that he had saved a space for one of those fancy pump organs. They had been talking about having one someday. The warmth from the fire burning in the fireplace gave a welcome feeling.

The door to the large back porch and the door to the large front porch finally stopped banging—-at last they were all moved in. The stove in the kitchen had been stoked up, and food was waiting. After the food was slicked up, the neighbors had said their good-byes, and the chores were all done, the family congregated in the parlor behind closed doors. This was the first of many evenings to be enjoyed in the parlor.

After all the excuses for lingering a little longer in the warmth of the inviting room were spent and before the children were sent to bed, the family knelt in prayer. Rocks and flat irons that were placed in the kitchen stove oven to heat were wrapped—-ready to tuck at their feet. The night before was spent in a friend's home where they found refuge along the way—-but tonight they had their own beds.

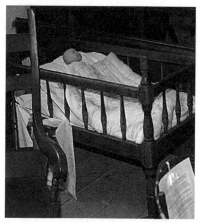
Similar cradle at the Rock Church

Don and Betsy carried the lit candles, and the others followed—-carrying footwarmers. The stairs creaked, and the bedrooms were cold. The ticks were so full of fresh straw that it was difficult to stay put in the beds. While shifting their footwarmers down a bit and nestling their feet in a nice warm spot, the Urie children snuggled under the heap of quilts until they stopped shivering and went to sleep.

Libby was left sleeping in her new cradle[5] in the parlor. The Indians painted it, too. The cradle was placed where John, if needs be, could stick out his foot and gently rock the baby back to sleep.

It was early to rise for all the family. There was breakfast to cook, chores to be done, and Zill, Net, and Mary had to be delivered to the one-roomed schoolhouse. Betsy didn't care much about going to school, so she stayed home. There was always the tending of wee ones, lots of cooking, housekeeping, and washing to help with—-besides Betsy liked to sew.

Priscilla toured the large lawn on the sides and front of the house. "The white picket fence," Priscilla thought, "would help

Side Lawn

keep Will out of harm's way." By the front gate under the lilac bush was a barrel that was filled with water dipped from the creek. Priscilla soon discovered when the chore was done that in the evening, the water by morning had time to settle and was much nicer to drink. She was adamant when she cautioned, "Dip the water upstream from the cattle crossing."

Being on the main road like they were, Priscilla soon noticed, brought many strangers to their door. The travelers were always willing to chop wood or some other chore for a bite of food. The weather was getting colder, and they stopped appearing so often, but Priscilla was sure that come springtime, she would be busy feeding extra mouths again.

John saw by the paper that the petition for amnesty to polygamists for past offenses was endorsed on the 19th day of December by "the governor, Arthur L. Thomas, and Charles S. Zane, who had again become chief justice, and many leading 'Gentiles.'"[6] John was starting to rest easier now. He was eager to see if the proposal would actually be accepted when it finally reached the senate.

The winter was long and cold, but Net, Mary, and Will thought it was fun walking over fences on the crusts of drifted snow. Christmas had been special this year. A piñon tree had been brought in and decorated with strings of popcorn and ornaments made in school. For the very first time, Priscilla's children had their father with them on Christmas Eve and even when they got up the next morning.[7]

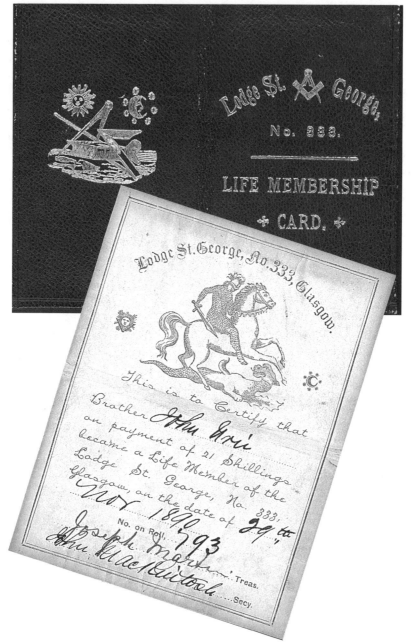

Mason Membership Card

CHAPTER 24

The Crowning Glory

It was a beautiful Sunday evening John and Priscilla were waiting on the front porch when the white-topped buggy, pulled by Jack's team, Mac and Coaly, arrived with Jack and his future bride Violet Lunt—-chaperoned by Lizzie, and the bride's mother, Mary Ann Lunt.

On the next morning, June 14, 1878, the entourage of Uries and Lunts proceeded to the St. George Temple, where the happy couple were sealed for time and all eternity.

When the bridal party returned to Hamilton's Fort, Priscilla was waiting with a modest dinner consisting of roast beef and cabbage—-for after-dinner visiting, she had popcorn and molasses candy prepared. Priscilla, while watching the enjoyment of the occasion, was wishing Sarah Ann could have lived long enough to celebrate the marriage of her last child.

It didn't take long for the bride to learn how particular her new father-in-law was about his own customs. Before "Aunt Priscilla" could warn her, while Violet was helping set the table according to the custom in her family, she had already placed the plates on the table upside down. When John saw what she had done, he said, "Lassie, what does this mean? Am I not to eat?"[1]

Violet learned other likes and dislikes of John Urie, too. When he and Aunt Priscilla came to visit in the Urie family home at Cedar City, Violet made sure the towels were hung just right, and remembered to never again turn her father-in-law's plate upside down.

With the celebration of the wedding behind her, this summer was going to be spent by Priscilla on the mountain. Priscilla missed going there for the last three years—-she was eager to see Tom's and George's new cabins. Getting everything ready for the families to go was always a hustle and bustle. George, Martha, and Agnes, Urie cousins from Salt Lake City, were making another annual trip down to go on the mountain, too.[2]

After a wonderful and productive stay on the mountain Priscilla dreaded summer's end. Life was moving along fast—-now that Don was almost seventeen it was time to think about his education. It had been discussed before about sending Don to Provo to attend the Brigham Young Academy, and this fall seemed like a good time for Don to go. John and Priscilla agreed that it would be good for Don to stay in a dormitory for boys.

Realizing his father was slowing down and figuring his mother was carrying another child, Don resisted going to Provo. After much consideration—-knowing Jack and the other boys would help while he was gone—-Don finally bent to his parents wishes.

The relationship between Priscilla and her sister, Betsy Ann, was better than ever. They enjoyed going together to Relief Society, quilting, participating in rag-tearing bees, and all sorts of things. Some of their friends had been going to Professor E. Koyle for what was called phrenological[3] chart readings. It seemed to be a fad going around, and they thought it sounded like lots of fun.

John scoffed at the idea of anybody being able to determine a person's character and intelligence just by feeling the person's head. With a chuckle, he suggested they would make just as much use of time by sticking to the reading of tea leaves.

Priscilla's report didn't turn out as great as she hoped it might, but she was content to believe she had a certain amount of high character and to discover she wasn't quite as dumb as she thought she was.

In the meantime, during this year 1892, feelings between John and his brother George were yet to be resolved. Whenever John had anything to write to George about, John's message went through his mother.

Letters from John's mother were sparse, but John continued writing to her and waited patiently for replies.

Violet Swan Urie, John's widowed sister-in-law, wrote a letter to John saying she had received word that his mother had passed away. Taking into consideration where the news came from, John presumed Violet was wrong and got a letter off to his mother with the news.

After waiting for what seemed like forever to John, he finally received a letter. Tom came out from town with the mail and handed his father an envelope with his mother's handwriting on it. John hurriedly opened the letter to read:

My dear Son John   1 November 1892
. . . . I do not know what terrified any person to telegram to Violet that I was dead, I felt hurt at it, I am in as good health at the present time as any old Mother can be and I am thankfull to our heavenly Father for his kindness to me. Your brother George is very kind to me and attentive.

You were right in thinking that I was still in the land of the living, able to write to you—-if God pleases to spare my life I will send to you what is your due on 11th November, but I thought that I would write you to let you know that I was still alive and not dead.

In reply to John's complaints of doom, his mother wisely counseled him with these words:

[I] was sorry to hear that your health was not so good as you would like it to be. You said that you was failing, of course you are getting older, you are in the border of sixty years of age and cannot expect to be so strong as when you were younger. Do not be cast down you will live a great many years yet, do be careful not to contract a cold to weaken your body, live well and take a little brandy occasionly—-but not too much. . . .

In closing, she added:

Your Brother George wishes you to write to him personaly and not through me. Please to write him a nice Brotherly letter. . . . I wish you both as Brothers to be agreeable with each other before I pass away it will be a comfort to me and make me much happier at death.
Your Mother
Agnes Urie
I will send to you 11th Nov what is your due in a bank draft.[4]

Priscilla was glad to see John's mother could perk him up. She couldn't help but notice a marked sparkle in John's personality after his mother's letter arrived. Priscilla noticed also that he spent time writing a long letter to his brother George—-"just like his mother asked him to," she thought.

Priscilla missed Don around the place. He was a tease at times, but he was good about encouraging his sisters with their studying. Don is the one who got Betsy going to school once in a while. Priscilla wished he wouldn't egg Net and Mary on so much about getting ahead of their neighbor friend, Lonie Brown, in their grades.

In Don's last letter to his mother and father, he asked for them to write to him a little oftener and commented: "I have had one letter from John [Jack] since I heard from you."

Priscilla guessed Don was getting along all right—-after reading he had gained fifteen pounds since he left home. John was proud of Don's eagerness to learn but figured Don needed more exercise. Both John and Priscilla were amused when Don commented: "This is the worst place I ever was in, it seames worse than Panaca ever did and it looks about like Panaca does."[5]

After reading Don's letter and seeing that the horses were getting fat and hard for him to handle, John, thinking maybe his son did know a bit about horses, told Priscilla, "I guess I'll take Don's advice about not feeding the horses grain—-it's likely they can live without it."

John was treating Priscilla with tender care, and she was taking her condition all in stride. She had gotten along at Panaca without Sarah Ann, and now she guessed she could get along just the same.

The tail end of winter came, and the roads were still muddy when word was sent to Dr. Forrester in Cedar City to get out to John Urie's, at Hamilton's Fort, as fast as he could. The day was Thursday, March 27, 1893. The doctor made it in plenty of time; the baby girl wasn't born until evening, so he stayed the night.

The baby was too young to be blessed on the coming fast Sunday. It was a good thing she was, with all the fuss going on about the Salt Lake Temple being dedicated. Lots of families headed for Salt Lake City early to get to conference and to be there on the 6th day of April for the big affair. Some of the Urie families went, but John stayed behind to be with Priscilla.

Forty years had lapsed since the cornerstones had been laid for the temple, and it was fitting that forty thousand people should congregate for the placing of the capstones.

John watched the newspapers with great interest to read about the dedication. He called Priscilla to sit in her chair next to him while he read:

> After the announcement from the architect from the top of the building that the capstone was ready, President Woodruff stepped before the people and said: "Attention, all the House of Israel, and all ye nations of the earth. We will now lay the top stone of the Temple of our God, the foundation of which was laid and dedicated by the prophet, seer and revelator, Brigham Young."
>
> He then pressed an electric button and the stone was laid. A mighty shout, of "Hosanna! Hosanna! Hosanna! to the God and the Lamb! Amen! Amen! Amen! under the direction of President Lorenzo Snow, went up from the people and was repeated three times.[6]

John and Priscilla wished they could have been there, but they were happy some of their family could witness the great event.

At the church house in Cedar City on the first Sunday of May during fast meeting, the building was filled to capacity. John proudly took his new daughter in his arms and stood at the head of a circle formed by his grown sons, sons-in-law, and the bishopric where he gave her a name and a blessing. She was to be known upon this earth as Jean Klingensmith Urie,[7] a namesake honoring both families.

John's waiting to see what would happen when the proposal on polygamy went before the senate was finally realized. His worries about his being caught and punished for his participation in polygamy were over after Benjamin Harrison, a Republican now at the end of his term as president of the United States, "who a short time before had visited Utah, on January 4, 1893, issued a proclamation of amnesty to polygamists for past offenses, limited to those who entered into that relation before November 1, 1890."[8]

For John, the crowning glory was when "The Utah commission, acting on the pardon of the President, ruled that the restrictions against voters in the territory should be removed."[9] Now John was going to work harder than ever to become a citizen of the United States of America.[10]

CHAPTER 25

Life at Hamilton's Fort

A considerable length of time passed before John started worrying about his mother. Being accustomed to long stretches between letters put him off guard. Agnes had been faithful and sent the usual November 11 allotment with a note conveying that she was well.

It was nearly March when Priscilla noticed John was stewing about something—-he went into town almost every day. When he came back, he wasn't smiling. He had his usual handful of newspapers and such. Finally, Priscilla broached the subject of his mother. John hated to admit he was worried but said to Priscilla, "I dinna know why I kinna hear from my dear old mother."

When the message by telegraph arrived on the 4th day of April, 1894, John knew why he had been so apprehensive. His mother had passed away. John wept bitter tears but consoled himself, knowing he had fulfilled one of his mother's last wishes. John was glad he had gone to Scotland before his mother died so she could see him "face to face."

The inheritance was now hanging in the balance, and John wondered what would become of it. The case was still before the courts in Scotland, but nothing much was happening.

By the time Jean Urie was born, Libby was making herself well known with her chatter. Will, because he was five years old now and because he was always around, was the big brother to the little ones. He was such a handsome boy, and his nature was as sweet as he was gentle. When Mary, the old-fashioned and motherly child, was home from school, she looked after them all.

For the older girls, Betsy, Zillie, and Net, harvest time was the busiest time of all. The Urie boys from the first family were always out to the farm and, together with Don and their father, were mowing and bailing lucerne, threshing grain, and, of course, bringing the sheep and cattle off the mountain. The cattle herd was usually taken south to the desert, where it was warmer for the winter. The robust young men burned off lots of energy and needed generous, nourishing meals to keep their strength up. Their father, however, stood by his tradition of eating two thick slices of day-old bread broken into a bowl of milk for his supper.

All the children liked to tease Priscilla when she got all decked out in her garb for extracting honey from the hives. It was a favorite time, too, because they enjoyed eating honey fresh from the comb.

Don worked hard through the summer of 1894 and, in the fall, left a lot of the work to his half brothers—-while he attended his second year at the Brigham Young Academy.

Before cold weather set in, the house had to be cleaned from top to bottom. Stovepipes and chimneys had to be swept, and the curtains had to be washed, starched, and stretched on prickly frames to dry. The beds were moved back from the middle of the room where they had been placed for better summer ventilation.

At the end of long, busy days, John and Priscilla found themselves sitting on the back porch taking in the beauty of the autumn sky and all that surrounded them. During one of these quiet moments, Priscilla thought about her eight living children and wondered how many more she would have. John was getting older—-he was fifty-eight when he sired Priscilla's last child.

The hope for more sons, even though John loved all his "bonnie lassies," was compelling. With all the attention John gave her, Priscilla was certain she would bear more children.

While Priscilla was in her world of thoughts, John was thinking on his pet subject. By keeping abreast of the political scene, John could see that laws were shaping up to where he and other immigrants would soon be in a position to become citizens of the United States.

During the fall of 1894, Priscilla's thoughts on the certainty of carrying another child was confirmed; and the following spring, on April 3, 1895, Priscilla beamed with joy when she gave birth to a son. This was a special birth and might be the last for Priscilla. John thought it was probably Priscilla's turn to choose a name. Well, Priscilla, thinking this was a generous gesture, agreed.

Pondering the position she was in gave Priscilla a feeling of importance. Knowing Alexander was a name found in John's ancestry would show some respect for his side of the family. From her side of the family, she wasn't certain, but Captain Alexander Fancher was a name which came to her mind often. When Priscilla decided on the name Alexander for their new son, John consented without any hesitation.

Priscilla was happy with her little son "Alex." To Priscilla, this baby was a semblance of her past. Through him, she could cling to the mystery of her innermost thoughts. Always wondering "To whom was I born?" and "Do I have brothers and sisters? What did they look like? Did any survive and remember me?" She clung foremost to the thought, "I know my mama and my papa loved me."

John seemed to sense Priscilla's yearning to know of her true link in life. Nothing could be done to change the terrible thing that had happened to her own parents. The best thing John knew to do was to encourage Priscilla to seek the ancestors of Philip Klingensmith and Betsy Cattle—-claiming them as her parents. John conveyed the importance of taking Klingensmith and Cattle names to the temple for their work to be done.

Priscilla, deciding that John was right, sent letters to relatives and finally hired a researcher in Pennsylvania to help find records on the Klingensmiths. Priscilla's mother's brother, William Cattle, was a friend, and he corresponded with Priscilla. Consequently, she gathered many names for her eternal progression.

While John was continually endeavoring to prepare names for the temple, he hadn't stopped pouring over the papers with avid interest to read articles written on his favorite subjects.

That fall, when the big election day came, on the first Tuesday of November 1895, John hitched up the buggy and took Priscilla to the polls. The gathering was exciting with all their friends speculating on who would win the election. When the votes were in, the long struggle for statehood ended. The act for adopting the Constitution of the United Sates had been approved, and Heber M. Wells was to become the first governor of the new state of Utah.

When the news came by telegraph that Utah was a state, word spread like wildfire. Throngs of people in Salt Lake City celebrated the affair in great style, while settlers of the outposts threw their hats in the air and hugged the ones closest to them—-joining in the great jubilee. In Cedar City, the moment news arrived, the ringing of the town bell, cow bells, and all other bells filled the air with revelry.[1]

Having looked forward to the inauguration day, to be held on January 8, John read with great interest from Sunday's Daily *Herald*, printed January 5, 1896, the proclamation signed by President Grover Cleveland:

Whereas, the Congress of the United States passed an act which was approved on the Sixteenth day of July, Eighteen Hundred and Ninety-four, entitled, "An Act to Enable the People of Utah to Form a Constitution and State Government, and to be Admitted into the Union on an equal footing with the original States," which act provided for the election of delegates to a Constitutional Convention, to meet at the seat of government of the Territory of Utah, on the first Monday in March, eighteen hundred and ninety-five, for the purpose of declaring the adoption of the Constitution of the proposed State and forming a Constitution and State government for such state;

And, whereas, delegates were accordingly elected, who met, organized and declared on behalf of the people of said proposed State their adoption of the Constitution of the United States, all as provided in said act:

And, whereas, said Convention so organized did, by ordinance irrevocable, with the consent of the United States and the people of said State, as required by said act, provide that perfect toleration of religious sentiment shall be secured and no inhabitant of said State shall never be molested in person or property on account of his or her mode of religious worship, but that polygamous or plural marriages are forever prohibited; and did also by said ordinance make other various stipulations recited in section three of said act:

And whereas, said Convention thereupon formed a Constitution and State government for said proposed State, which Constitution, including said ordinance, was duly submitted to the people thereof at an election held on Tuesday next after the first Monday of November, eighteen hundred and ninety-five, as directed by said act;

And, whereas, the return of said election has been made and canvassed and the result thereof certified to me, together with a statement of votes cast and a copy of said Constitution and Ordinance, all as provided to said act, showing that a majority of votes lawfully cast at such election was for the ratification and adoption of said Constitution and ordinance;

And, whereas, the Constitution and government of said proposed State are republican in form, and said Constitution is not repugnant to the Constitution of the United States and the Declaration of Independence; and all provisions of said act have been complied with in the formation of the said Constitution and government.

Now, therefore, I, Grover Cleveland, President of the United States of America, in accordance with the act of Congress aforesaid, and by authority thereof, announce the result of said election to be as so certified, and do hereby declare and proclaim that the terms and conditions prescribed by the Congress of the United States to entitle the State of Utah to admission into the Union on an equal footing with the original states is now accomplished.

In testimony whereof, I have hereunto set my hand and caused the seal of the United States to be affixed.

Done at the city of Washington this fourth day of January, in the year of our Lord one thousand eight hundred and ninety-six, and the Independence of the United States of America the one hundred and twentieth.

(Signed) Grover Cleveland.
By the President:

(Seal.)   Richard Olney,
                                        Secretary of State.

Later, while he was reading the papers after conference held April 6, 1896, John shook his head with disgust in light of all the contention going on over the new Manifesto presented at conference, which clearly defined the division of church and state.

Arguments seemed to be inevitable because of potential conflicts between church and state. Since the beginning, when the territory was first settled, men holding political positions also held high church positions and continued to hold them in 1896. The affiliation as a Democrat or a Republican also threw fuel on the fire.

Who was right or wrong didn't seem to concern John, but he kept himself knowledgeable on the subject. He was leaning toward a Republican disposition, and that was where he decided to put his support.

John was still strong in The Church of Jesus Christ of Latter-day Saints when, on June 24, 1896, he was advanced in the priesthood. On this honorable occasion, a private meeting was held in the office of the stake presidency, where his sons who held the priesthood stood in a circle and President F. M. Lyman ordained John Urie to the office of High Priest.

Priscilla and the rest of the family witnessed the ordination. Afterwards, it was announced in church meetings, and congratulations were given. The afternoon was enjoyed with a lovely dinner prepared by the Urie women at Hamilton's Fort.

Having reconciled himself because he knew his close ties to Scotland were gone, John decided to proceed with his wish to become a naturalized citizen. Priscilla and all of John's children accompanied him to Parowan, where he appeared before the Fifth Judicial District Court of the state of Utah. While abandoning his homeland, John took the required oaths and was admitted by the court as a citizen of the United States of America. The seal of the court was affixed on the 18th of September, 1896, and signed by Silas J. Ward, clerk, and by W. L. Cook, deputy clerk.

John had mixed emotions about giving up his homeland and becoming a citizen of the United States, but he was happy with the prospects of being able to vote in the next Presidential election.[2]

CERTIFICATE OF CITIZENSHIP.

United States of America,   *State of Utah, S.S.*

Be it Remembered, That on the _Eighteenth_ day of _September_ in the Year of our Lord One Thousand Eight Hundred and Ninety _Six_ _John Urie_ late of _Scotland_ in the Kingdom of _Great Britain_ at present of _Hamilton Fort, Iron_ County, in the State aforesaid, appeared in the _Fifth_ JUDICIAL DISTRICT COURT of the State of Utah, and applied to the said Court to be admitted to become a CITIZEN OF THE UNITED STATES OF AMERICA, pursuant to the directions and requirements of the several Acts of Congress in relation thereto. And the said _John Urie_ having thereupon produced to the Court such evidence, made such declaration and renunciation, and taken such oaths as are by said Acts required; thereupon it was ordered by the said Court that the said _John Urie_ be admitted, and he was accordingly admitted by the said Court to be a

Citizen of the United States of America.

IN TESTIMONY WHEREOF, *The Seal of said Court is hereunto affixed this* 18 th *day of* _September_ *in the Year One Thousand Eight Hundred and Ninety* _Six_ *, and in the Year of our Independence the One Hundred and* _twentieth_

BY THE COURT:

Silas J. Ward
Clerk.

By _W. H. Cook_
Deputy Clerk.

No. D 5.   SKELTON & CO'S Legal Blanks. Provo. Utah.

CHAPTER 26

From Don's Full Jug

One evening in the late fall of 1896, John felt the call of the prairie. Remembering the taste of potatoes wrapped in blankets of mud and tucked and baked in the hot embers of a fire taunted his taste buds.[1] His memory was sparked when he watched Don emptying a bucket of hot ashes from the fireplace onto the midden[2] in the back yard.

He wouldn't partake of such a treat after his bowl of bread and milk, but he wanted his children to experience the enjoyment. The family congregated reluctantly at first but finally pitched in to help. After washing their hands, they all waited eagerly as they watched the embers on what Priscilla called the trash pile. Turning the potatoes over now and then while the family waited kept their interest. After what seemed like forever, the potatoes were dug out of the embers with a stick and left to cool a bit.

Peeling away the mud and charcoal-covered skin surrounding the potatoes revealed a scrumptious meal. Globs of butter, mixed with charcoal, dripped from the wee ones' fingers as they juggled the hot potatoes in an effort to get a bite. Don felt he had one up on the rest of his siblings of eating his potato—-which he held on a stick—-without making a mess. He had learned this skill from being out on the range with the older Urie boys.

Violet Swan Urie

On the next day, the memorable evening turned into sadness when news of the tragic death of Viotet's son, George Lovett Urie, arrived. All of John's children knew George because of his trips to the mountains with them.

When the newspapers arrived, the Urie children shuddered when the vivid details of his death were described. Their cousin suffered a horrible death—-he slipped between two moving cars of a train. "The remains were nothing but a pulp"[3] George had been in the navy, and when he came out, he found employment with the Rio Grande Western as a brakeman.

George had a young wife, Maggie White, whom he had been married to for about a year and a half before the incident. It was John's judgment that when the Urie estate was settled, in all probability, Maggie would not get her husband's share of the inheritance. John was thinking, "It was only the kindness of my dear mother's heart that Sarah Ann and Priscilla ever got any portion—-and now she is gone."[4]

John and Priscilla noticed their twenty-two-year-old son, Don, was going into town more often than usual. The name Naomi Perkins came up often, too.

They figured that now he was all grown up, Don must be courting. John decided that before things got too serious, it was time for a mission.

For a while, this was to be Don's last summer going up on the mountain. Zillie, Net, and Mary were going to go, too. Priscilla was staying home with John and the rest of the family, while she and Betsy did the sewing to get Don ready for his mission.

Naomi Perkins

Donald Urie

Because Don was going to the Southern States Mission, loving hands made him some nice wool underclothing and some suits. While Priscilla and Betsy were sewing, John kept them up on the news from Salt Lake City.

With new statehood and good feelings prevailing among the people of Zion, a big celebration was being planned. "Governor Heber M. Wells recommended in one of his messages to the legislature, that the state hold an inter-mountain fair, or jubilee, during the month of July, 1897, it being fifty years from the entrance of the pioneers into the Salt Lake Valley."[5]

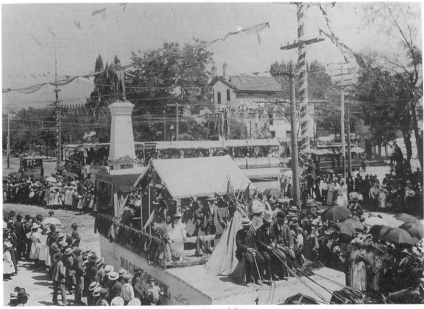

This is the Place Monument
(Utah State Historical Society)

John judged it would be an extravagant undertaking. A monument honoring Brigham Young and the pioneers was going to be placed right smack in the middle of the intersection on Main Street and South Temple. All the surviving pioneers of 1847 were going to be the honored guests. John said to the women, "Fancy this, they are even going to be given a badge fashioned out of gold."

The unveiling and dedication by President Wilford Woodruff was to be on the 20th so the 24th of July parade could be a separate part of the celebration. John guessed some of the folks from Cedar City would go to the celebration and the return to tell the Uries all about it. Don for sure would see the monument when he went to mission headquarters in the city.

October came, and the Sunday before Don left for his mission proved to be a special day. At church, friends and relatives bid him well—-slipping him a little cash. Dinner was extra nice and Priscilla tried not to cry. When the day came for Don to leave, Will pleaded to ride with his father to deliver his brother to the train station in Milford. The thoughts of Will seeing his first train and waving goodbye to Don were used for persuasion. At the station, John remembered the early morning he and his son David left for their missions. As the train pulled out, John wished he were young enough to go with this son, too.

John and Will, like their old horse Gipps, were pretty well used up by the time they got back to Hamilton's Fort. Priscilla anticipated their arrival with a hot meal. When the family came to the table, they couldn't help but notice how eager young Will was to take Don's place at the table.

John wasn't going to let on, but he found it hard on him emotionally to have his oldest son gone. John could see Priscilla was having a hard time too. Keeping busy was the only answer to staving off the loneliness. This wasn't hard to do with all that was left undone. Taking Zillie and Net into harness to help him husk corn for the crib occupied part of John's time. John knew Don hadn't had time to get the husking done and thought Tom and Jack would see it through.

When Don's first letter arrived, the Urie family was ecstatic. He made it to Salt Lake City where he wrote: "We are in good health and spirits . . . . We met Joseph F. Smith, Pres.[6] who told us to put our trust in the Lord & hold a stiff upper lip." With devotion and a hint of homesickness, Don added: "I would not live here for anything, our country place is worth all Salt Lake City for my use."[7]

The mission headquarters was in Chattanooga, Tennessee. In the beginning, Don was comfortable and well taken care of. His first companion, Elder Needham, Don thought, was "a good young man" and seemed "intelligent."

Love and support from the entire Urie family was felt by Don from the very beginning of his mission. In answer to their letters, he wrote: "I am very much pleased to know you like the spirit of my letters, and of course, I know you be anxious to hear from me. I can assure you it was as much pleasure almost for me to write, as it was for you to read."

Before ending his letter, Don wrote: "Well, I often wonder if my place at the table is missed. But Will can take it till I come back, then I shall be proud, to again occupy that position if my mission is fulfilled honorably before God and man."

The Republicans came on strong in this 1897 election year. John, while supporting Don with letters and means, turned his attention to being actively engaged in campaigning—-talking it up with his friends and all. His report to Don was, "Politics high, democrats very much divided in this County. . . . There is bread and butter in office now-a-days, a great many are anxious to serve the dear public."[8]

Priscilla went about her business of trying to keep in touch with everybody who was dear to her. She visited with her father's third wife, Margaretha Unthank,[9] in Cedar City a few days before news came that Margaretha had passed away.[10] It hadn't been unexpected. Although Margaretha was only sixty-one years-old, she had endured a hard life.

After Margaretha's well-attended funeral, her son Alfred took the opportunity to visit with his half sister, Priscilla. Words spoken at the funeral stirred up thoughts about his father and the Mountain Meadows incident. For a long time, Alfred had been thinking about riding out to the meadows. Now seemed like a good time to ask Priscilla if she wanted to go.

Alfred noticed Priscilla, all of sudden, was pale. She passed it off by telling him she didn't feel very well and said she guessed she wouldn't be able to go with him.

At times, Priscilla felt Alfred understood where she came from. "What could ever possess him?" she thought, "to think I could ever walk on the meadow." Finally, it dawned on Priscilla that he didn't know, and she wasn't going to tell him now. Sometime—-maybe—-but not now.

Alfred let it go, wondering what all of a sudden came over Priscilla. She changed the subject—-asking Alfred how long it had been since he saw their father. He told her, "Not since that time I went down on the Colorado." This remark affirmed Priscilla's notion—-believing Philip Klingensmith was dead after all.

The January day was cold, and John was waiting patiently for Priscilla to come along. Bidding Alfred goodbye, she tossed over her shoulder the words, "Don't be a stranger." Letitia, Alfred's wife, was also waiting patiently.

Letitia Dover K.

Reading letters that arrived often from the mission field kept the Uries in touch. The family learned that walking the rails to the nearest town by Don and his companions, sometimes as far as seventy-five miles or more, wasn't uncommon. Sometimes, they knocked on as many as a dozen doors before they could find a place to rest their heads. At other times, they slept outdoors or on the floor of the building where they last preached.

One time, Don thanked his father for the dime he sent.[11] Another time, he asked for the Lord's blessings because he needed them so much. Don had $1.60 left in his pocket and was going to soon give it to elders who were traveling a long distance.

As he found opposition and challenges by ministers of other churches during this, his first experience with prejudice toward the Mormons, Don's thoughts were: "Of course all their assaults spring from such 'scripture' as 'The Manuscript Found' and 'The History of John D Lee.'"[12]

In one of his letters, Don wrote:

> Father I have not had very much experience in the field yet, but I have had enough to convince me that the more we study about the Gospel the more we can see the beauty of it and the necessity of living so as to know that our course in life is approved by the Giver of all good. I have been striving for that spirit of love for mankind that so characterized our Lord & Savior, but you know that it [is] so hard to love those that hate and dispise you. I did not know that we were so much the victim of such feelings until I came here, but I do not care how much I am hated, for the Gospels sake, that hatred does not condemn me unless it exists in my own heart. Our Savior tells us to love our enimies, and to pray for them that dispitfully use you, and unless we do this we can't expect to enjoy the full extent of His spirit.
>
> Keenly now do I reliaze the fact that (you have told me off many times), you can't pour water out of an empty jug, the testimony I have convinces me that I am right, but that won't convince others, we must prove to them by the scriptures that we are teaching the true gospel.
>
> I hope and pray that I may be able to explain the Gospel to the people, by the aid and assistance of the Lord.[13]

Priscilla's emotions got the best of her when Don wrote: "Some times I would like to pop in upon you unaweres and see what you would say—-wouldn't it be fine to catch you all around the fire place injoying home life, I almost believe that I ment to stay at home allways, but I guess not. I am ready to do what ever I am called upon to do, whether at home or abroad."[14]

In a time of frustration for Don, taking back words that had been spoken years ago could never be. Priscilla wished they could when she read, "Mother always told me that I was selfish, that I knew, but there is one thing I have found out here, that is, if I ever wish to be excepted by God I must step out of self."[15]

Elizabeth, William, Jean

CHAPTER 27

"Do Your Duty, Sir"

The new year, 1898, found Priscilla enjoying her children and breathing a sigh of relief that her baby, Alex, was almost three years old. His father called him "Sandie" and thought he was quite a "daisy,"[1] now that he was wearing pants and had all his curls cut off.

Priscilla's arms ached for babies, but she was content to watch her children grow. After all, she had given birth to eleven children; and she had kept nine of them alive.

Sixty-three-year-old John, even though he himself hadn't doubted his potency, surprised Priscilla when she discovered she was carrying their twelfth child. Priscilla thought that forty-three, for herself, was beyond a time to bear another being for John's posterity.

When Priscilla told John of the coming event, his eyes lit up, and a smile was on his face. Priscilla countered his obvious delight with, "But John, I'm much too old to be having another baby."

With a broader smile yet, John answered, "But, my bonnie lass, ye kinna turn back now."

With another heir on the way, the business of John's inheritance was more important than ever. According to the law of the land, Priscilla had given birth to only two legal heirs, Jean and Alex. John, wanting the rest of his children to have a fair share too, started proceedings in their behalf.

According to provisions of the will, the suit was to be settled, even though the beneficiaries were not of legal age. While the suit was pending and in accordance with it, the money for John Urie's heirs was being held and accumulated until the number of his issue could be determined.

Thoughts of Don were always in the hearts of the Urie family. They watched for his letters intently.

Priscilla felt bad she hadn't written as often as John. When she did write, in her mind she was thinking, "Did I spell that word right?" or "Why am I such a dumbbell?"

Don always welcomed his mother's letters. Priscilla's words of encouragement and love buoyed him up. She usually tucked in a few stamps and kept him up on the news of his relatives. Priscilla was also good about abiding by any request—-like sending flowers and seeds to women who were temporarily taking her place. On her own, handkerchiefs with beautifully tatted edges were sent.

In her last letter, best regards were sent from the Klingensmith uncles and aunts—-Philip, John, and their wives, Lizzie and Clara. Aunt Jane had written and sent her regards, too. Priscilla knew Don always wanted to hear about her sister, Besty Ann, and "Uncle Johnnie Hamilton."

Priscilla's letter beginning, with "My Dear Son Donald," included:

Your Father is shucking corn every day . . . . I guess you will think this is a funey letter, but I have been so buisy putting up fruit we have got such a nice lot of botteled peaches, I wish you could just see them . . . . Your Father has gone to Cedar today to take Zillie to the normal School there is no Church School this winter. Betsy went up with them. Nettie, Mary, Willie, Libbe, Jean, are all to School so you see Alex an myself are all that is at home today. . . . I feel that we have been blessed every way and am thankfull to my hevenly Father that I have a Son that is worthy of being a honord servent of God if I can only rais all of my children to be good laterday saints it will be the comfort of my life.

In the empty space at the bottom of her letter, Priscilla wrote for Alex:

Dear Donald I send you a lock of my hare. Mama cut it of and I am in pants wont I be big boy when you come back? Papa got me a new red wagon and I hall wood for Betsy. I will sleep with you when you come back. I send you lots of kisses x x x x x x x x x x.[2]

The oldest Urie children understood the words of the gospel that Don wrote and were proud he was so filled with the spirit of his mission—-they had been brought up on most of it from their father. The little ones missed him but had a difficult time getting caught up in his preaching.

Priscilla was happy for her little ones when a letter from Don, which had been written on the first day of June 1898, arrived with a special little note for each of them. The whole family gathered around while the letter was read aloud.

To Betsy, who was now twenty-one years old, he wrote: "Do not wait for me to answer your every letter, remember where I am and what I am doing and write often, take an active part in Sunday School, and your Young Ladies Meetings, they belong to you young folks and you must help to make them interesting."

Nineteen-year-old Zillie, whom Don admired for her diligence in learning, he wrote: "I am glad you write often and thank you from the depths of my heart. I hope you are studying hard, both in your school books and the books that treat upon the gospel."

Nettie, now fifteen years old, was the one Don figured took his place on the farm. He always tried to encourage her in her learning: "Write often Nettie, and let me see how nicely you get along in your composition. You are improving, be a good girl and don't forget to read the bible and have your prayers."

To his twelve-year-old, tender-hearted sister, he wrote: "Mary, How are you? I would give a dollar to see you if I had it. Is the cats and kitten's fat and gentle, be a good girl and teach your older sisters how to be kind by your example, write to me and tell every thing you can think of."

The once-gentle little brother had now reached the rowdy age of ten and needed a challenge: "Willie you are getting [to be] a large boy I expect, I hope you are doing what Father and Mother tells you, study your books hard and see if you can't be as smart as Pa."

Don reminded seven-year-old Libbie, who had been sick of late, that he had been looking for her letter and added: "[Y]ou are well are you. . . . [B]e a good girl and dont fight with Will if he does make you mad once in a while, just take know notice of him and he will be sorry for every thing he does to you."

Don figured five-year-old Jean had become everybody's girl by now—-his love for her was plain: "Well sweetie Jeanie kiss Alick [Alex] for me. I liked your letter very much, do you play around in the mud with Alick when papa is watering the garden, does you and Alick have your naps. Be a good girl."

And to all of his siblings, he wrote: "If you my sisters and brothers want to advance rapidly in all your lawfull undertakings, humble yourselves before the Lord and ask him in faith, and keep His commandments and he will help you. Study the will of the Lord and see what is required of you and you will injoy happiness, peace, and joy in doeing it."[3]

To his father, Don wrote: "Write soon and tell me all about Thomas, John [Jack], Dave, George, and all the girls. I write to John and wrote to Albert[4] also the other day. I wish all my brothers were called to perform a mission of some kind."[5]

The closer it came to a year's time on his mission, the more discouraged Don became. When he made a plea for more letters, he claimed: "A letter from home in this foresaken place, is just as sweet as a gleam of sunshine in a Russian dungeon."

After busily "climbing up and down . . . rough and rocky mountains seeking for the honest in heart and if they were found [they] did not know it," Don felt inclined to write his parents of his gratitude:

I feel truely to prais the Lord, that my parents were humble honest souls hungering and thrusting after truth. A man to except the gospel in this land has to swim aginst the current of openion, and wade down the creek of scofs and scorns.[6]

While thinking of ending his mission after serving a year and knowing it would not be an honorable decision, Don made this plea in his last letter home: "When you write, give me some encouragement, father; you know how to do it, you also know how it renews ones spirits, gives them fresh energy, and a firmer determinednation."

John didn't take long to send back a lengthy letter to his son filled with encouragement and rebuffing:

Your pride, or your independance, or whatever you call it, needs taking down a peg or two. . . . Among whom you travel be they rich, or poor, you must be humble . . . . To be refused your hire as one of Christs Ministers is no sign of something wrong on your part, always providing of course that you put your trust in God. Should you have to sleep out at night sometimes is a trial for yourself. Never mind my boy, put your trust in God and all will be well, no matter what comes along, as my father told me once while on a mission "Do your duty sir if you are a Mormon Missionary." Father was an honorable man, he cared not for religion of any sort.

In all your ministrations among the people, "Be as harmless as a dove, and as wise as a serpent."

And then his father, among all the rest of his words of encouragement, added: "We say, do your duty sir and you will fill our hearts with joy and peace knowing that we have a son who is blessed of God."

Before signing his letter with "'Guid Nicht' an 'God be wi ye' is the prayers of your Father & Mother,'" John wrote: "You have heard of President Woodruff's[7] death no doubt."[8]

After fasting with prayer and carrying the words of his father in his heart, Don went for an interview with his conference president, Benjamin E. Rich. Don came away with the resolve he would stay in the field and serve for another year.

While noticing many young men were leaving their missions after laboring only one year, John was indeed proud—-his son chose to tough it out and serve an honorable, two-year mission.[9]

CHAPTER 28

𝒟𝒾𝓈𝓅𝓊𝓉𝑒 𝒪𝓋𝑒𝓇 𝒥𝓃𝒽𝑒𝓇𝒾𝓉𝒶𝓃𝒸𝑒

Family Group at Hamilton's Fort. Far left: Will (William). Back row: John Hamilton, Mary, Betsy, Net (Janet), Betsy Ann Hamilton, Priscilla, Zill (Priscilla), young girl standing in front of Net is unknown, next to her is Libby (Elizabeth). Jean is with the bicycle & Aleck (Alexander) is holding the lamb. John Urie is sitting.

Don was delighted when he received a letter with a snapshot of the whole family. They were lined up in front of the porch. His father was the central figure, sitting in his front-porch chair. Don got a chuckle over Alex holding the lamb and Jean showing off her bicycle. Will looked right smart wearing a suit, hat and all. It was good to see a likeness of his "ma," sisters, Aunt Betsy Ann, Uncle Johnnie and their kids, and their faithful dog, Coaly.

Time wasn't flying fast enough for Don to get home and see them all. The mission was hard. Spiritual revivals were going on with gangs causing trouble. A commotion stirred up over remnants of old news about B. H. Roberts, who was elected in the November 8, 1898, contest as one of Utah's Democrat representatives in Congress. Because Roberts was a polygamist, he was denied the seat, which contributed to resentment toward missionaries, the contention being that the "Mormons" violated their pledge with the government.

According to Don:

[I]t seems that Satan must have had a well organized secret service which burst forth all at once, but it is only a few Elders who are suffering, & not all by any means, probably only one or two pairs out of each conference covers the extent, or is the limit. This is the time of religeous revivals, & this Southern blood when hot is hell, therefore we are keeping low till revivele time passes. When I say low I mean we are not holding as many public meetings.[1]

It was with great interest John watched the well-oiled wheels of the Church. During the spring of 1899, President Lorenzo Snow passed through Hamilton's Fort on his way to St. George. This was a particularly dry year when President Snow, who always emphasized the law of tithing, inaugurated a reform of the principle among members of the Church.

By August, John received a letter from Don with these questions about tithing:

Lorenzo Snow

A question: Do I owe tithing on the money you have given, to sustain me in the Missionary field? You have paid tithing on it once, that was your just dues to the Lord. Now you gave to me money, which was a blessing of the Lord to me, I am a member of the Church and am under its laws, the laws is one tenth of the increase, this money given to me was increace, therefore it comes under the law of tithing, and I find myself about twenty dollars behind in my just dues to the Lord. . . . My duty was to have paid my dues as I received this money, but I did not understand the law as perfectly as I do now. . . . I wish to pay my just tithing to the Lord that I may have claims upon his blessings.[2]

Don was taught from a very young age the principle of tithing. Back home, Don had helped prepare the ground, plant seeds, water and cultivate, watch the crops grow, and help bring in fall--harvests the best of which were loaded on to a wagon, with what was considered a goodly load, to be taken as tithing to the bishop's storehouse in Cedar City.

John did his part in teaching Don, and now President Snow reinforced his teaching of this important law of the Lord. While John was proud to have raised such a son, he was surprised Don hadn't written the family a sermon on the law of the fast.

Priscilla missed Don and read his letters with great interest. Pangs of worry increased when, in September, Don wrote about an added difficulty, which Priscilla very well knew was tough:

Eld. Peterson & I are well as far as bodily strength is concerned, but we have that "Certain Disease" which we are compelled to cease laboring in order to rid ourselves of the same. If you can send some of the old fashioned sheep dip' please do so by next mail if possible. About 4 or 5 oz.'s will be enough.[3]

John, seeing how worried Priscilla was, didn't take long to send Don's package off—-hoping it would do the trick. Content that all else was going well, John was looking for the soon-to-be arrival of the baby when word came from Scotland announcing his only living brother, George,[4] was dead. George, at times, had been a canker and at times a blessing in John's life. Even though emotions were mixed, John was feeling a great loss.

Three days after John received news of his brother's passing, on November 29, 1898, Priscilla gave birth to another son. John hardly had time to grieve over his brother and be happy over the birth of his son when after Priscilla had done everything she could, the baby died also.

The local newspaper carried this news to all their friends throughout Iron and Washington Counties: "The infant child of Mr. and Mrs. John Urie of Hamiltons Fort, whose birth we chronicled last week, succumbed to an attack of convulsions on Monday. Dr. Middleton was summoned but arrived only a few minutes before it died."

A nod and a look of knowing from the doctor prompted John, before the baby took his last breath, to give him a blessing and the name Lillias Urie, a male synonym that John felt was appropriate and that was given in honor of the one who gave him birth.

Priscilla just knew it was her bad milk again and swore she would never give birth to another baby to die from the cause of it.

John, having failed to talk her out of her notion and resigning himself to the fact that there would be no more heirs to his father's fortune, decided to proceed with settlement of the inheritance.

When a letter with the decision on the inheritance money finally arrived, John was disappointed with the outcome. Upon examination of the contents of the letter, he found several of his children would not receive a share.

When David, George, and Sarah Ann discovered they were left out of the will, they went to Hamilton's Fort to confront their father about the unfairness of it all. To go up against a full-blooded Scotsman was a brave undertaking, but the children had enough Scotch and Irish blood in them to take on the task.

John, even though he was sorry about it, hated the thoughts of his children coming to him to stir up the controversy of the "Old Country Money." The Scotch law was clear; they had been left out of the will because their mother's divorce from Ferril hadn't become legal until after they were born.

This didn't set very well with David, George, and Sarah Ann because they didn't believe it was true. Besides, they couldn't understand why their cousins,

Martha and Agnes, were getting so much. They recoiled a little when their father said, "Kin ye not understand that your Uncle James' quarter share is separate from my quarter share?"

"But," they argued, "they get all of that money for just two and you have so many children." Their further contention was, "We are your children too, and our brothers and sisters aren't willing to share what rightfully belongs to us."

The bickering went on and on without much resolve. Priscilla was glad when they finally left[5].

Priscilla found John in the parlor with his head in his hands. When John heard Priscilla approaching, he raised his head and said, "I dinna what to do Priscilla—-it was my father and his stubbornness that caused all this grief." Tapping his cane on the floor, he exclaimed, "Why, oh why, dinna my father let things be?"

John knew if his father had left him a full share of the inheritance, to deal with as he saw fit, he would not have had this trouble. John's hands were tied—-the courts of Scotland ruled.

Trying to explain the best he could, John went to his desk and wrote a letter to Betsy, who had gone to Salt Lake City to work as a nanny and housekeeper:

> I received the other day a letter from Scotland stating that everything is settled and that your portions is 76 pounds or $365.00 payable on your signing a receipt which I have received. The above amount is the accrued interest since your grandmothers death. An additional $60 will be paid you next December, and annually thereafter until Alex is 21 years of age. Donald, Zill Jean and Sandie [Alex] will also get the same as you and at the same time, that is they get their $363 and their $60 on signing the receipts, all of which I have. . . . Tom, Jack, Agg [Agnes], Jessie and Eliza also get the same as you. Dave, George and Sarah receive nothing, neither Net, Mary, Libbie and Will.
>
> Your mothers family will get a little over $1800 just as soon as I send for it and $300 next December and the same yearly thereafter, that is $300 yearly until Sandie is 21 when the principal about $2500 each will be given. I think I have sufficiently explained things so you can understand it.
>
> Tom and the rest of them refuse to divide with Dave George and Sarah which I am sorry for. Keep this business to yourself, do not boast of your good luck to anyone as they are doing in Cedar making great asses of themselves.[6]

John sent a similar letter to Don to which Don replied: "I will leave everything to you. My confidence in my father is as firm as the rock. You know more about this affair than I do. You have my full confidence, and do with my portion as you think best."

After John's oldest children from his first family started a law-suit making claim to their share, the treacherous Salt Lake *Tribune* caught wind of the proceedings. John was badly shaken when he read the headlines: "Complicated Will Case—-Scotch Suit Involving Numerous Utah People—-A Father's Attempt to Disinherit His Son, Who Had Joined the Mormon Church and Moved to Utah."[7]

John tried to keep peace, knowing the lawyers would eat up the inheritance. The law-suit ended up costing $10,000 in lawyer fees. Feelings were hurt, and when Don heard about it—-not wanting to have anything to do with the dispute—-he said he didn't want any part of the money.

Watching John go through all the turmoil of the estate gave Priscilla feelings of regret that there was ever any money to squabble over.

This thing about polygamy seemed foolish to Priscilla. She knew, after watching John grieve over the loss of Lillias, it wasn't so much having a large posterity for him that was important. The important thing was having little ones to love and care for. All the money in the world could not fill the place of any one of his children.

Wherever the affluence of the Urie family came from, whether inheritance or the hard labor and ingenuity of John, the family felt well cared for. John had plenty of land. Often, when he returned home from town, he brought material by the bolts for the women to sew with. In the fall, flour was put into the bins by the ton.[8]

Dark Fruit Cake (5 pounds)

1 lb. Radiant Mix
1 lb. seedless raisins (3 cups)
1 lb. seeded dates (3 cups)
½ lb. (2 cups) nuts
¼ cup molasses or honey
¼ cup sherry wine or dark fruit juice
1 cup butter
1¼ cups brown sugar
4 eggs
2 cups sifted flour
¼ tsp. baking soda
¼ tsp salt
1 tsp cinnamon
½ tsp. cloves & mace, each

Mix fruits & wine, nuts, molasses
cream butter & sugar – beat in eggs
add fruits then flour
275° for 2½ hours.

Jean Urie Duncan

CHAPTER 29

The Good Old Times

When Don heard the railway was going to pass through Cedar City, he wrote, "I certainly would like to ride into Cedar City on the vestibule and I think that will be the case. Let us hope so any how, for I do not relish the idea of bumping over Minersville Ridge in the dead of winter."[1]

Priscilla's waiting finally ended—-she had her oldest boy home. It was like celebrating the Christmas holiday all over again. Scotch fruit cakes that were made with lots of nuts, citron, figs, dates, currants, and raisins and that had been baked and dribbled with rum were wrapped in cloths and stored to age for Don's return. Steamed suet puddings, to be served with lemon sauce, were on the menu for dessert, too.

Betsy Urie

Betsy welcomed and bid Don goodbye at the train station in Salt Lake City—-she couldn't leave her employment just yet. Zillie was home from school for the weekend. All the Uries were eager to hear about Don's mission; but, most of all, the siblings wanted to bundle up and dash over the beautiful, fresh, drifted snow on a bobsled—-just like old times.

Upon their return, the Urie children gathered with John and Priscilla, who were waiting in the parlor with popcorn ready to pop. A tray of honey, which had been cooked, pulled, and twisted into ropes of yummy candy, was brought from the kitchen. Sitting by the warmth and glow of the fireplace with his family was what Don had been yearning for.

Mary and the lambs.

Don felt joy in seeing the familiar, unchanged things he left behind. Adjusting to the loss of watching his sisters and brothers grow filled Don with thoughts of being robbed—-of time that never could be reclaimed. While Don was gone, Betsy, Zillie, Net, Mary, Will, Libby, Jean, and Alex had been making memories of their own.

So many changes had been made—-Betsy

living in Salt Lake; Zillie getting higher learning in Cedar City; Net growing big enough to help with genealogy; and tender-hearted Mary becoming a patient shepherdess of orphan lambs. Will had developed a determined personality of his own. Libby seemed so smart—-Don was sure she was going to be a school teacher. When Don left, Jean was having tea parties with her little friend from across the street. Now, with Alex as a sidekick, Jean was playing cowboy and Indian with Jimmy Jake—-who claimed he would be an Indian chief when he grew up.[2]

Don noticed how his brothers and sisters had grown in stature—-and in appetite. Much more food was prepared. Stacks of pies were stored in the cold shed. Steaks were cut for breakfast from beeves hanging in storage there, too. Don's own appetite was satisfied when he helped eat the loaves of bread and large pans of biscuits.

Priscilla watched the lives of her family move forward. While the old century was left in history, the turn of a new century was rung in with high hopes and expectations.

L to R, front row: Mary, Jean, Janet. Back row: Elizabeth, Betsy, Priscilla

Don's courting was resumed. Naomi Perkins became his bride in the St. George Temple on December 4, 1900.

John's interest in politics continually kept him stirred with emotion. Rushing to the house after his trip to town and handing Will the reins to his team, he called, "Priscilla Lass, where are ye?"

Priscilla came rushing from the house thinking something terrible was wrong.

"That vile *Tribune* will ne'er be in oor hoose."

It wasn't anything new to hear John go on about the newspaper. After following John in silence to the chairs on the back porch, Priscilla listened.

John lit up his corncob pipe. After taking a few puffs to calm himself, he commenced to air his feelings.

Conversations on the subject had been had before. The problem years ago with B. F. Roberts being barred from the U.S. Senate was bad enough—-now it was Senator Reed Smoot whom Congress wanted to oust from the Senate. The untrue claim that Smoot was also a polygamist was another excuse to attack the Mormon Church.

John's ire was up when the "*Tribune* maliciously cartooned, and wickedly vilified President Joseph F. Smith in its columns in a manner that would not have been tolerated anywhere outside of Utah."[3]

The newspaper had been fed by retaliation of the wealthy mining man, Thomas Kearns, who had been elected by the legislature to the U.S. Senate. When Kearns was denied support from Joseph F. Smith—-which meant the Church, Kearns' hate campaign began.

After the "American Party" had been formed by Kearns—-and men of his same disposition for the excuse of investigating the Reed Smoot case—-political conditions became intolerable. The appearance of daily attacks on Joseph F. Smith were met, by him, with these words:

> I feel in my heart to forgive all men in the broad sense that God requires of me to forgive all men, and I desire to love my neighbor as myself; and to this extent I bear no malice towards any of the children of my Father. But there are enemies to the work of the Lord, as there were enemies of the Son of God. There are those who speak only evil of the Latter-day Saints. There are those—-and they abound largely in our midst—-who will shut their eyes to every virtue and to every good thing connected with this latter-representation against the people of God. I forgive them for this. I leave them in the hand of the just Judge.[4]

John and Priscilla had many conversations concerning this political circus—-until the anti-Mormons sickened of the situation and teamed with other citizens to end the goings-on.

The subject around the Urie household was on a happier note when John came back from town with the Sears, Roebuck & Company catalog—-which claimed to be the cheapest supply house on earth. Dreams of things wished for in the past began to come true. Page 240 showed a picture of a magnificent cottage organ. The regular price of $50.00 was a bargain at $33.50--with a

OUR NEWEST STYLE COTTAGE ORGAN

GUARANTEED FOR 25 YEARS.
LONGEST, STRONGEST AND MOST BINDING EVER GIVEN WITH AN ORGAN.

THE IMPROVED PARLOR GEM

A REGULAR $50.00 ORGAN FOR ..... **$33.50.**

No. 21924
Order by Number.

IN DESIGN SO PERFECT, IN STYLE SO NEW, IN TONE SO POWERFUL AND EXQUISITELY PURE, AND IN PRICE SO LOW THAT NO COMPETITION CAN STAND THE TEST OF COMPARISON.

Remember Our ... 25 Years' Binding Guarantee.

BRAINARD'S NEW METHOD ORGAN
SEARS ROEBUCK & CO. CHICAGO ILL.

OUR $1.00 WITH ORDER PLAN.
You can send us $1.00 with your order and we will ship you our Improved Parlor Gem Organ C. O. D., subject to examination. After examination you can pay the balance and freight charges, otherwise you can return the instrument to us, and we will cheerfully refund your deposit.

OUR FREE TRIAL PLAN.
As fully described in the introduction of this department you can deposit the price of the instrument with your local banker and have the Organ taken to your own home for a free trial. The banker will send us the money at the end of 30 days, unless you have pronounced the Organ unsatisfactory and not as represented, in which case you return the Organ to the freight agent and upon presenting the bill of lading to the banker he will refund your money to you.

DESCRIPTION.
5 Octaves, 11 Stops, 2 Octave Couplers, 1 Tone Swell, 1 Grand Organ Swell, 4 Sets Orchestral Tened Resonatory Pipe Quality Reeds, 1 Set Exquisitely Pure and Sweet Melodia of 37 Reeds, 1 Set Charmingly Brilliant Celeste of 37 Reeds, 1 Set Rich, Mellow, Smooth Diapason of 24 Reeds, 1 Set Tuneing, Soft, Melodious Principall of 24 Reeds.

NAMES OF 11 STOPS, Diapason, Principal, Dulciana, Melodia, Celeste, Cremona, Bass Coupler, Treble Coupler, Diapason Forte, Principal Forte and Vox Humana.

THE ACTION
in this Organ consists of the Celebrated Newall Reeds, which are only used in the highest grade instruments. This Organ is fitted with Hammond's Couplers and Vox Humana, also the best Dolge felts, leathers, etc.

THE CASE.
This is one of the handsomest Cases ever used on an Organ at anything like the price. It comes in solid oak or solid black walnut, beautifully carved, ornamented and decorated, as shown in the illustration. It is especially constructed to develop the acoustic properties of the organ, forming a qualifying chamber which gives a pipe like quality to the tone, hitherto obtained in the finest reed organs. The wood used in the case is thoroughly seasoned and will stand any climatic change. It is highly finished, has a 10x14-inch French plate mirror, nickel plated pedal frames, and every modern improvement. The sides are 1⅛-inch lumber, and below the key board it is finished in panels. The new and handsome marquetry designs on each side of the mirror are not found in any other organ.

THE TONE.
That most important and quality in an organ is faultless. The depth and breadth, without sacrificing sweetness of tone by the sounding chamber, together with the finely tempered metal used in the reeds, secure a purity of tone which can only be equaled by the soft pipe of the Church Organ. These pipe-like qualities cannot be procured from any other manufacturer at any price.

DIMENSIONS:
Height, 72 inches; length, 44 inches; width, 23 inches.

Weight, boxed for shipment, about 200 pounds.

Our efforts in the past to render greatest possible value in musical instruments have received the commendations of THOUSANDS OF DELIGHTED CUSTOMERS.

REMEMBER OUR LIBERAL TERMS.

$1.00 WITH ORDER, balance C. O. D. after satisfactory examination.   SEND NO MONEY. JUST DEPOSIT PURCHASE PRICE WITH YOUR BANKER.   FREE THIRTY DAYS' TRIAL in your home.

A HANDSOME STOOL AND VALUABLE INSTRUCTION BOOK FURNISHED FREE WITH THIS ORGAN.

twenty-five-year guarantee. The space left for an organ—-so many years ago—-was filled, and a piano was added to dreams, too.

Alex Urie

While all the Uries enjoyed listening to rhythmic melodies, none but Jean was inclined to play. Through the years, it was she who filled the house with music.

Don was the one who strived for his brothers and sisters to pursue higher learning—-all of them, that is, except Alex, who was more interested in becoming a sheep rancher. Libby, Mary, and Jean attended the Branch Agriculture College in Cedar City—-striving to become school teachers.

Zill made her home in Cedar City after marrying Samuel "Bud" Fife Leigh on September 19, 1907, in the St.

"Bud" Leigh

George Temple.

Thirty-two-year-old Betsy was considered a spinster. The idea of being ugly still nagged at her. More than once, Betsy was told, she looked like her father—-who she thought wasn't quite so handsome anymore. Betsy left and returned home a number of times. In Salt Lake City, she became a dressmaker. John encouraged her in a letter, written July 13, 1909, by saying:

> The wage is small and room, boarding &c is high. However it is a change from the everlasting tread, tread of the sewing machine at home. It is also a change of scenary. An out is what you need & I hope will benifit you in many ways. Of all things take care of your health & dont forget that God is whom you must trust. . . . Your mother is writing giving all the news. God bless you.
>
> Your Father

John also relayed news about the weather and her brother's work, by writing: "It is very warm down here, no rain, very little wind & work is on, hauling hay, watering &c&c." Priscilla, feeling tired and not seeing all she accomplished, wrote:

> I dont know how you stand to work all day while it is so hot—-for I am as lazy as I can be—-if I had a boss and had to—-maby I wouldn't be so

lazy. I have just finished making 13 boxes of soap—-10 for Zill and 3 for me—-it is damd hot work . . . tomorow we will wash. Libbie is up to Dons yet. What with runing after cows & calves, chickens, turkeys troting around, I dont do any thing. . . . I havent been to Cedar but once since you left. . . . Libbie will get some curents while she is up there.

Mother

Elder Wm. Cattle Urie

During November 1911, the weather was cold and snow was on the ground. John shook his hat and brushed his shoulders before he and Priscilla entered the house. Hanging his hat on the hall tree as he passed, John went into the parlor. Priscilla stood for a moment, watching to make sure John was all right, before she took off her bonnet and coat.

It was another sad day for John—-his son David was taken swiftly by pneumonia.[5] "Some time alone is what John needs," Priscilla thought as she went about getting a bite to eat. They had eaten with the family in town hours earlier—-after the funeral—- but spent time visiting with the crowd.

A smile came to John's face as Priscilla entered the room. John was remembering the last time they stopped by Dave's home. Dave was holding a grandson on his knee—-entertaining the lad by blowing smoke rings with his corncob pipe.

From Hamilton's Fort on March 26, 1912, John—-full of the dickens—-wrote to Betsy in Cedar City:

Dear Betsy

What do you think Will is called to go to the Southern States on a mission to be in Salt Lake May 8th, ready to start.

Don't tell Will he has not seen the letter yet, but say you had a "dream" about his leaving on a mission in the month of May &c.

Rain, hail, snow & wind all last night

God bless you
Father

Will had grown into a lovable and almost favorite child of the whole Urie family. Letters written by Will arrived from Kentucky and Tennessee to the grown-up Urie children—-including the first family. Being among the youngest of the children, Will didn't feel the responsibility of filling his letters with gospel doctrine.

Remembering how long two years were, Priscilla found it harder to let her second son leave on a mission. Will was treated much the same as Don had been. Some people treated him grand, and others still had the same old prejudices.

When Betsy sent her letter from Will along to her parents in Hamilton's Fort, Priscilla thought, "I just wish people would learn to be decent and treat my boy right." In the letter, she read:

> [And] while making these walks we was able to get our breakfast but there wasn't much to it—-a few fried apples and a little pig and some tomatoes and the hot, so called biscuts. We got some stuff at the little country stores but when we buy anything in a country store the people soon find out that we had money or we could not buy. Yesterday we were standing in front of a house waiting for the train, while standing there we dug down in our pockets to see if we had money enough to ride with. After counting our nickles over, we heard the people that was in the house say, "I thought them Mormons traveled without purse or script." Then they had a big laugh over it.

Priscilla wept a little when she commented to John about the way people were treating their boy. John responded from his comfortable chair, sitting next to her in the parlor, with, "What are they doing to Will now Lass?"

Priscilla read aloud:

> A week ago tonight we held meeting in a school house and had a very good time. But after meeting the people all rushed out of the house and left us there—-not one of them ask us to go home with them—-well after the people were all gone I steped out of the school house door to have a look at the weather. I was standing a few feet from the door and here came a large rock flying through the air. It struck the earth a few feet from where I was standing. I steped in the house and there was another rock or two thrown but did no damage. They were thrown by some smart boys. After things had quited down we spread a newspaper on the floor and went to bed but not to sleep much.[6]

While Will was away on his mission, eighteen-year-old Alex—-figuring he was all grown up and not needing a mission—-decided to get married. Young Ruth Pryor and Alex went on their own to the County Courthouse in Parowan on May 1, 1913, to take their vows.

After Will returned from his mission in 1914, two more weddings took place.

Ruth Pryor

While working in Victor, Emery, Utah, Betsy met a lawyer who asked for her hand in marriage. Betsy, now thirty-seven years old, followed in her mother's footsteps by marrying an older man, too. Fifty-eight-year-old John Westly Warf took Betsy to the Salt Lake Temple to be married on July 2, 1914. Betsy made her home with John and his five daughters—a ready-made family, in Victor.

In a return letter to John W. Warf, Priscilla wrote:

August 23 1914
Dear brother Warf I hope you are well as this leaves us all. I am glad you think so much of Betsy & that she & you are so happie. It is me that knows the worth of her for she has been a dutifull daughter & I know she will be just as good a wife as she has been a daughter. . . . Please excuse pencil with love & best wishes to you all from Mother

John W. Warf

While attending college at Utah State, Libby became engaged to William Angus Stephensen from Holden, Utah.

Libby, wanting Angus to know about her childhood, told him how she "loved to ride horses, roaming the hills, visiting the sheepherders, eating fried mutton and sour-dough biscuits with them, picking wild flowers, finding gum from the pine trees and gathering pinenuts in the fall."

Libby was a little proud when she claimed, "Will was always willing to let me ride his best horses because I didn't spoil them, I loved to work in the garden and fields." About her home, she said, "In my leisure time I'd curl up in Father's big red plush chair and read books from his library—over three hundred volumes."[7]

William Angus
Stephensen

After Libby and Angus were married on September 3, 1914, in the Salt Lake Temple, they went to Fort Collins, Colorado, where Angus completed his course in veterinary medicine.[8]

CHAPTER 30

Mary's Dream

"Was it fair?" John was thinking. "To have married my young bonnie lass so many years ago."

With the fading years, John's tummy was now like St. Nicholas—-could pass for him, too. John's bushy beard and hair were snowy white. The noise John made, while he slept at night, was so loud Priscilla had to move to another bedroom.

John, having chopped his lot of wood for the day, was sitting in the sun with his granddaughter, Mona, and faithful Coale beside him. Jean saw her chance to catch a picture of the two with her new camera. Jean coaxed her father to pose

John & Priscilla

with an ax by his side. Mary, having noticed the picture taking, brought Priscilla away from bottling fruit long enough to have her picture taken, too.

With his train of thoughts broken, John went to the house and cooped up in his comfortable room. Soon, his thoughts turned to Betsy—-wondering how she was getting along. With pen in hand, he wrote:

September 8, 1914

Dear Betsy,

Perhaps you may think I have forgotten you. Not so. The girls & your Mother write quite often & no doubt tell you all the news. I am just as good in health as when you left. My appetite is good and I sleep well. I eat well, but I am getting older all the same. My hips & legs forbid me knocking around much. I chore a bit & chop all the wood. I must do something, I can't sit in my chair & read all the time. . . . Your mother of course is as busy as can be, her health is good. . . . Will & Sandy are busy & have but little spare time to write.

John continued his letter with news about each of the children, Aunt Betsy Ann, and Uncle Johnnie, who was on his death bed. Before closing, John included his usual good advice:

No doubt you enjoy your married life, be a good wife to your husband & children and the Lord will bless you. Dont forget your duty as a L.D.S.—-in doing so the Lord will bless you . . . Give my respects to your good man & tell him I would like to have a look at him some of these days. The mail is waiting.

God bless you Betsy
Father

All members of the Urie family were good about writing letters back and forth. In Will's letters to Betsy, he liked to tease her a little bit. Sometimes, Will wrote about being in love with a girl—-just to see if Betsy would bite. In one of Will's letters, he wrote:

I just got done writing to my little girl friend. I have been trying to shake her for some time, but she dont shake—-she is a sticker. I am getting tired of the girls here, so I guess I will have to come and work for you this winter and see how the girls sute me over there. What about it? . . . With a lot of love and best wishes to you and husband. Will[1]

Early in the following year when the snow was hardly off the ground, John started hearing plans for his eightieth birthday. He had no control over the fuss his family was making.

The ward hall was reserved for Wednesday night, April 28, 1915. With so many children, spouses, grandchildren, and great grandchildren, 247 relatives and friends turned out for the reunion.

According to the *Iron County Record*:

The program consisted of songs, recitations, reminiscences of early days, dancing and refreshments.

The great grandchildren of the honored guest presented him with a gold headed cane and a gold handled umbrella. Eight of the smaller great grand children were hitched to a small wagon on which was mounted a gigantic birthday cake, the wagon being profusely ornamented with bunting and flags. The driver was a small grandson of the patriarch. A procession followed of 25 other grand-children. After marching about the hall the cake was drawn up in front of Mr. Urie and the presentation remarks were made by Miss Mona Urie,[2] a grand-daughter, who made a neat and pleasing speech.

Relatives from St. George, Parowan, and other places were present at the celebration, which was a pronounced success.

John was done in from the big to-do, but he agreed with the newspaper when it reported: "The honored guest was very much pleased and thoroughly enjoyed every minute of the entertainment."

A year and a half later, an incident happened that horrified the entire Urie family.

As usual, Alex came down from Cedar City to help Will bring the crops in. The last load of hay was ready to be unloaded. Dawn was breaking, and it was a beautiful day. "Will was on top the load using a Jackson derrick fork on the east side of the barn. Alex was running the horse, Will's old Hetty, on the south side of the barn and through the corral bars. Mary was standing by the bars to keep about eight milk cows from going out."[3]

When Alex and Mary heard a blood-curdling scream from Will, they hurried around the barn to where they saw Will, streaming with blood, running toward the house. By the time they got to Will, with Coale barking at their heels, Dick Middleton was there to help carry him to the house where they laid him on the kitchen table.

When John and Priscilla looked at Will, they could see where the fork pierced his shoulder—-blood was gushing from the wound. Will, feeling his life slipping away from him, murmured, "No need to send for a doctor—-it will all be over in a few minutes." Within eight minutes after he was called, Dr. A. N. Leonard was there to take Will to the hospital.

Ross Urie

Will lingered in a near-death state until 10:30 p.m. the next day, Thursday, October 26, 1916. The fork had pierced his heart. Grief stricken, the Urie family stood weeping. Taking his small son, Ross, by the hand, Don moved quietly from the room—-feeling his heart had been pierced, too. Now, the brother Don had prayed for so many years ago, and the plans Will had for running a farm at Lake Point, where he purchased several acres of land and put in two wells, were gone.

Priscilla's feelings about Will were conveyed to Betsy in a letter written on November 9, 1916:

I thot we would of had a letter from you befor this. We are all well but I miss poor Will more every day if I was to give way I feel like I couldent stand it—-every thing I look at puts me in mind of him but I have a lot to be thankfull for—-for he was such a good principled boy—-for a long time he wouldent even take a drink of tea or coffe—-he was the only one that wouldent drink ether of them up to the dippen pen & there was about fifteen men. . . . With a bushel of love Mother

Mary Urie

Priscilla asked Net to finish writing—-her thoughts left her. When Net took over, she was having trouble, too, while she wrote: "Mother wanted me to finish out the paper but I dont know what I can say to you." Net wrote everything she could think about—-ending the letter with: "Mother is sending you this handkerchief of Will's."

Comfort finally came when, one month to the day after Will died, tender-hearted Mary saw and talked with Will in a dream. Feeling the importance of the dream, Mary put it on paper.

Priscilla, pondering why it was Mary that Will appeared to, finally understood. Seeking the patience and wisdom of John always helped Priscilla figure things out. Reading the last portion of the dream to John gave her further understanding of the dream:

Will said, "How is Alex getting along?" I said, "Oh, he is getting along pretty well, but it is so lonesome at home without you." I then started to cry. Will said, "Don't cry and feel bad about it, because I am so happy and everything is so nice, and I am busy where I am." He started to tell me about where he is and he smiled and seemed so happy all the time that I could not but feel it was alright. I awoke crying.

John consoled Priscilla by explaining the dream was a message--she should try harder to feel happy for Will. Priscilla tried, but everyday experiences refreshed memories of her precious son. Will's picture was to remain on the fireplace mantle from now on.

Placing a proper memorial upon the grave of Will was John's way of dealing with his grief. The $300 granite stone was magnificent and was to have, in time, besides Will's name, John's and Priscilla's names chiseled on opposite sides. Paying homage to the closest place John could be to his son was a common occurrence.

In the early years, the streets of Cedar City were lined with trees and watered by ditches that ran around the blocks for irrigation. Now the shade of these trees was a blessing during warm summer days. On most days, a gentle breeze or strong wind stirred the air. It was on one of these warm summer days, after visiting the cemetery, when John Urie dropped by the printing office.

For amusement purposes, this story was printed in the newspaper:

Not many days ago, Uncle John Urie of Hamilton's Fort was in the *Record* office "swapping lies" with our reporter, and conversation drifting upon his age and physical condition, the old veteran remarked: "I, I, Mun; I am eighty-two years old, and I can sleep well, eat a good meal's victuals, and chop a stick of wood."

"Well, what more do you want?" remarked the reporter.

"What more do I want? I dinna kin what more a mon could want. I dinna want all that. I could do very weel without the choppin' of the wood." Which goes to show that Brother Urie has not lost his keen Scotch sense of humor yet.[4]

"Old Folks Party"

This picture was taken in the Tabernacle at Cedar City, Utah, just after dinner on October 15, 1907, at 5:00 p.m. Total: 98 present in 1907. By 1933 there were only 12.

Cedar City Tabernacle

CHAPTER 31

Shadow of The Temple

In 1918, World War I and the dreaded influenza that raged during the reign of the war finally ended—-its dark shroud had taken its toll. United States President Woodrow Wilson made this declaration on November 11, 1918: "My fellow countrymen: The armistice was signed this morning. Everything for which America fought has been accomplished. The war thus comes to an end."[1]

Soon after the armistice, on November 19, 1918, President Joseph F. Smith of the Mormon Church passed away. Heber J. Grant was his successor.

While President Joseph F. Smith was head, "The Church was placed in a position to command the respect of all honest men. Prejudice was overcome, and the great men of our nation commenced to look upon the Latter-day Saints with more kindly feelings."[2]

The twilight of John Urie's life was creeping in—-but his wit and keenness of mind continued to entertain many a stranger and friend—-weather permitting—-on his front porch.

Tales of the "auld country" gathered John's grandchildren around his knees. John began by saying, "When I was there in 1891 the 'Auld Hoose,' was still just as it was 100 years ago. I went inside and knew it as I did sixty-five years since. I particularly eyed 'The Hole in the Wall'[3] where my mother was born and where Grandfather and Grandmother died. I also visited 'Granndy Kehead' a farm of sixty acres—-the home of my grandparents and their parents before them, and for 100 years before them."[4]

John's heritage was deep in his soul. Spending hours of preparing names for the temple and writing the things he felt--activities that could be meaningful in the lives of his posterity--were behind him. His May 14, 1919, letter to Betsy brought him to the reality of his present condition:

We are all well at home. My legs & hips are getting weaker & weaker. I can walk with great difficulty, but I can eat & sleep pretty well. I can chop a stick yet by taking lots of rest. They wont let me do anything & I have set in a chair most all the time. I have worn out the hinderend of 3 or 4 pair of pants. I read a good deal, but I get tired of it. Yet I am thankful I can spend the time in that way. It is very seldom I go to Cedar, once in 2 or 3 months. Your Mother & Net are well, they have plenty to do.[5]

The celebration for John's eighty-fifth birthday, on April 28, 1920, was spent attending the St. George Temple.

1920 CEDAR CITY, April 28. John Urie, who is 85 years old today, can trace his posterity to the fourth generation through seven members of his family. The accompanying picture shows just one of the seven lines. The son is Thomas Urie, the grandson Thomas Roy Urie, and the great-grandson Ernest Urie.)

John was old, but he was still respected and honored as head of the Urie family. Jean, who was now teaching school in Meadow, Utah, knew that when"Charlie"[6] asked her to marry him, he must write for permission from her father.

Jean and Charlie had set a date for May 20 to be married in the Manti Temple. This letter was promptly sent to Jean's parents:

Meadow, Utah
April 11, 1920

Dear Bro & Sister Urie, I am asking you perhaps what you little expect after so long a time. And that is what I consider "Gods best gift," your baby-girl for a wife and helpmate.

Jean and I have had quite a long time to get acquainted and I only hope we have both chosen well. My intentions are to make her happy and contented. By both doing our part, being congenial & considerate of each other I think we will be successful.

You will have to forgive me if I'm not able to pay you a honey-moon visit. For if I get away long enough to get married that will be all that is possible, but we will try and spend part of next holidays with you. Perhaps I can let Jean visit you a few days this summer. Still I can't part with her for very long. Ha!

I have seen your photos several times so I know quite well who I am writing to. But for you if any it hasn't been even a natural picture. So all you have is our word for it.

I hope to be all that I represent and prove worthy of the girl for whom I'm asking.

Hoping to soon receive the expected answer.

I am your friend and intended son

Chas

Charles E. Duncan

Jean K. Urie

When the letter of consent was sent back to Meadow, the couple proceeded with their wedding plans.

As the days passed, John's hips could carry him no more—-he was confined to bed. When John's appetite left him, Priscilla could see it was time to call the children together to comfort John in his last days. To Jean and Charlie, Priscilla wrote:

Dear Children
Meadow, Utah

Just a line to tell you that your father does not improve gradtely getting weaker. Tom & John are here all of the time & Donald will be here to day Can't take any thing but watter   Mother[7]

When Jean reached her father's bedside, his only spoken words to her were, "Are ye stout?" Jean's reply was, "Yes." Jean could see her father was at peace and happy that she was going to have a wee one. John's peace came with the knowledge he was going to a "wonderful, heavenly home where there is neither pain nor sorrow—-to receive his reward for a well-spent life of usefulness and to meet his loved ones who had gone on before."[8]

On Friday February 11, 1921, at 2:00 p.m., John Urie, at the age of eighty-six, closed his eyes forever.

The *Iron County Record* gave this account:

"Pioneer of Iron County Passes at Hamilton's Fort"

Word is received of the death of John Urie Sen. of Hamilton's Fort this afternoon. Funeral services will be held in the Cedar City tabernacle Sunday afternoon at 2:00 P.M. An account of Brother Urie's life will be published in the *Record* next week.

Sunday was one of those most perfect, early spring days. Priscilla was prepared with the clothes she lovingly made for John—-four years earlier. Priscilla added John's real Irish linen shirt, which he brought from his homeland long ago. His clothes all fit perfectly. After they were carefully pressed by Betsy, Priscilla "and the boys dressed John. According to his own desire, Gordon Matheson took him to his old residence in Cedar City where his numerous posterity and friends viewed his body."

For the funeral, "the tabernacle was crowded, even in the gallery." The entourage to John's final resting place was impressive. "According to John's wish, he was taken to his final resting place by a pair of beautiful Clydesdale horses driven by his grandson, Arthur Nelson. After which followed the pallbearers, Kenneth and Roy Webster, Wood Urie, and Urie Williams who were some of the older grandsons. . . . Fourteen cars followed the remains to the cemetery."[9]

It was a year and a half before Priscilla was to be left in the house alone. Net finally consented to marry an older man, too, Albert Fisher Andrew, who had been interested in her for several years. The couple were married in the Salt Lake Temple and made their home in Salt Lake City where Albert, a carpenter by trade, completed a lovely home on 200 East 1700 South.

Albert Andrew

When Priscilla decided to live with Mary in an apart-ment in Murray, where Mary was teaching school, Alex brought his family to live in the Urie home. After a year of apartment living, Priscilla decided she should buy a house.

Priscilla found a cute little one bedroom house, located down a lane on 161 North Almond Street, Salt Lake City. Priscilla and Mary moved in on August 25, 1924. Via a short cut, the house was only one-half block from the temple. It didn't take long for Priscilla and Mary to plant climbing roses on the front of the house. The two women bought a china cupboard and filled it with pretty dishes, and then the house was a home.

Betsy moved to the city and was running an apartment house at 318 C Street First Avenue. Priscilla missed Hamilton's Fort but was content to be where three of her daughters were living close by. Priscilla spent every day she could working in the temple and embroidering temple aprons.

When Priscilla was invited to a party honoring the pioneers, she wore the paisley shawl John brought home to her from Scotland. Priscilla wore the shawl proudly over her shoulder, securing it with the beautiful anchor pin. Mr Auerbach, who owned the large department store, Auerbach Brothers, was so taken with the shawl he offered to buy it. Priscilla was flattered but declined.

Albert, Priscilla's son-in-law, loved to visit with Priscilla--just so he could rile her about the Mountain Meadows Massacre. Albert was always taunting Priscilla about being Philip Klingensmith's daughter. Finally, one day, Priscilla could stand no more and blurted, "I am not a Klingensmith." Her words fell on deaf ears.

Priscilla needed John because John could always comfort her. He was the only one she could talk to about where she really came from.

After Albert left with his wide eyed-son, Urie, who couldn't understand what was going on, Priscilla, while trying to pull herself together, recalled how it was after John died.

After John's funeral was over and all the family was gone, Priscilla remembered how all alone she felt. The days that followed

Albert Urie Andrew

passed slowly. It was still cold out, and the song birds hadn't returned to sing their songs. All her children were married but Net and Mary. Mary was away teaching school.

Priscilla remembered finding herself going about aimlessly and thinking, "What is the use, my dear John is gone."

In search of some consolation, Priscilla remembered going to her trunk. With the lid open, her eyes went to the stack of letters tied with a faded silk ribbon. Soon, she was smiling; and the tears were wiped away. She found what she was looking for. John had such wisdom! After all these years, the words he wrote while on his last trip to Scotland meant more to her that day than when she first received his letter. It was then she knew she could go on.

Bringing herself back to the present, Priscilla searched her little trunk and found John's letter. She slowly reread his counsel:

Dear Priscilla,

In all your reflective moments be sure and seek the good spirit, that will comfort you and make you triumphant over all the ills of life, you have a clear conscience, I am proud to say, & you have patiently stuck to me as a wife and the mother of my children, let gossip, which is born of ignorance go to the four winds, your life is an honest and a pure one, this should be satisfactory to you, it is to me. May God help me, not only in being a father to the children, but a husband to you.[10]

Priscilla laid the letter down—-remembering loving thoughts of so many years ago when she whispered, "Thank you John, you were helped by God, and it was through Him that you were a good husband to me. I am content now—-you will always be near me."

Priscilla

John Urie

Front row: Bud Leigh, Lenore, Alice, & Scott Urie. Second row: Jack Leigh, Ernest Urie, John Urie, Winnefred Urie, Alice Leigh Back row: Helen Leigh, Elizabeth & Priscilla in the background.

Jean Urie at Glenwood teaching school.

Mary Urie sitting on front row (wearing a white hat).

Elementary school in Cedar City. Jean Urie is teacher.

Thomas Urie home in Cedar City

Front: Thomas Urie. Second: Jim Bryant.
Back left: unknown. Back right: Al Thorley

Sarah Ann McMillan Urie's Daughters. Front row, L to R: Agnes Urie Nelson, Agnes Eliza Heyborne Macfarlane, Eliza Ann Urie Webster. Back row: Sarah Jane Urie Hunter, Jessie Urie Williams, Teresa Ann Farrel Urie Duncan.

"Jack" Urie

Eliza Urie

John Webster

Violet Swan Urie & Family

Daughter Agnes Urie Coppin and children on the left. Martha Urie Folland and children on the right.

Henry Folland's Auto 1902 (1st locomobile in SLC)
Sid, Reta, Lorin, & Ruth Folland

APPENDICES

FAMILY GROUP CHART WITH NAMES OF CHARACTERS IN BOOK

George & Agnes Main Urie

George Urie, b. 11 Feb. 1811, Airdrie, Lanarkshire, Scotland; d. 30 June
1885, Glasgow, Scotland; father: John Urie; mother: Janet Graig;
George married: Agnes Main, b. 6 July 1813, Airdrie, Lanarkshire,
Scotland; d. 14 April 1894, Glasgow, Lanarkshire, Scotland; father:
Thomas Main; mother: Janet Forsyth.

CHILDREN

John, b. 28 April, Airdrie, Lanarkshire, Scotland; d. 11 Feb. 1921,
Hamilton's Fort, Iron, Utah; m. 5 April 1856: 1 Elizabeth Hutcheson;
2 Sarah Ann McMillan Farrel; 3 Priscilla Klingensmith.

Thomas, b. 28 April 1837, Glasgow, Lanarkshire, Scotland; d. 28 June
1887, Glasgow, Scotland; m. abt 1855: Mary Cowan.

Agnes, b. 3 Feb. 1841, Glasgow, Lanarkshire, Scotland; d. May 1841,
Glasgow, Lanarkshire, Scotland.

George, b. 21 Feb. 1843, Glasgow, Lanarkshire, Scotland; d. 26 Nov.
1898, Glasgow, Lanarkshire, Scotland; m. abt 1861: Elizabeth
McLellan.

James, b. 28 Sept. 1847, Glasgow, Lanarkshire, Scotland; d. 30 Jan.
1883, Glasgow, Lanarkshire, Scotland; m. 1 June 1868: Violet Swan.

David, b. 30 June 1850, Glasgow, Lanarkshire, Scotland; d. 11 Mar.
1862, Glasgow, Lanarkshire, Scotland.

John & Elizabeth Hutcheson Urie

1 John Urie, b. 28 April, Airdrie, Lanarkshire, Scotland; d. 11 Feb.
1921, Hamilton's Fort, Iron, UT; father: George Urie; mother: Agnes
Main; John m. 5 April 1856: Elizabeth Hutcheson, b. 9 Nov. 1841,
Cuilhill, Lanarkshire, Scotland; d. 16 Mar. 1857, Cedar City, Iron,
Utah; father: David Hutcheson.

NO CHILDREN

John & Sarah Ann McMillan Heyborn Ferril Urie

2 John Urie [see above] m. 12 Jan. 1858: Sarah Ann McMillan Heyborne
Ferril; b. 2 Oct. 1826, Waterford, Wexford, Ireland; d. 14 Sept. 1891,

Cedar City, Iron, Utah; father: William McMillan; mother: Elizabeth Smith; Sarah Ann m. 1: 13 Sept. 1842, John Heyborn, Newport, South Wales, England; m. 2: 1853, Ferril, Australia.

CHILDREN

David, b. 3 Nov. 1858 (twin), Cedar City, Iron, Utah; d. 12 Nov. 1911, Cedar City, Iron, Utah; m. 30 April 1883: Zelphia Wood.

George, b. 4 Nov. 1858 (twin), Cedar City, Iron, Utah; d. 25 April 1932; m. 16 Oct. 1881: Alice Jane Perry.

Sarah Jane, b. 20 Dec. 1869, Cedar City, Iron, Utah; d. 20 Nov. 1940, Cedar City, Iron, Utah; m. 8 Oct. 1879: David Hunter.

Thomas, b. 19 Jan. 1863 (twin), Cedar City, Iron, Utah; d. 28 Sept. 1924, Cedar City, Iron, Utah; m. 20 April: Katherine Gower.

Agnes Main, b. 19 Jan. 1863 (twin), d. 1 Sept. 1940, Cedar City, Iron, Utah; m. 1 Jan. 1880: Peter Albert Nelson.

Eliza Ann, b. 11 Dec. 1864, Cedar City, Iron, Utah; d. 12 June 1939, Cedar City, Iron, Utah; m. 30 Jan. 1883: John J. G. Webster.

Jessie, b. 21 Dec. 1867, Cedar City, Iron, Utah; d. 5 Mar. 1951, Cedar City, Iron, Utah; m. 22 April 1890, Richard W. Williams.

John Jr., b. 19 Jan. 1870, Cedar City, Iron, Utah; d. 2 Dec. 1936, Cedar City, Iron, Utah; m. 14 June 1892: Violet Lunt.

John & Sarah Ann McMillan Heyborn

1 Sarah Ann McMillan [see above] m. 14 Sept. 1842, Newport, South Wales, England: John Heyborne, b. 1 Aug. 1811, St. Giles without Cripplegate, London, England; d. 23 Nov. 1852, Badlam, Sydney, New South Wales, Australia.

CHILDREN

Robert William, b. 19 Dec. 1843, Kilkenny, Kilkenny, Ireland; d. 5 June 1907, Cedar City, Iron, Utah; sld. 9 Oct. 1866, Salt Lake City, Salt Lake, Utah: Margaret Bladen.

Agnes "Tillie" Eliza, b. 16 Feb. 1846, Sydney, New South Wales, Australia; d. June 1906, Cedar City, Iron, Utah; m. 9 Oct. 1866, Salt Lake City, Salt Lake, Utah: John Menzies Macfarlane.

Charles McMillan, b. 21 June 1848, Lanceston, Tasmania, Australia; d. 27 Dec. 1935, Cedar City, Iron, Utah; m. 30 Oct. 1866, Salt Lake City, Salt Lake, Utah: Mary Ann Leigh.

John James, b. 28 Jan. 1850, Sidney, New South Wales, Australia; d. 24 July 1866, Cedar City, Iron, Utah.

Frederic, b. 30 Oct. 1851, Sidney, New South Wales, Australia; d. Sept. 1854, Sidney, New South Wales, Australia.

John & Sarah Ann McMillan Farrel

2 Sarah Ann McMillan [see above], m. John Farrel, Sidney, New South
Wales, Australia.

CHILD

Teresa Ann, b. 27 Jan. 1854, Sidney, New South Wales, Australia; d. 9
May 1935, Cedar City, Iron, Utah; m. 27 May 1872, Cedar City,
Iron, Utah: John Chapman Duncan.

John & Priscilla Klingensmith Urie

3 John Urie [see above] m. 24 Nov. 1873: Priscilla Klingensmith, Salt
Lake City; b. 20 Mar. 1855, Cedar City, Iron, Utah; d. 26 Oct. 1924,
Salt Lake City, Salt Lake, Utah.

CHILDREN

Kathleen, b. 27 Aug. 1874, Cedar City, Iron, Utah; d. 27 Sept. 1874,
Cedar City, Iron, Utah.

Donald Clyde, b. 29 Oct. 1875, Cedar City, Iron Utah; d. 9 Mar. 1948,
Provo, Utah, Utah; m. 4 Dec. 1900: Naomi Perkins, St. George,
Washington, UT.

Betsy, b. 24 Nov. 1877, Cedar City, Iron, Utah; d. 16 June 1979, Salt
Lake City, Salt Lake, Utah; m. 2 July 1914: John Westley Warf, Salt
Lake City, Salt Lake, Utah.

Priscilla, b. 10 Dec. 1879, Cedar City, Iron, Utah; d. 29 June 1970,
Cedar City, Iron, Utah; m. 19 Sept. 1907: Samuel Fife, St. George,
Washington, Utah.

James, b. 2 Aug. 1882, Cedar City, Iron, Utah; d. 25 Aug. 1882, Cedar
City, Iron, Utah.

Janet Forsyth, b. 14 Dec. 1883, Cedar City, Iron, Utah; d. 23 May 1962,
Salt Lake City, Salt Lake, Utah; m. 12 Oct. 1922, Salt Lake City, Salt
Lake, Utah: Albert Fisher Andrew.

Mary Main, b. 3 July 1886, Cedar City, Iron, Utah; d. 18 Dec. 1963,
Salt Lake City, Salt Lake, UT; sealed 26 Mar. 1954: Alonzo Pratt
Kesler.

William Cattle, b. 10 Sept. 1886, Cedar City, Iron, Utah; d. 26 Oct.
1916, Hamilton's Fort, Iron, Utah.

Elizabeth Hutcheson, b. 10 Feb. 1891, Panaca Lincoln, Nevada; d. 1 May
1979, Henderson, Sands, Nevada; m. 3 Sept. 1914, Salt Lake City,
Salt Lake, Utah: William Angus Stephensen.

Jean Klingensmith, b. 27 Mar. 1993, Hamilton's Fort, Iron, Utah; d. 3
Mar. 1957, Salt Lake City, Salt Lake, Utah; m. 12 May 1920, Manti,
Sanpete, Utah: Charles Edwin Duncan.

Alexander, b. 3 April 1895, Hamilton's Fort, Iron, Utah; d. 16 May

1985, Grand Junction, Mesa, Colorado; m. 1 May 1913, Parowan,
Iron, Utah: Ruth Pryor.

Lillias, b. 19 Nov. 1898, Hamilton's Fort, Iron, Utah; d. 3 Dec. 1898,
Hamilton's Fort, Iron, Utah.

Philip & Hannah Henry Creemer Klingensmith

1 Philip Klingensmith, b. 3 April 1815, Brush Creek, Westmoreland,
Pennsylvania; d. unknown; father: Philip Klingensmith; mother: Mary
Anderson; Philip m. 28 Feb. 1841, Tippecanoe County, Indiana:
Hannah Henry Creemer, b. 14 April 1826, near Columbus, Franklin,
Ohio; d. 11 Mar. 1891, Panaca, Lincoln, Nevada; father: Jacob
Creamer; mother: Ann Elizabeth Reed; Hannah div. Philip: 22 May
1871; m. between 1875-1880: Adolphe Londrush.[1]

CHILDREN

Sarah Ann, b. 20 Feb. 1842, Tippecanoe County, Indiana; d. 23 Sept.
1899, San Bernardino, California; m. 27 Jan. 1855, Charles Carter.

Mary, b. 6 Feb. 1844, Betrand, Berrien, Michigan; d. 10 July 1845,
Nauvoo, Hancock, Illinois.

Moroni, b. 14 July 1845, Nauvoo, Hancock, Illinois; d. 16 July 1867,
Parowan, Iron, Utah; m. 16 May 1867, Cedenia Dalton.

Hannah Henry, b. 30 Oct. 1847, Council Bluffs, Iowa; d. 24 Nov. 1911,
Los Angeles, Los Angeles, California; m. 6 Dec. 1861, Thomas
Marion Mathews.

Nancy, b. 17 July 1849, Pacific Springs, Mountains; d. 1938, buried at
Forest Lawn Cemetery in Glendale, California; m. 13 May 1867,
William Newman, div.; m. George Albert Cook.

Keziah, b. 29 Aug. 1851; d. between 1871/1873; m. Feb. 1865, John
Mark Coombs. Philip and Hannah attended the temple for their
marriage. After Keziah died John remarried twice. One woman was
Ellen Sophrena Pratt. John was b. 1846 and d. 1906.

Lavina, b. 8 Jan. 1853, Cedar City, Iron, Utah; d. 13 June 1940, La
Crosse, L. C., Wisconsin; m. 16 April 1870, Allan McDougal.

Donna Isura, b. 3 Oct. 1855, Cedar City, Iron, Utah; d. 4 Jan. 1856,
Cedar City, Iron, Utah.

---

[1]"Federal Census, Nevada, Lincoln County, Meadow Valley Wash, enumerated; 1,2,3, day of
June 1880, listed Adolphe Londrush, age 53, farmer, b. Michigan, Hannah H., age 53, wife,
keeping house; Ellen A., age 12, daughter, at home; Hellen A., age 12, daughter, at home; William
Butler, age 8, grandson; Eliza L., age 6, granddaughter; Hannah S., age 3, granddaughter."

The John Henry Butler children were raised by Hannah after their mother, Donna C.
Klingensmith, died on 25 August 1878. The father gave the youngest child away before Hannah
arrived to fetch her grandchildren home.

Donna C., b. 9 Dec. 1856, Cedar City, Iron, Utah; d. 25 Aug. 1878,
Silver Reef, Lincoln, Nevada; m. 17 May 1870, John Butler.

Philip, b. 22 Dec. 1858, Cedar City, Iron, Utah; d. 31 Jan. 1928,
Huntington Beach, Orange, California; m. 24 June 1885, Clara M.
Logan.

John Henry, b. 22 Dec. 1858, Cedar City, Iron, Utah; d. 28 Jan. 1908,
Salt Lake City, Salt Lake, Utah; m. 10 Nov. 1882, Elizabeth Mathews.

Eliza Ann, 18 Jan. 1860, Beaver, Beaver, Utah; d. 4 Mar. 1891, Cherry
Creek, White Pine, Nevada; m. 27 Feb. 1875, Lewis Sharp II.

Melissa Mariah, b. 1 Mar. 1862, Toquerville, Washington, Utah; d. 3
Aug. 1867, Parowan, Iron, Utah.

Ellen Adelia, b. 14 Oct. 1867, Parowan, Iron, Utah; d. 4 Aug. 1928,
Reno, Washoe, Nevada; m. 17 Aug. 1881, Martin Mathews.

Hellen Amelia, b. 14 Oct. 1867, Parowan, Iron, Utah; d. 24 Dec. 1936,
Panaca, Lincoln, Nevada; m. 16 Jan. 1882, Charles, Mathews.

Philip & Betsy Cattle Klingensmith

2 Philip Klingensmith [see above] m. 21 Jan. 1846, Cedar City, Iron,
Utah: Betsy Cattle, b. 9 April 1838, Foleshill, Warwickshire, England;
d. 16 Mar. 1867, Cedar City, Iron, Utah; father: William Cattle;
mother: Elizabeth Dagley.

CHILDREN

Priscilla, b. 20 March, 1855, Cedar City, Iron, Utah; d. 26 Oct. 1942,
Salt Lake City, Salt Lake, Utah; m. 24 Nov. 1873, John Urie.

Mary Alice, b. 19 Mar. 1857, Cedar City, Iron, Utah; d. 27 April 1937,
Parowan, Iron, Utah; m. 24 Nov. 1878, John Benson.

Betsy Ann, b. 9 July 1859, Cedar City, Utah; d. 14 Mar. 1926,
Hamilton's Fort, Iron, Utah; m. John C. Hamilton.

Margaret Jane, b. 5 Mar. 1863, Cedar City, Iron, Utah; d. 24 Dec. 1936,
Los Angeles, Los Angeles, California; m. Alma Spillsbury.

William Cattle, b. 16 April 1865, Cedar City, Iron, Utah; d. 22 Aug.
1866, Cedar City, Iron, Utah.

Philip & Margaretha Elliker Klingensmith

3 Philip Klingensmith [see above] m. 21 Jan. 1857, Cedar City, Iron,
Utah: Margaretha Elliker, b. 25 Dec. 1835, Kusnacht, Zurich,
Switzerland; d. 8 Jan. 1898, Cedar City, Iron, Utah; father: Hans
Elliker; mother: Margaretha Studer; Margaretha m., 22 May 1871:
William Unthank; they had four children.

CHILDREN

Alfred, b. 20 Dec. 1858, Cedar City, Iron, Utah; d. 17 Nov. 1943, Cedar

City, Iron, Utah; m. Leah Letitia Dover. Alfred chose to spell his name: Klingonsmith.

Margaret Alice, b. 20 Oct. 1861, Cedar City, Iron, Utah; d. 19 Dec. 1943, Cedar City, Iron, Utah; m. 21 Oct. 1882, Benjamin Smith.

Elizabeth, b. 15 Jan. 1863, Cedar City, Iron, Utah; d. 1 Mar. 1951, Cedar City, Iron, Utah; m. 10 June 1888, James Humphries.

John Henry, b. 29 Jan. 1869, Cedar City, Iron, Utah; d. 9 Oct. 1874, Cedar City, Iron, Utah.

VICTIMS OF MOUNTAIN MEADOWS MASSACRE[2]

On September 15, 1990 a Mountain Meadows Memorial dedication ceremony was held in the Centrum at Southern Utah State College, now a University, in Cedar City, Iron, Utah. The following list of those believed to have been killed at or near the Mountain Meadows was provided in a pamphlet, by Roger V. Logan and the late Lee Oertle, that was printed for the occasion:

William Allen Aden, 19
George W. Baker, 27
Manerva A. Beller Baker, 25
  Mary Lovina, 7
Wards of George and Manerva
Baker:
  Melissa Ann Beller, 14
  David W. Beller, 12
John T. Baker, 52
  Abel, 19
John Beach, 21
William Cameron, 51
Martha Cameron, 51
  Tillman, 24 [Tilghman]
  Isom, 18 [Ison]
  Henry, 16
  James, 14
  Martha, 11
  Larkin, 8
William's niece:
  Nancy, 12
Allen P. Deshazo, 20
Jesse Dunlap, Jr., 39
Mary Wharton Dunlap 39
  Ellender, 18
  Nancy M., 16
  James D., 14
  Lucinda, 12
  Susannah, 12

  Margarette, 11
  Mary Ann, 9
Lorenzo Dow Dunlap, 42
Nancy Wharton Dunlap, 42
  Thomas J., 17
  John H., 16
  Mary Ann, 13
  Talitha Emaline, 11
  Nancy, 9
  America Jane, 7
  William M. Eaton
Silas Edwards
Alexander Fancher, 45
Eliza Ingrum Fancher, 32
  Hampton, 19
  William, 17
  Mary, 15
  Thomas, 14
  Martha, 10
  Sarah G., 8
  Margaret A., 7
James Mathew Fancher, 25
Frances "Fanny" Fulfer Fancher
Robert Fancher, 19
Saladia Ann Brown Huff
  William
  Elisha
  Two other sons
John Milum Jones, 32

---

[2]According to the "History of the Carlock Family," a Coker family from Arkansas was also slain. The number in the family is unknown.

Eloah A. Tackitt Jones, 27
  daughter
Newton Jones
Lawson A. McEntire, 21
Josiah (Joseph) Miller, 30
Mathilda Cameron Miller, 26
  James William, 9
Charles R. Mitchell, 25
Sarah C. Baker Mitchell, 21
  John, infant
Joel D. Mitchell, 23
John Prewit, 20
William Prewit, 18
Milum L. Rush, 28

Sebron, 18
Matilda, 16
James M., 14
Jones M., 12
Pleasant Tackitt, 25
Armilda Miller Tackitt, 22
Richard Wilson
Solomon R. Wood, 20
William Wood, 26
Others unknown
Charles Stallcup, 25
Cynthia Tackitt, 49
  Marion, 20

The following children survived and were returned to their families in nortwest Arkansas in September 1859. Additions and corrections are by author:

Children of George and Manerva Baker
  ["Betty"] Elizabeth, 5
  ["Sallie"] Sarah Frances, 3
  William Twitty, 9 months
Daughters of Jesse and Mary Dunlap
  ["Becky"] Rebecca J., 6 [8]
  Louisa, 4
  Sarah E., 1
Daug. of Lorenzo Dow & Nancy Dunlap
  Prudence Angeline, 5
  Georgia Ann, 18 months
Children of Alexander and Eliza Fancher
  Christopher "Kit" Carson, 5
Triphenia D., 22 months

Daughter of Peter and Saladia Huff
  Nancy Saphrona, 4
Son of John Milum and Eloah Jones
  Felix Marion, 18 months
Children of Jos. and Matilda Miller
  John Calvin, 6
  Mary, 4
  Joseph, 1
Sons of Pleasant and Armilda Tackitt
  Emberson Milum, 4 [7]
  William Henry, 19 months
At least [four] other survior[s]
remained in Utah. [including Priscilla]

LIST OF KNOW PARTICIPANTS AND ALLEGED PARTICIPANTS
of
THE MOUNTAIN MEADOWS MASSACRE

This list of names is written, not as an embarrassment to descendants of the participants, but as a matter of history. The names have been found on various records and were compiled by the author into one list. Known participants and alleged participants are not distinguished. Some spelling is questionable.

George W. Adair
Samuel Adair
Ira Allen
Benjamin Arthur [George]
William Bateman
----- Behunin
Thomas Cartwright [Enos]
John W. Clark
Joseph Clews
Ezra Curtis
Jacob Durfey [Jabez]
Tom Edwards
Will Edwards
Joseph Elang
Columbus Freeman
Isaac C. Haight
Elias Oscar Hamblin
Richard Harrison
John Hawley
William Hawley
John M. Higbee
Charles Hopkins
John Humphreys
George Hunter
----- Ingram
Erwin Jacobs
John Jacobs
Nephi Johnson
Samuel Jukes
Philip Klingensmith
Samuel Knight
Dudley Leavitt

Samuel Leavitt
John Doyle Lee
Samuel Lewis
A. Loveridge
[Alexander H.]
F. C. McDulange
Daniel Mcfarlane
John Mcfarlane
Samuel McMurdy
James Mangum
John Mangum
Sims Matheney
James Mathews
John Mathews
Jabez Nomlen
Harrison Pearce
James Pearce
Samuel Pollock
James Price
William Riggs
Joseph Smith
Carl Shirts
Dan C. Shirts
William Slade, Sr.
William Slade, Jr.
Anthony Stratton
Arthur Stratton
William C. Stewart
----- Tate
----- Thornton
----- Tyler
John Urie

Hamilton Wallace
John West
Joel White
Samuel White
Robert Wiley

Alexander Wilden
Elliott Wilden
John Willis
William Young

Notes

CHAPTER 1

1. Documentation and further details of the massacre are found in chapter 4.
2. Referred to as John throughout the rest of the book.
3. Letter from John Urie to his cousin, Herschell Main.
4. According to *Webster Dictionary*: an agreement of Presbyterians in Scotland in 1648 to oppose episcopacy: also called *National Covenant*.
5. Betty Evans, MS, "Martha Swan Urie Folland, Native Daughter of the Utah Pioneers," in authors collection.
6. "Agnes Main Urie was baptized in Airdrie, Lanarkshire, Scotland, by David Moffat between the months of September and October in the year 1849, and was confirmed at the water's edge on the same date. She does not know who confirmed her. Can't find any record of this baptism in the books of the Airdrie Branch of the Glasgow conference. She had the gift of interpretation of tongues." (John Urie)
7. Mary Urie, MS, *John Urie History*.
8. David Drummond baptized and confirmed John Urie on that same day.
9. This chapter is based on actual history and the writing of John Urie. Quotes without footnotes are part of the drama.

CHAPTER 2

1. George Bowering journal, 19 [37-38-39].
2. Train captains mentioned in Haight's journal are [David] Wilkin, [John W.] Cooley, [Jesse W.] Crosby, [Moses] Clawson, [Jacob] Gates, John E. Forsgren [Freeman], Eggleston [Henry Ettleman], [Vincent] Shurtliff, [Cyrus H.] Wheelock, [Claudius V.] Spencer, Appleton [M.] Harmon, John Brown, Daley, Steward, and William Parry, who replaced [Joseph] W. Young because of Young's poor health. (Southern Utah State University, "Biographical Sketch of Isaac C. Haight;" LDS Church emigration list.)
3. A story related to the author by his daughter, Elizabeth Urie Stephenson.
4. All quotes from the letter written by John to his parents in Scotland are actual. This chapter is based on true history and the writings of John Urie, George Bowering, and Isaac C. Haight.

CHAPTER 3

1. From Sacramento to San Francisco was 91 miles, where he took shipping to San Pedro, known as Los Angeles, which accounted for the distance.
2. A story related to the author by her mother, Jean Urie Duncan.
3. He was a participant in the Mountain Meadows Massacre, he signed the first affidavit telling about the crime, and testified at the first John D. Lee Trial.
4. The share, or cutting blade, of a moldboard plow.
5. Luella Adams Dalton, ed. and comp., *History of Iron County Mission*, 1956,

165-166.

6. Anna Jean Backus, *Mountain Meadows Witness, The life and times of Bishop Philip Klingensmith*, (Spokane: The Arthur H. Clark Co.) 1995, 89-90.

7. She was the daughter of David Hutcheson, born November 9 [24], 1841, Cuilhill, Lanarkshire, Scotland.

8. While John was in Salt Lake City, on March 21, 1857, he entered the House of the Lord to receive his endowments and was ordained an elder the same day by Dr. Sprague.

CHAPTER 4

1. Parley P. Pratt, who was ordained an apostle in 1835 by Joseph Smith, Oliver Cowdery and David Whitmer, was in jail with Joseph Smith in Missouri. Pratt was an explorer and missionary for the Church. He delivered a speech at the laying of the cornerstone of the Salt Lake Temple.

2. According to Richard F. Burton, an English traveler who was in Salt Lake City in 1860, "[T]he death of Apostle Pratt figured in the accusations then being made against the Mormons over the Mountain Meadow massacre. . . . [T]he skeptics said the Arkansans were killed by Mormons in revenge for the murder of the Apostle Pratt in Arkansas. . . . Mrs. McLean had become one of the apostle's plural wives." (Wallace Turner, *The Mormon Establishment*, 1966, 301.)

3. Hubert Howe Bancroft, *The Works of Hubert Howe Bancroft, Vol. XXVI*, 546-47; n7, "This account of Parley's murder is based on the testimony of Geo. Higginson and Geo. Crouch, whose letter, dated Flint, Arkansas, May 17, 1857, was first published in a New York paper. Copies of it will be found in the *Millennial Star*, xix. 478."

4. "The Postmaster General . . . annulled the contract held by certain Mormons for the transportation of the monthly mail to Utah, ostensibly on account of non-perfor-mance of the service within the stipulated time, but really because he was satisfied the mails were violated either enroute or after arrival at Salt Lake City." (Harold Schindler, *Orrin Porter Rockwell, Man of God, Son of Thunder*, 1966, 249, n64; *New York Tribune*, writing in *The Atlantic Monthly*, "The Utah Expedition," Vol. III (1859), 367.)

5. Most of the families were Methodists. "There was a Methodist minister in the party, and prayers were said morning and night." (*History of the Carlock Family*, "Mountain Meadows Massacre in 1857," 133, copy in possession of author. The Fanchers belonged to the Methodist Church. (See Paul Buford Fancher, 1993, *Richard Fancher (1700-1764) of Morris County, New Jersey, Richard Fancher's Descendants 1764-1992, Fancher-Fansher-Fanchier-Fanshier.*)

6. According to Rebecca Dunlap, the oldest surviving child of the massacre, "[T]here were a lot of rough acting young men that joined them in Salt Lake City." (Told by Rebecca Dunlap to her granddaughter, Isabel Minnie Evins Kratz, who corresponded with the author.)

7. "[T]he company was headed by a man familiarly known as 'Uncle Jack of Crooked Creek, Carroll Co., Ark.'. . . He was a warm friend and a bitter enemy; was possessed of good property, land, negroes, &c. He started with a drove of cattle, intending to return and move to California, if he liked the country; he leaves a wife

and several children in this county." *Daily Arkansas Gazette*, "Extract from a letter
Carroll Co.," *Arkansas State Gazette and Democrat*, 18 February 1858, 2/2.)
Document used by compliments of author, Will Bagley.

8. A fact known by the author--given through stories of her Great Grandfather
James Duncan, who lived in Meadow, Millard, Utah, during this time period.

9. "Wednesday, 1st of September, 1847. . . . there are some new peas and corn in
tassel in our fields. . . . Sunday 19th . . . This evening a meeting was held for to
herd our cattle or guard the grain . . . a thing they never done. Company after
company [of Saints] came in and turned their cattle loose and devoured about 40 acres
of grain in one field and 20 in another and among the rest eat up to me 1 1/4 acres of
buckwheat and corn, beans and peas, and devoured all that I had for to live upon
through the winter for my family, consisting of four." (John Steele, Jr., *Diary of*,
25.)

10. Captain Alexander Fancher was known to be the train master; George Baker
was captain of the herd.

11. "At the time of the Mountain Meadow Massacre, September 1857, David
[Wilson Tullis, born 3 June 1833], was working for Jacob Hamblin, who owned the
Meadows and had given permission for the Missourians to stop, came and fed their
stock there. . . Two of the men who were later massacred, came to talk to David a
few days before it happened, to try and find a place to stay and feed their cattle, since
David was the man who took care of Jacob Hamblin's business. . . . David had found
out that the massacre was being planned and that men were being rounded up to help
with the killing. He did not want to take part in it, so with the aid of three of his
friends, Sister Harrison, Sister Thornton and Sister Knell, he formed a plan to keep
from going. They put him to bed with hot bricks around him and put hot packs on his
head. By the time the men came for him he had the appearance of having a high
fever. So this and a few well timed groans, were enough to convince them that he
was in no condition to go." (Mrs. Milo Tullis, "The Life Story of David Wilson
Tullis and Martha Eccles," 5 August 1953. History given to author by David Clayton
Bishop, grandson of David Wilson Tullis.)

12. This story about the wranglers leaving may or may not be true. This author has
not been able to document this fact.

13. According to David Wilson Tullis, in words to his son John, things that
happened there, "Were too bad to tell, I won't repeat them as it was too terrible."

14. "On the 13th of January. My self [Thomas Hugo Hickman] and William
Huntington (afterwards Post Master at Springville, Utah) as we neared the Mountain
Meddows went on ahead of the Teams to view the Battle ground, there had been a
light snow. We found 40 human heads some with the flesh and hair on, they where
all women, and girls heads from 80 years down to young girls a few years old--all on
a space of 4 square rods, such was what we saw of the remains of the Massacree."
(The diary written by Thomas Hugo Hickman was found in a shoe box that had been
hidden within the wall of a closet. It was discovered when a house in Marysvale,
Utah was torn down in the 1970s. The authors copy of the diary is by compliments of
Laura McConnell.)

Elizabeth Carlock Fancher, daughter of Isaac Carlock of Missouri, who married
James Fancher, a close blood relative of the slain Fanchers, adds another family to
the list of those slain in the massacre: "One of the Coker families of Arkansas. The

wife was a descendant of Isaac Carlock of Missouri. This Coker family who lived in Arkansas were all slain." Elizabeth was closely related to the Coker family. (The authors copy of the "History of the Carlock Family" is by compliments of her cousin, Samuel Leigh.)

15. "Later some of the older ones were killed. Sister Thornton, raised one who was 7 years old, for awhile." It was learned later, after she was returned to Arkansas that "They never would have taken her if they had known how bad she felt to leave Thornton's." (Tullis)

16. "Sam Dukes was one of the men who Murdered the Emigrants, he told me all about it." (Hickman) See Appendix for list of known victims of the massacre and list of the known men who participated.

17. All quotes are from Hickman's diary.

18. "[T]hat girl was afterwards secretly Murdered she knew to much." (Hickman)

19. Letter sent from Salt Lake City written by George A. Smith to William H. Dame in Parowan, on 6 September 1857, states: "About 1600 footmen started for Utah, 500 of them has deserted before Br. Murdock passed them about 100 miles below Laramie. . . . The prospects are that the grand army will not arrive here before the next September." (BYU, W. H. Dame Collection.)

20. "[A]ccording to early missionaries, the Presbyterian Church first gained a foothold in Parowan because there were many who were upset over Mountain Meadows. The Parowan Church was merged into the Cedar City Church in the early part of the 20th century." (Letter sent to author from Cedar City, written by Rev. C. Jeffrey Garrison, 16 January 1996.)

21. The shame and sorrow that hung over the participants and their loved ones passed on to succeeding generations. This chapter is based on actual history; the writing of John Urie; the book by the author, Anna Jean Backus, *Mountain Meadows Witness*, 1995; and all others mentioned in footnotes.

CHAPTER 5

1. Sarah Ann McMillan Heyborne Farrell was the daughter of William and Elizabeth Smith McMillan, born in Waterford, Ireland, 2 October 1826.

2. Evelyn Webster, MS, "Sarah Ann McMillan Heyborne Urie."

3. See John Urie's "History of Cedar City." Found in *Mayors of Cedar City, and Histories of Cedar City, Utah*, by Evelyn K. and York F. Jones, 1886, 477.

4. Ibid.

5. On July 31, 1859, Philip Klingensmith was released as bishop and was replaced by Henry Lunt.

6. Robert Glass Cleland and Juanita Brooks, ed. and annotation, *A Mormon Chronicle, The Diaries of John D. Lee, 1848-1876*. Vol. I, 301-304.

7. Teresa Ann F. Urie Duncan, "Teresa Ann F.[Farrel] Urie Duncan, 1859," Kate B. Carter, *Our Pioneer Heritage*, Vol. 9, 1966, 430-431.

8. The true date of John's parents coming to America and the offer of a home anyplace in America are the bases for this dramatized story.

9. Based on a story written by Alva Matheson, *Cedar City Reflections*, 1974, 53-54. Most of this chapter is based on true history.

CHAPTER 6

1. Called *conference* because it was not a fully organized district of the LDS Church; it was about the size of a small ward.
2. "The line was completed in 1855 at a cost of $8,000,000." (*The World Book Encyclopedia, Vol. 14*, 1961, 106.)
3. Stories about "Johnnie" and the wheat are from Teresa Ann's history.
4. Evelyn K. and York R. Jones, *Mayors of Cedar City*, 1986, 90.
5. The boxes from Scotland were larger than trunks.
6. This entire chapter is based on true history.

CHAPTER 7

1. Haycock, Thomas James., ms, "Mary Alice Klingensmith Benson--my Grandmother."
2. See *Mountain Meadows Witness*, p 18.
3. James A Little, "Jacob Hamblin," in George Q. Cannon, *Fifth Book of Juvenile Instructor, The Faith-Promoting Series* (Salt Lake City: Juvenile Instructor Office, 1881).
4. True statement made to Priscilla by her father.
5. Most of this chapter is dramatized and is based on true dates, stories and events.

CHAPTER 8

1. Betsy Urie Warf, MS, "Priscilla Urie."
2. Direct quote from Priscilla's writing.
3. Margaret Jane Klingensmith, MS, "Story of Life of Margaret Jane Klingensmith," (Salt Lake City, Utah, Nov. 27, 1929), 2.
4. Taken from copy of the actual letter.
5. Copy of actual letter.
6. Mary Main Urie, Priscilla's daughter.
7. Cloth woven from yarn spun with a combination of wool and cotton or linen.
8. Record found among Priscilla's papers.
9. Luela Adams Dalton, *History of Iron County Mission and Parowan*, (Parowan: Privately printed, 1956), 452.
10. All of this chapter is based on true history.

CHAPTER 9

1. The Salt Lake City *Daily Tribune*, 4 August 1881.
2. Rev. John Parson Newman was President Grant's minister and was also chaplain of the United States Senate. (*Essentials in Church History*, 551)
3. Margaret was nicknamed "Maggie" and was the daughter of Betsy Cattle's sister, Mary.
4. This chapter is based on true history, John's letter to Scotland, and was interpreted in drama through the intuition felt by the author about her grandmother's life.

CHAPTER 10

1. Quote from John's letter to his parents in Scotland.

2. Evelyn Webster, MS, "Sarah Ann McMillan Heyborne Urie."

3. John Jr.

4. Statement appearing at the end of Philip Klingensmith's trial testimony. Testimony was transcribed by the author from papers found within one of the four boxes of Lee papers located in the LDS Archives during 1975.

5. This chapter was all dramatized by the author concerning true and imagined events in the lives of the characters.

CHAPTER 11

1. "The Lee Trial," Beaver Utah, September 15, Salt Lake City, *Deseret News*, 16 September 1876.

2. "Scotch Suit Involving Numerous Utah People," Salt Lake City *Tribune*, 1898. (Clipping found in John Urie scrapbook.)

3. David Wilson Tullis, and his son James, who witnessed the execution of John D. Lee, claim Lee was sitting on a plank across his coffin which was up in a wagon box. Samuel Worthen, of Panguitch, where Lee was buried, claimed that Lee's body was dumped out of his casket into a grave that was not covered with dirt for many years afterwards. The stench of his body became unbearable. (Related to the author by Tullis' grandson, David Clayton Bishop.)

4. Transcribed from copy of original letter.

5. Joseph Fielding Smith, *Essentials in Church History*, (Salt Lake City: Deseret News Press, 1946), 578-579.

6. This chapter was dramatized around actual events. It is easy to believe Priscilla longed to go to Scotland.

CHAPTER 12

1. Children belong to James Urie (John's brother) and his wife Violet Swan. They most always stayed two weeks.

2. Hurschell G. Urie, MS, "A Biography of Thomas McMillan Urie."

3. Margaret Jane Klingensmith Spilsbury, *Story of Life of Margaret Jane Klingensmith*, November 27, 1929.

4. First Minute Book, 1, Thursday 20 November 1856, Cedar City, Utah. (William R. Palmer collection, SUSU.)

5. Story based on *Deseret News* article: "Mass Meeting of the Ladies of Cedar City, Iron County, Utah, Jan. 15th, 1879," 5 February 1879.

6. The couple left soon after to join the Pioneer Company leaving for the Hole in the Rock Mission. David and Sarah Jane Urie Hunter left with them.

7. Drama of the love story for this chapter took place during true events.

CHAPTER 13

1. Taken from the carefully kept diary of John Urie.

2. The city was called *Cove* until 1849. Then, during the British occupation of Ireland, it was named *Queenstown* in honor of Queen Victoria. The government renamed it *Cobh*, the Gaelic spelling of Cove, in 1922, after Ireland became free from British rule. (T. W. Freeman, *The World Book Encyclopedia*, Chicago: Field Enterprises Educational Corporation, 1961, 597.)

3. "Arrival of missionaries--Elders John Urie and David Urie, missionaries from Utah to Great Britain, arrived in Liverpool on the *S. S. City of Berlin* on Monday, October 4th. Both were in good health and spirits, and had a pleasant trip from home." (*Millennial Star*; Vol. 42, page 649.)

4. Based on John Urie's diary and letters.

CHAPTER 14

1. "The 'Destroying Angels' Accomplish a Mission They are set to do," printed in the *Pioche Daily Record*, dispatched to the *San Francisco Call*, circulated on July 30, 1881, titled "A Mormon Bishop Murdered;" *Daily Tribune*, August 4, 1881, "Klingensmith, He is Supposed to Have Been Murdered by Mormons;" *Deseret Evening News*, August 16, 1881, "A Farfetched Assumption."

Destroying Angels did not belong to an organized group, perse. Any worthy man could be called, by an authority, to be a Destroying Angel to take the life of an offender. It was not considered a crime by Mormon standards.

2. According to the diary entry on, February 26, 1875, by George Hand, a Tucson saloonkeeper from the years 1875-1878, "Jack Klingenschmidt came in from Sonora today. He was near being killed there last year by a Mexican in his employ." (*Whiskey, Six-guns & Red-Light Ladies*, compiled and edited by Neil Carmony, published by High-Lonesome Books, Silver City, New Mexico.) Quote is by compliments of Sharon Cunningham, Associate Editor for Pioneer Press, Union City, Tennessee.

3. John Urie's diary.

4. Story came from *History of Iron County Mission and Parowan Utah*, ed. and comp. by Luella Adams Dalton, (Parowan: Privately printed 1956), 139.

5. Ibid.

6. The paisley shawl is in the possession of Priscilla's granddaughter, Helen Stephensen McBain.

1. The drama in this chapter is based on true history and the diary of John Urie.

CHAPTER 15

1. John Urie journal.

2. Bancroft, 772.

3. *Tribune*, 1898.

4. This chapter was based on Jane's history and family genealogy, depicting life lived in polygamy as it really was. The story about David and Zelpha is true. Letters to and from Scotland, the inheritance, the story revolving around the death of George, and John's trip to Scotland are all true.

CHAPTER 16

1. Alfred chose to spell his last name with an "o".

2. Joshia F. Gibbs, *The Mountain Meadows Massacre*, (Salt Lake City: Salt Lake Tribune Publishing Co., 1910), 43; BYU SCL, *Americana*, F 826, G532, 1966.

3. Laurs A. Pederson, "History of Philip Klingensmith," MS.

4. *Holy Bible*, King James Version, Matthew 7:12; *Book of Mormon*, 3 Nephi 13:12.

5. See "John D. Lee's Lost Gold Mine" by Charles Kelly, *The Desert Magazine*, August, 1946, 9, for a possible connection between Lee and Klingensmith's prospecting together.

6. Maribah Amelia Mathews Amberson, MS, "Life History of Helen Amelia Klingensmith Mathews," 1959-1960, 1.

7. Letter to author from Norman Rose, a descendant of Philip Klingensmith.

8. All of Priscilla's thoughts and actions are dramatized. This chapter, although at times, events are out of sequence in time, is based on actual history.

CHAPTER 17

1. L. W. Macfarlane, *Yours Sincerely, John M. Macfarlane*, (Salt Lake City: privately, 1980), 229.

2. Macfarlane, 229-230.

3. No relation to John D. Lee.

4. Alma Platte Spilsbury was captured and charged with polygamy, along with ten other Mormons, spending six months in the Yuma Territorial Prison located in Arizona. It may be this is where Alma was during this time.

5. This is a critical insight to what has happened to many records.

6. A word commonly used for the marshals. Webster's Dictionary: "a person of outstanding worth or importance: often used humorously."

7. Letter from John Urie to Priscilla, Cedar City, 3 July 1890, Panaca, Nevada. This chapter is based on true history. The dramatized life of Priscilla in Panaca is supported by letters.

CHAPTER 18

1. Letter from Agnes Urie to John, Cedar City, 16 July 1890, from Glasgow Scotland.

2. Saint Martin's day, a church festival held on November 11.

3. Letter written: 16 July 1890.

4. This chapter is dramatized true history.

CHAPTER 19

1. Letter from John Urie to Priscilla, Panaca, Nevada, 2 October 1890, from New York.

2. Letter from John Urie to Priscilla, Panaca, Nevada, 8 November 1890, from Glasgow, Scotland.

3. Ibid.

4. Ibid.

5. Ibid.

6. Letter from John Urie to Priscilla, Panaca, Nevada, 14 November, from Glasgow, Scotland.

7. Letter from John Urie to Priscilla, Panaca, Nevada, 20 December 1890, from Glasgow, Scotland.

8. Based on letter from John Urie to Priscilla, Panaca, Nevada, 14 November 1890, from Glasgow, Scotland.

9. Ibid.

10. Letter from John Urie to Priscilla in Panaca, Nevada, 29 November 1890, from Glasgow, Scotland.

11. *Deseret News*, 11 October 1890.

12. Letter from John Urie to Priscilla, Panaca, Nevada, 29 November 1890, from Glasgow, Scotland.

13. Letter from John Urie to Priscilla, Panaca, Nevada, 20 December 1890, from Glasgow, Scotland.

14. Letter from John Urie to Priscilla, Panaca, Nevada, 13 December 1890. from Glasgow, Scotland.

15. Letter from John Urie to Priscilla, Panaca, Nevada, 29 November, 1890, from Glasgow, Scotland.

16. Letter from John Urie to Priscilla, Panaca, Nevada, 20 December 1890, from Glasgow, Scotland. This chapter was dramatized into a love-story that was easily drawn from letters.

CHAPTER 20

1. Elizabeth Hutcheson was born 10 February 1891, at 6:30 p.m. in Panaca, Lincoln County, Nevada. Blessed in the same place by Bishop Milton L. Lee, 15 March 1891.

2. Letter from John Urie to Priscilla, Panaca, Nevada, 1 January 1891, from Glasgow, Scotland.

3. Ibid.

4. Ibid.

5. Letter from John Urie to Priscilla, Panaca, Nevada, 20 December 1890, from Glasgow, Scotland.

6. This true story was related as told by John's grandson, Ross Urie.

7. Based on letter from John Urie to Priscilla, Panaca, Nevada, 12 May 1891, from Cedar City.

8. Ibid.

9. Ibid.

10. *Webster*: "grippe, a contagious virus disease like a severe cold, characterized by fever, bronchial inflammation, catarrhal discharge, and intestinal disorder; influenza: also spelled grip."

11. Based on letter from John Urie to Priscilla, Panaca, Nevada, 13 December 1890, from Glasgow, Scotland.

12. Based on letter from John Urie to Priscilla, Panaca, Nevada, 20 December 1890, from Glasgow, Scotland.

13. Ibid.

14. Based on letter from John Urie to Priscilla in Panaca, 12 May 1891, from Cedar City.

15. The drama of this chapter has brought the author to believe it really happened. John's letters bring credence to how they felt about each other. John did travel through snow to get to Priscilla. Births, names and dates are accurate.

CHAPTER 21

1. Letter from Don Urie to Priscilla, Panaca, Nevada, 14 February 1891, from Cedar City.

2. Slang for being reminded or approached.

3. Letter from John Urie to Priscilla, Panaca, Nevada, 12 May 1891, from Cedar City.

4. Slang for not cutting yourself short.

5. Letter from John Urie to Priscilla, Panaca, Nevada, 8 July 1891, from Cedar City.

6. Letter from Don Urie to his mother [Priscilla], Panaca, Nevada, 10 June 1891, from Cedar City.

7. Based on letter written by John Urie to Priscilla, Panaca, 26 June 1891, from Cedar City.

8. Ibid.

9. Ibid.

10. This chapter is dramatized by using letters to depict true history.

CHAPTER 22

1. Joseph Fielding Smith, *Essentials in Church History*, (Salt Lake City: Deseret News Press, 1946), 609.

2. Based on letter from John Urie to Priscilla, Panaca, Nevada, 26 June 1891, from Cedar City.

3. "Nuggets of Truth," Salt Lake City *Herald*, Semi-Weekly, 2 November 1892.

4. "Duty of the People," *Semi-Weekly Herald*, Salt Lake City, Utah: October 1892.

5. Based on letter from John Urie, to Priscilla, Panaca, Nevada, 14 November 1890, from Glasgow, Scotland.

6. Based on letter from John Urie to Priscilla, Panaca, Nevada, 26 June 1891, from Cedar City.

7. Letter from John Urie to Priscilla, Panaca, Nevada, 7 September 1891, from Cedar City.

8. Letter from John Urie to Priscilla, Panaca, Nevada, 7 September 1891, from Cedar City.

9. Based on letter from John Urie, to Priscilla, Panaca, Nevada, 11 September 1891, from Cedar City.

10. She and her husband, Richard, cared for one of the surviving baby boys from the massacre until the boy was sent back to Arkansas.

11. Philip Klingensmith's third wife, who, with advice from the Church, married

William Unthank, after Philip left Cedar City.

12. Letter from John Urie to Priscilla, Panaca, Nevada, 18 September 1891, from Cedar City.

13. This chapter is based on history taken partially from newspaper clippings from John Urie's scrap book and letters. The drama surrounds true history.

CHAPTER 23

1. Letter from John Urie to Priscilla, 18 September 1891, Panaca, Nevada, from Cedar City.

2. Ibid.

3. Now in possession of the author.

4. Admired by many of their grandchildren.

5. The author, her siblings, and her daughters were rocked in the same cradle.

6. *Essentials in Church History*, 609.

7. Drama based on true dates, events, letters, and stories told to author by her mother and cousins. It is true that Panaca did not harbor many families who lived in polygamy.

CHAPTER 24

1. "Violet Urie," written by herself.

2. They usually spent two weeks every summer.

3. A system by which an analysis of character and of the development of the faculties can allegedly be made by studying the shape and protuberances of the skull. (*Webster*, 1103)

4. Letter from Agnes Urie to John, Hamilton's Fort, Utah, 1 November 1892, from Glasgow, Scotland.

5. Letter from Don Urie to his mother and father, Hamilton Fort, 7 November 1892, from Provo, Utah.

6. *Essentials in Church History*, 610.

7. The author's mother, who grew up to marry Charles Edwin Duncan. She gave birth to Faust Urie, Charles Homer, Anna Jean, and William Craig.

8. *Essentials in Church History*, 609.

9. Ibid.

10. The drama of this chapter depicted true history.

CHAPTER 25

1. Story adapted from "At Parowan," by McGregor. (Daughters of Utah Pioneers, Lesson for September, 1996, Compiled by Jean S. Greenwood.)

2. This chapter was drawn from true history. The setting allowed the author to interject the turmoil that she sensed her grandmother went through.

CHAPTER 26

1. Drawn from the memory of the author, who was taught by her mother.

2. A kitchen trash heap that was common in Scotland.

3. Newspaper clipping found in John Urie's scrapbook.

4. Quote from a letter.

5. *Essentials in Church History*, 613.

6. First counselor to President Wilford Woodruff.

7. Letter from Don Urie to his father and mother, Hamilton's Fort, 18 October 1897, from Salt Lake City.

8. Letter from John Urie to Donald, 24 October 1898, mission field, from Hamilton's Fort.

9. Margaretha Elliker Klingensmith Unthank.

10. Margaretha Elliker Klingensmith Unthank died on 8 January 1898.

11. His father as a gesture put the dime in his letter. At mission headquarters, John Urie kept money in a fund that Don could draw on.

12. Based on a letter from Don Urie to his family, 27 August 1898, from Pafftown, North Carolina.

13. Letter from Don Urie to his parents, Hamilton's Fort, 19 December 1897, Hamilton's Fort, from Evansville, North Carolina.

14. Letter from Don Urie to Betsy Urie, 24 February 1898, Hamilton's Fort, from Hunting Creek, Tennessee.

15. Letter from Don Urie to his parents, Hamilton's Fort, 23 June 1898, from Hunting Creek, Tennessee. This chapter was based on letters and actual history. It isn't known whether Will went to the train station. The drama of Alfred and Priscilla's conversation is the author's imagination. The spelling in Don's letters is unchanged.

CHAPTER 27

1. Slang for something outstanding or notable.

2. Letter from Priscilla Urie to Don on his mission, 16 September 1898, from Hamilton's Fort.

3. Letter from Don Urie to his brothers and sisters, Hamilton's Fort, 1 June 1898, from Elkville, North Carolina.

4. Peter Albert Nelson, who married Agnes Main Urie.

5. Letter from Don Urie to his father, Hamilton's Fort, 19 March 1898, from Brushy Mountains, North Carolina.

6. Letter from Don Urie to his parents, Hamilton's Fort, Utah, 23 June 1898, from Hunting Creek, North Carolina.

7. The death of President Woodruff was 2 September 1898 at the home of Colonel Isaac Trumbo in San Francisco. According to the line of procession, eleven days after the death of President Wilford Woodruff, at the October conference, eighty-five-year-old Lorenzo Snow was unanimously sustained as President of the Church.

8. Letter from John Urie to Donald in the mission field, 12 September 1898, from Hamilton's Fort.

9. This chapter is dramatized from letters to tell the story.

CHAPTER 28

1. Letter from Don Urie to his Father, Hamilton's Fort, 22 August 1899, from New Tazewell, Claiborne, Tennessee.

2. Letter from Don Urie to his Father, Hamilton's Fort, 8 August 1899, from Johnson City, Union, Tennessee.

3. Letter from Don Urie to his Father, Hamilton's Fort, 14 September 1899, from Bright Hope, Tennessee.

4. George Urie died on 26 November 1898 in Glasgow, Scotland.

5. The Urie family did quarrel over the money but, this quarrel was drawn from the author's imagination.

6. Letter from John Urie to Betsy, Newland, Lincoln, Nevada, 10 April 1899, from Hamilton's Fort.

7. Newspaper clipping found in John Urie's scrapbook.

8. This chapter is based on true history.

CHAPTER 29

1. Letter from Don to his sister, Priscilla [Zillie], Cedar City, 28 March 1899, from Johnson City, Tennessee.

2. He was Jean's playmate and did become an Indian chief.

3. *Essentials of Church History*, 629.

4. Ibid., 628-629.

5. David was fifty-two years old when he died 12 November 1911.

6. Letter from Will Urie to his sister (Betsy), Salt Lake City, 3 August 1912, from Acton, Taylor, Kentucky.

7. "Life Sketch of Elizabeth Hutcheson Urie Stephensen," written by herself.

8. This chapter was dramatized from true history depicting stories heard by the author.

CHAPTER 30

1. Letter from Will Urie to Betsy W. Warf, Victor, Utah, 9 July 1915, from Hamilton's Fort.

2. Don and Naomi Urie's daughter.

3. Taken from a short story written about the incident by Mary Urie.

4. Dramatized from letters and stories to portray actual events.

CHAPTER 31

1. Francis A. March, In Collaboration with Richard J. Beamish, Special War Correspondent and Military Analyst, *History of the World War* (Chicago: The United Publishers of the United States and Canada, 1919), 19.

2. *Essentials in Church History*, 636.

3. The place for a bed.

4. Based on letter from John Urie to his cousin, Herschell Main.

5. Letter from John Urie to Betsy, Murray, Utah, 14 May 1919, from Hamilton's Fort.

6. Charles Edwin Duncan, a World War I veteran and father of the author.

7. Postcard from Priscilla to Mrs. Charles E. Duncan, Meadow, Utah, February 1921.

8. Taken from family history titled "Death of John Urie," author unknown.

9. Based on family history of John Urie's death.

10. Letter from John Urie to Priscilla, Panaca, Nevada, 20 December 1890, from Glasgow, Scotland.

BIBLIOGRAPHY

PUBLISHED WORKS

Backus, Anna Jean. *Mountain Meadows Witness, The life and times of Bishop Philip Klingensmith*. Spokane: Arthur H.Clark Co., 1995.

Bancroft, Hubert Howe. *Works, Vol. XXVI, of History of Utah 1540-1886*. San Francisco: History Co., 1889.

Book of Mormon. Salt Lake City: The Church of Jesus Christ of Latter-day Saints, 1981.

Brooks, Juanita, ed. *Journal of The Southern Indian Mission; Diary of Thomas D. Brown*. Logan: Utah State Univ. Press, 1972.

Carlock. *History of the Carlock Family*. Arkansas.

Carmony, Neil, ed. and com. *Whiskey, Six-guns & Red-Light Ladies*. Silver City, New Mexico: High-Lonesome Books.

Cleland, Robert Glass and Juanita Brooks, ed. and annotation. *A Mormon Chronicle, The Diaries of John D. Lee, 1848-1876*. Two Vol. San Marino: Huntington Library, 1955. Salt Lake City: University of Utah Press, 1983.

Dalton, Luella Adams, ed. and comp. *History of Iron County Mission*. Parowan: Privately printed, 1956.

Duncan, Teresa Ann F. Urie. "Teresa Ann F. Urie Duncan, 1859." Kate B. Carter, *Our Pioneer Heritage*. Salt Lake City: Daughters of Utah Pioneers, Vol. 9, 1966.

Gibbs, Joshia F. *Lights and Shadows of Mormonism*. Salt Lake City: Tribune Pub. Co., 1909.

--------. *The Mountain Meadows Massacre*, Salt Lake City: Salt Lake Tribune Publishing Co., 1910; BYU SCL, Americana, F 826, G532, 1966.

Holy Bible. Authorized King James Version with explanatory notes and cross references to the standard works of the Church of Jesus Christ of Latter-day Saints. Salt Lake City" pub. by the Church, 1979.

Jones, Evelyn K. and York F. *Mayors of Cedar City, and Histories of Cedar City, Utah*. Salt Lake City: Woodruff Pntg. Co., 1886.

Macfarlane, L. W., M.D. *Yours Sincerely, John M. Macfarlane*. Salt Lake City: privately, 1980.

March, Francis A., Ph.d., In Collaboration with Richard J. Beamish, Special War Correspondent and Military Analyst. *History of the World War*, Chicago: The United Publishers of the United States and Canada, 1919.

Matheson, Alva. *Cedar City Reflections*. Cedar City: Southern Utah State College Press, 1974.

Schindler, Harold. *Orrin Porter Rockwell, man of God son of Thunder*. Salt

Lake City: University of Utah Press, 1966.
Smith, Joseph Fielding. *Essentials in Church History*. Salt Lake City: Deseret News Press, 1946.

PAMPHLETS AND PERIODICALS

Kelly, Charles. "John D. Lee's Lost Gold Mine," *The Desert Magazine*, August, 1946.
Matheson, Alva, *Cedar City Reflections*. Cedar City: Southern Utah State College, 1974 (SUSU since 1991).
Mountain Meadows Memorial Dedication Ceremonies, Sept. 15, 1990, Centrum, SUSU, Cedar City, Utah. (Roger V. Logan, Jr., Judge, Harrison, Arkansas, and Lee Oertle of Beaver, Utah, provided list of those believed to have been killed at or near the Mountain Meadows in 1857).

NEWSPAPERS

"Cleveland's Proclamation." SLC *Herald*, Daily, 5 January 1896.
"Duty of the People." SLC *Herald*, Semi-Weekly, October 1892.
Letter to the editor from John Urie. SLC *Deseret News*, 17 July 1871.
"Mass Meeting of the Ladies of Cedar City, Iron County, Utah, Jan. 15th, 1879." SLC *Deseret News*, 5 February 1879.
"Nuggets of Truth." SLC, *Herald*, Semi-Weekly, 2 November 1892.
"Scotch Suit Involving Numerous Utah People," SLC, *Tribune*, 1898.
"The Urie Family Holds a Reunion," Cedar City *Iron County Record*, April 1915.
"The Lee Trial," Beaver Utah, September 15, SLC, *Deseret News*, 16 September 1876.

UNPUBLISHED WORKS

Collections:
LDS Archives

John D. Lee Collection, containing transcript of Philip Klingensmith's trial testimony.

Private Collections:

Amberson, Maribah Amelia Mathews, MS, "Life History of Helen Amelia Klingensmith Mathews, 1959-1960.

Auger, Bernon J., copyright holder for George Bowering Diary, closed record in LDS Archives.

Evans, Betty, MS, "Martha Swan Urie Folland, Native Daughter of the Utah Pioneers."

Haycock, Thomas James, Jr., MS, "Mary Alice Klingensmith Benson--my Grandmother."

Hickman, Thomas Hugo, "Diary."

Lunt, Violet, MS, "Violet Urie."

Pederson, Laurs A., MS, "History of Philip Klingensmith."

Spilsbury, Margaret Jane Klingensmith, *Story of Life of Margaret Jane Klingensmith*, November 27, 1929.

Stephensen, Elizabeth Hutcheson Urie, MS, "Life Sketch of Elizabeth Hutcheson Urie Stephensen."

Urie, John, journal, letters and diary, in authors collection.

Urie, Mary Main, MS, "Priscilla Urie."

Urie, Hurschell, MS, "A Biography of Thomas McMillan Urie."

--------, MS, "A Brief Sketch of the Birth Place and Life of John Urie."

Warf, Besty Urie, MS, "A Short Sketch of the Life of Priscilla Urie."

Webster, Evelyn, MS, "Sarah Ann McMillan Heyborne Urie."

Southern Utah State University:

Palmer, William R., MS, Haight, Isaac Chauncy, "Biographical Sketch of Isaac C. Haight;" Minutes for, "Organization Meeting Female Benevolent Society," 20 November 1856, Cedar City, Iron, Utah.

———

LETTERS

All letters from John and Priscilla Klingensmith Urie collection are transcribed by author, unless otherwise stated.

Smith, George A., to William H. Dame, Parowan, Utah, 6 September 1857, from Salt Lake City, Utah.

Smith, PK, to daughter [Priscilla], Cedar City, Utah, 28 March 1870, from Smith Ville, Nevada [?].

Urie, Agnes, to John, Cedar City, Utah, 16 July 1890; 7 August 1890; 1 November 1892, from Glasgow Scotland.

Urie, Agnes, to Priscilla, Cedar City, Utah, 18 May 1886; 17 February 1887; 16 May 1887; 15 November 1887, from Glasgow, Scotland.

Urie, Don, to Betsy Urie, Hamilton Fort, 24 February 1898, from Hunting Creek, Tennessee.

Urie, Don, to Brothers and Sisters, Hamilton's Fort, 1 June 1898, from Elkville, N. C.

Urie, Don, to Mother [Priscilla], Panaca, Nevada, 14 February 1891; 10
June 1891, from Cedar City, Utah.

Urie, Don, to Father, Hamilton's Fort, 19 March 1898, from Brushy
Mountains, N. C.; 14 September 1899, from Bright Hope, Tenn.; 8
August 1899, Johnson City, Union, Tenn.; 22 August 1899, New
Tazewell, Clairborne, Tenn.

Urie, Don, to Father and Mother, Hamilton Fort, 7 November 1892, from
Provo, Utah; 18 October 1897, from Salt Lake City; 19 December 1897,
from Evansville, N. C.; 8 May 1898, from Boomer, N. C.; 27 August
1898, from mission.

Urie, Don, to Priscilla [his sister, Zillie], Cedar City, 28 March 1899, from
Johnson, Tenn.

Urie, John, to Betsy, Victor, Emery, Utah, 8 September 1914, from
Hamilton's Fort; 29 November 1920, from Hamilton's Fort; Murray,
Utah, 14 May 1919, from Hamilton's Fort.

Urie, John, to Donald, mission field, 12 September 1898; 24 October 1898,
from Hamilton's Fort.

Urie, John, to Mother [Agnes Main Urie], Glasgow, Scotland, 2 June 1891,
from Cedar City, Utah.

Urie, John, to George and Agnes Main Urie, Glasgow, Scotland, 28
February 1873, from Cedar City, Utah.

Urie, John, to George [his brother] Urie, Glasgow, Scotland, 12 May 1878,
from Cedar City, Utah.

Urie, John, to Priscilla, Panaca, Nevada, 2 October 1890, from New York.

Urie, John, to Priscilla, Panaca, Nevada, 15 May 1889; 3 July 1890; 12 May
1891; 8 June 1891; 26 June 1891; 7 September 1891; 11 September 1891;
18 September 1891; from Cedar City, Utah.

Urie, John, to Priscilla, Panaca, Nevada, 8 November 1890; 14 November
1890; 29 November 1890; 13 December 1890; 20 December 1890; 1
January 1891, from Glasgow, Scotland.

Urie, Priscilla, to Don in mission field, 16 September 1898, from Hamilton's
Fort, Iron, Utah.

Urie, Priscilla, to Mrs. Charles E. Duncan, Meadow, Utah, February 1921,
from Hamilton's Fort, Iron, Utah.

Urie, Priscilla, to John W. Warf, Victor, Emery, Utah, 23 August 1914,
Hamilton's Fort, Iron, Utah.

Urie, Will, to Betsy Urie, Salt Lake City, Utah, 3 August 1912, from Acton,
Taylor, Kentucky.

Urie, Will, to Betsy U. Warf, Victor, Emery, Utah, 9 July 1915, from
Hamilton's Fort, Iron, Utah.

Rose, Norman, to author, Orem, Utah, 27 April 1990, from Torrance,
California.

INDEX

Through Bonds of Love
has been produced in an edition of 2000 copies,
of which 200 are specially bound, numbered,
and signed by the author.
The book was designed
by
Anna Jean Backus.